THE STRUGGLE FOR
SUPREMACY IN GERMANY
1859–1866

THE STRUGGLE FOR
SUPREMACY IN GERMANY
1859–1866

BY

HEINRICH FRIEDJUNG

TRANSLATED BY

A. J. P. TAYLOR

AND

W. L. McELWEE

NEW YORK / RUSSELL & RUSSELL

1966

Der Kampf um die Vorherrschaft in Deutschland,
1859 bis 1866 was first published in 1897.
This abbreviated translation was made from
the Tenth Edition, published in 1916 – 17,
and was first published in England in 1935

REISSUED, 1966, BY RUSSELL & RUSSELL
BY ARRANGEMENT WITH A. J. P. TAYLOR
L.C. CATALOG CARD NO: 66—13169
PRINTED IN THE UNITED STATES OF AMERICA

TRANSLATORS' NOTE

Der Kampf um die Vorherrschaft in Deutschland takes up
two large volumes in the original and it has been necessary
to abbreviate considerably in order to compress it into one
volume for the English public. Our general principle has
been to preserve in full the political and diplomatic matter,
but to keep only so much of the military history as is necessary for an understanding of the general account. Thus we
have included practically every detail of the Prussian and
Austrian mobilisations, because they determined the course
of diplomatic events in April and May 1866; we have
abridged the account of the battle of Königgrätz, but we
have nevertheless accorded it considerable space, because
of its crucial importance. On the other hand, the war in
the Tyrol, which takes up ten pages in the original, is dismissed in a sentence, and the battle of Lissa, which takes
up sixty pages, in a paragraph. By such drastic excisions
we have, we hope, been able to preserve all that is most
valuable from the political and diplomatic point of view in
Friedjung's account.

We hesitated long before we decided to add some supple-
mentary notes of our own. It is not our desire to bring
Friedjung up to date or to attempt to write a new book on
the ruins of the old. *Der Kampf um die Vorherrschaft* can
tell its own story without any assistance from us. But certain points which Friedjung found mysterious have since
been elucidated by the opening of the Austrian archives
after the war, and it would have been pedantic to omit
matter which we may be sure Friedjung would have himself

included had he lived a year or two longer. Some of this material comes from our own researches in the Austrian archives, some of it is taken from Professor Redlich's *Das Österreichische Staats- und Reichs-Problem*, to which we make the most sincere acknowledgement. We wish also to thank Professor L. B. Namier for invaluable assistance and advice.

The translators are jointly responsible for the translation, the omissions, and the additional notes. A. J. P. Taylor is responsible for the Introduction.

CONTENTS

INTRODUCTION

HEINRICH FRIEDJUNG, the author of this book and perhaps the greatest of Austrian historians, was born at Rostchin in Moravia, of Jewish parents, on January 18, 1851, and died in Vienna on July 14, 1920. He was the author of numerous historical works—*The Emperor Charles IV and his Share in the Intellectual Life of his Time* (1876); *The Struggle for Supremacy in Germany* (1897–98); *Benedek's Literary Remains* (1901); *The Crimean War and Austrian Policy* (1907); *Austria from 1848 to 1860* (incomplete: the first volume, 1909; the first part of the second volume, 1912); *Historical Essays* (1919); and *The Age of Imperialism*, which was completed after his death by Professor A. F. Přibram (1920–22).

The Struggle for Supremacy is undoubtedly Friedjung's greatest work, for in it he combined the accuracy and the gift of vivid narrative, which stamps all his work, with a deep emotional comprehension of both parties in the struggle. His account is impartial, but the impartiality is not due to aloofness; it springs from the fact that Friedjung sympathised with both combatants—he was on both sides at once. For Friedjung was by conviction a passionate German Austrian, proud of the great traditions of Germany, but equally proud of the great traditions of Austria. The War of 1866 laid the foundations of a united German Empire, such as German patriots had aspired to for years, and Bismarck, its architect, became the national hero of all Germans. Friedjung was no exception—he felt as German as any Prussian or Bavarian—and Bismarck is clearly the hero of *The Struggle for Supremacy*. But Friedjung was also

ix

an Austrian and, while he rejoiced that Germany had achieved unification, he could not but grieve that it should be achieved at the expense of Austria. It was impossible for Friedjung to find an Austrian statesman whom he could set against the titanic figure of Bismarck, for, though he made some attempt to turn Benedek into his hero, he was too clear-sighted to believe that there was anything of a real hero in that conscientious, second-rate officer. What Friedjung sets against the personal greatness of Bismarck is the impersonal greatness of the Austrian tradition and of the cause of the German Austrians.

The essence of the German Austrian position had been the desire to have the best of both worlds—to occupy the leading position in both Germany and the Austrian Empire. This dualism enabled Friedjung to write a great book, but in political life it bound him to a cause without a future. As Friedjung says, the German Austrians were the real losers in the War of 1866. The German Austrian problem was a direct outcome of the rise of nationalism at the beginning of the nineteenth century; until then there had been nothing paradoxical or unusual in the German Austrians being part of Germany (or rather the Holy Roman Empire) and at the same time being connected with other nationalities outside it. But the belief that states ought to have a national basis, that tremendous legacy of the French Revolution, struck at the very root of the German Austrian position. Metternich realised clearly that nationalism would destroy the Austrian Empire, and for this reason he persuaded the Emperor Francis to refuse the crown of Germany when it was offered to him in 1815; quite deliberately Metternich was preparing the way for a non-national Austrian Empire, contrasting with and so preventing the national German state. The liberals who sat in the Austrian Parliament of 1848 were equally realistic: caring for Austria as much as Metternich did, they too recognised that the survival of the Austrian Empire was only possible on a non-

national basis, and that basis they found in a free co-opera-
tion between the races, a co-operation which produced the
Kremsier Constitution of 1849. Nor did on the other hand
those German Austrians, who refused to abandon their
German nationalism, shirk the conclusion that this and the
Austrian Empire were incompatible; the destruction of the
Austrian Empire was the price for the achievement of the
national ambitions and that price they were prepared to pay.

But after the failure of the revolution of 1848 the German
Austrians made their great, their disastrous, mistake. They
gave up the struggle against the dynasty and began to co-
operate with it. The success of the dynasty had been everywhere so overwhelming that it seemed useless to stand out
against it; with short-sighted subtlety the German Austrians
now supported the Empire in the hope that they would one
day become the heirs of the Habsburgs as completely as the
French Revolution had been of the Bourbons. Henceforth
they believed that it was in their interests to support the
dynastic claims. They allowed their national feeling to be
diverted into the dynastic quarrel with Prussia and their
liberalism dwindled into an acceptance of the imperial theory
that the revolution had destroyed all the traditional rights
of the other nationalities. The central parliament, which
Schmerling set up in 1861, was as illegal and as artificial as
the absolutism it supplanted; but the Germans participated
in it because they believed that the parliamentary game,
weighted as it was in their favour, would give them supremacy
throughout the Empire. Similarly they supported Francis
Joseph's claim to supremacy in Germany in the belief that
Habsburg supremacy would mean supremacy for them.

There was a brief moment when Schmerling seemed to be
on the point of realising the German Austrian ambition of a
Germany united under Austria and an Austria united under
the Germans. But Schmerling's failure was complete even
before the War of 1866. The Meeting of the Princes at Frankfort in 1863 was the end of Austria s attempt to satisfy

German national feeling instead of the beginning, and hence-forth Austria confined herself to a conservative insistence on her traditional rights. Equally great was Schmerling's failure in Austria: in 1865 Schmerling was dismissed, the central parliament he had established was "suspended", and his successor Belcredi planned to remodel Austria on a federal basis. The decline of the German Austrians was confirmed and accentuated by the War of 1866. The leadership of Germany passed irrevocably to Prussia and the German Austrians were excluded for the first time from the national fold. Almost simultaneously they were dethroned from their predominating position in the Austrian Empire—Hungary was entirely removed from their influence and the Germans in the Vienna Parliament were allowed merely to acquiesce in the Compromise, after the negotiations between the Emperor and the Magyars had been completed. Under this double shock the German Austrians moderated their ambitions: they no longer hoped to rule all Germany and all Austria, they would be content if they could remain predominant in the western, non-Hungarian, half of the Austrian Empire. But soon their position was challenged even here—at first a German Ministry was in power, but in 1879 Francis Joseph broke with the German nationalists and appointed Count Taaffe, a German conservative, as Prime Minister, with a policy favourable to the Slavs. Francis Joseph disliked the liberalism of the Germans; moreover he believed that they would remain loyal whatever happened, whereas the Slavs needed conciliating if they were to be kept within the Empire.

Friedjung was one of the first victims of the new policy. In 1873 he had been appointed Professor at the School of Commerce in Vienna, and he combined his academic duties with active participation in politics. In a pamphlet on the Compromise with Hungary, published in 1877, he argued that the Austrian Empire was too much under the domina-tion of the Magyars and that Austrian policy should be

directed rather to a close co-operation with the German
Empire, and to conciliation of the Germans at home. This
pamphlet met with the disapproval of the new Ministry,
despite the conclusion of the alliance with Germany, and in
1879 Friedjung was dismissed. Thus forced into political life,
Friedjung played a leading part in the discussions on future
policy which now took place among the German Austrians.

The German Austrians were still shaken and bewildered
by their defeat; they could no longer drift on without examining their position, and it was increasingly necessary for
them to decide exactly what they desired in the future.
They had lost their dominating position in the Austrian
Empire, but they still reaped the advantages of being members of a great empire and they were not yet ready to see
that empire destroyed in the name of German nationalism;
moreover the worst that could befall them within the Empire
was the possibility of being put on an equality with the
Czechs in Bohemia, whereas in a united German Reich there
was the certainty of being subordinated to the Prussians.
The German Austrians still wanted to preserve the Empire,
but they were not prepared to sacrifice their nationalism in
favour of the imperial idea and become Austrians pure and
simple, co-operating with other Austrians of whatever race.
Centuries of German predominance could not be so easily
dismissed and the German Austrians still tried to make the
best of both worlds. The crude assertion of cultural superiority to the other races of the Empire was modified; the
German Austrians now claimed the task of educating their
fellow Austrians in modern ideas of liberalism and freedom.
But that education was to be conducted by the method of
entrusting the state to German nationalists and securing a
permanent German majority in Parliament.

In 1880 Friedjung, in co-operation with Georg von
Schönerer, later on the leader of the extreme Pan-Germans
in Austria, and Viktor Adler, subsequently the founder
of the Austrian Social Democratic party, produced the

xiv STRUGGLE FOR SUPREMACY IN GERMANY

Linz programme as a basis for the future policy of the German Austrians. It is ironical that of these three German nationalists two—Adler and Friedjung—were Jews, particularly ironical in Friedjung's case because he laid such emphasis on his being a German. Friedjung had no desire for the Jews to continue as a separate people; he believed that they should be absorbed into the nationalities among whom they lived. But Friedjung's race did in fact influence and warp his political career, for it made him overrate the ease with which the Germans could dominate and control the other races of the Empire. Friedjung regarded himself as a German, but he was only a German by adoption: he had become a German, because he valued German culture, and the process was no less deliberate for being subconscious. He therefore tended to expect a similar subconscious recognition of German superiority from the other races and he could not understand the reluctance of the Czechs, the Slovaks, or the Croats to follow his example.

The Linz programme set out to revive the primacy of the German Austrians in the Empire by securing for them the backing of Germany. Galicia and Dalmatia, the two extreme provinces of the Empire, were to be given a separate position within the Monarchy; the rest of the Monarchy west of the Leitha (that is excluding Hungary) was to be made more liberal and more centralised, with a suffrage so arranged as to secure a permanent German majority; the entire Monarchy was then to be bound to Germany by a tariff union, a common coinage, and a perpetual alliance, voted by the parliaments of both countries. "The two empires of the German nation are to be united as the firm bulwark of European peace." The German Austrians would not recover the dominant position in Germany and Austria to which they had once aspired, but they would be the hyphen, the essential link, between the two empires, and their divided loyalty would be no longer a source of weakness, but the very force which would hold the whole structure together.

The Linz programme, the work of Friedjung more than of any other one man, was in 1882 adopted by the new German Nationalist party as its statement of policy with the addition of the single clause—"No Jew can be a member of the German Nationalist party". Despite this, Friedjung co-operated with the party and in 1885 actually became for a short time the editor of the *Deutsche Zeitung*, the party paper. But the new party was very far removed from Fried-jung's idealism; it was a nationalist party pure and simple, and it objected to Friedjung not only for being a Jew, but almost as much for being a liberal. It was not long before Friedjung was driven from his editorial post and for the rest of his life he earned his living as a free-lance journalist, mostly with contributions to the German press. Friedjung did not cease to be a convinced German Austrian, but he no longer took part in day-to-day politics; the loss of his regular employment gave him more time for historical work and it was in the years immediately after his retirement that *The Struggle for Supremacy* was planned and written.

Friedjung had at first intended to write a history of parlia-mentary life in Austria since the establishment of the Dual Monarchy in 1867 — little more in fact than a glorified political pamphlet; but the fortunate chance of access to new sources of information—Benedek's private papers, and the archives of the War Office, thrown open by an excep-tionally enlightened minister—diverted Friedjung's atten-tion to the struggle between Austria and Prussia, and he supplemented this written material with interviews with the surviving participants in the period—Bismarck, Moltke, Rechberg, and others. It was another stroke of fortune that Bismarck had just been dismissed from office, and Friedjung therefore found him eager to give the fullest details of his policy before the War of 1866. It is true that certain sources remained closed: no information was forthcoming from Bel-credi or from the family of Esterhazy—on the ground that they were unwilling to reveal any secrets so long as Francis

Joseph lived—and the archives of the Foreign Office were inaccessible. These archives are now open and it is here that Friedjung's account stands in greatest need of supplement; but research has shown that, while the new material can add much of value to Friedjung's narrative, it does nothing to alter the general outline.

The Struggle for Supremacy was primarily a great piece of historical research, but it was also a continuation of Friedjung's political work in another form. For it was designed partly as a plea for the rehabilitation of the German Austrians and it was published in 1897, just at the crisis of their fate. The Taaffe Ministry, which had come into power in 1879, had set out to achieve a parliamentary majority by balancing the nationalities against one another; as Taaffe said, it was his object to keep all the nationalities in an equal state of moderate dissatisfaction. This was a policy of expediency, which made no attempt to provide for a future when the dissatisfaction would cease to be moderate; but it was at any rate a parliamentary policy—it was based on the assumption that Austria was now a constitutional country and that the government of the day must have the support of a parliamentary majority, even though this majority was often created by questionable means. So long as the Taaffe Ministry existed, there was still a hope that the national problems would be fought out within the limits of a parliamentary struggle and that parliament would represent a central, imperial authority which the nationalities would respect. But the bases of parliamentary life in Austria were becoming increasingly frail—the national parties turned more and more to an attitude of destructive opposition, and in 1893 a coalition of Czech conservatives and German nationalists placed the Taaffe Ministry in a permanent minority. Taaffe's resignation could have led to a better system if the coalition had been itself able to form a government; but the Czechs and Germans hated each other even more than they hated Taaffe, and had combined against him only because he had not been prepared to subordinate his policy to either of them.

For thirty years Francis Joseph had ruled Austria as a constitutional monarch; he had never believed in parliament, but it had given him the control of the army and of foreign policy, which was all he desired. But now the parliamentary system seemed to have broken down and no stable government could be built up. Francis Joseph therefore determined to break with the system of parliamentary government and to appoint a minister who would impose order on the nationalities from above, by imperial, not parliamentary, authority. Such a system of imperial centralism (though on a greater scale, for it had included Hungary) had already been attempted in Francis Joseph's reign by Alexander Bach. Then the Germans had grumbled at the denial of constitutional rights, but their opposition had been half-hearted, since Bach was a German pursuing a German policy. The man chosen now by Francis Joseph was Badeni, a Pole, who had acquired as Governor of Galicia the reputation of a "strong man". To be dictated to by a Pole was more than the Germans could stomach, and they would have opposed Badeni whatever his actual measures. But Badeni challenged German nationalism directly by the language ordinance, issued in 1897, by which Czech was placed practically on an equality with German as an official language in Bohemia. The Germans were thus threatened with complete exclusion from the civil services in Bohemia, for, whereas the Czechs were bilingual, few Germans would condescend to learn Czech.

The idea underlying the language ordinance was the same as that which underlay the Taaffe Ministry—that the Czechs needed conciliating if they were to remain loyal, whereas the Germans would have to remain loyal in any case for fear something worse befell them. The Germans had indeed often insisted that they were the one race loyal to the Empire as such, and this necessarily implied loyalty even when the Empire acted against their particular interests. Even now the Germans claimed that German was the Austrian "state language" (a doctrine which Friedjung attempted without much success to defend historically), and that in fighting the ordinance they were fighting for the Austrian "state idea". In actual fact, what the Germans meant by the "state idea" was that the Germans were a superior people to whom Austria in some way belonged; the other nationalities were to give up their national claims for the sake of Austria, this supernational entity, but the Germans were to preserve their national privileges intact. The contradictions of the German Austrian position were thus revealed: if Austria was a German state, the other nationalities could not be expected to remain loyal; if it were not a German state, the Germans must stand on an equal footing with the rest.

No doubt the Germans genuinely cared for the Austrian "state idea", but their struggle against the language ordinance went far to wreck the Austrian state altogether. For the Germans, the founders and upholders of the parliamentary system, broke with the traditions of parliamentary opposition and thus set a most damaging example to the other nationalities. In parliament the Germans resorted to the most violent obstruction; police had to be called in and there was a wild scene of free fights in the Chamber itself. Great crowds demonstrated in the streets of Vienna and in the other German towns; German Austria as a whole was almost in a state of rebellion. These demonstrations achieved part of their aim—Badeni was dismissed, but the language ordinance was not recalled (though it was later modified); and the Badeni period left to the Empire a most disastrous legacy.

If Badeni had succeeded, parliamentary life would have been destroyed, but the Empire would have been immeasurably strengthened; it would have shown itself to be stronger than the nationalities, the balancing and determining force, which Joseph II and Schwarzenberg had meant it to be. If, on the other hand, Badeni had been defeated by a coalition of convinced constitutionalists, then parliament would have been established once and for all as the vital and central force of the whole Empire. Neither of these things happened. Parliament did indeed remain in existence right up to 1914, but it was an empty form, and, under the guise of emergency decrees, Austria was governed bureaucratically and despotically. Parliamentary government had been destroyed, and destroyed by the Germans, its originators; henceforth there was no chance of a compromise between the nationalities. Nor did the Emperor gain what the parliament lost; Badeni's failure convinced Francis Joseph that any active, constructive policy would arouse opposition and would probably bring the whole imperial edifice to the ground. Francis Joseph was now an old man and his main anxiety was to make the Empire last his time; by pursuing an unobtrusive policy of expedients he did indeed keep the Empire in being, but it was little more than an empty shell, which would fall in the first storm.

The Struggle for Supremacy was concluded just after the fall of Badeni, and it is no detraction from its greatness as a work of history to suggest that much of it was written with the events of the Badeni period in mind. The emphasis which Friedjung lays on the unshakable loyalty and self-sacrifice of the Germans in 1866 is only to be expected; but Friedjung goes further and places the entire responsibility for the defeat of 1866 on the reactionary policy pursued by the dynasty ever since the time of the Counter-Reformation (with a certain interruption in the eighteenth century). Friedjung shared the German nationalist view that the terms liberal and German were synonymous: when he is criticising the anti-liberal policy of the Austrian Government he is thus censuring it for its refusal to depend solely on the Germans, and is implying that a Government based on the Germans would have prevented the catastrophe.

Friedjung's convictions appear still more clearly in his judgement on individual statesmen: his appraisal of them is determined by how nearly their policy approximates to the Linz programme. Rechberg comes in for an undue share of praise (perhaps the one grave misjudgement in the book) simply because his timorous avoidance of a conflict with Prussia inclined him towards a co-operation of the two German powers such as Friedjung desired. Schmerling is criticised for his hostility to Prussia, but on the whole he escapes lightly because his domestic policy was based upon a German predominance throughout the Empire. The full weight of Friedjung's censure is reserved for the forerunners of Badeni, who rejected both liberalism and German nationalism,—for Belcredi's "Ministry of Counts", and above all for Esterhazy. The low estimate Friedjung makes of the ability of these statesmen is thoroughly justified—and Badeni was of even poorer quality than Belcredi or Esterhazy. But one has an uneasy feeling that, if they had been abler, Friedjung would have disapproved of them still more. These feudal conservatives were no doubt ruling in the interest of their class; but the best of them recognised (what Friedjung never did) that Austria could not be based upon nationalism, whether German, Magyar, or Czech, and supported a political feudalism because they saw in it the only means of holding the Empire together. It is easy to dismiss Metternich and his conservative followers as pure reactionaries, but it is also false. They hated liberalism because it attacked their own position; but they hated it also because it threatened the Austrian Empire, which, they believed, had still important functions to perform. The Empire had lost its original justification—the defence of Europe against the Turk; and the alternative provided by Metternich, the defence of Europe against France and the Revolution, was rendered unreal (if it ever had been real) by nineteenth-century political developments. The Empire needed a new function, and enlightened Austrians believed that they had found that

function in a policy of economic amelioration. That this
policy was not altogether illusory is shown by the support
it received: even the German Austrians were attracted, even
Friedjung was tempted to become an Austrian pure and
simple.

By 1897 the German Austrians had moved far from
the dominating position and overweening claims of the
Schmerling epoch. Their domination was gone, and they
were finding it difficult to resist complete equality with the
other races of the Empire. In despair the more extreme
Germans, under the leadership of Schönerer, abandoned the
idea of Austria altogether and subordinated everything to
their nationality. The Habsburgs, the Austrian Empire, and
the Roman Catholic Church—everything that stood in the
way of complete absorption, cultural and political, into
Germany—were to go. The German nationalists evolved the
slogan, *"Ein Reich, ein Kaiser, eine Religion"*, and Schönerer
infuriated the Austrian Parliament by answering the address
of loyalty to Francis Joseph with a cry of "Long live the
house of Hohenzollern!" Such extreme nationalism could
have but a limited appeal; it was strong only on the cultural
frontiers—in Bohemia and Styria—where everything was
overshadowed by the daily contact between German and
Slav. In Vienna the differences between Austria and Germany could not be so easily ignored; Vienna was still the
capital of a great empire, with all the advantages which
that implied, and the inhabitants had no inclination deliberately to depress Vienna to the status of a provincial town.
The events of 1897 had shown beyond mistake that insistence on German nationality would wreck the Empire, and
that was a price which many Germans were unwilling to
pay. Rather late in the day they drew back and some of
them began to turn half-heartedly to an imperial policy,
which should transcend nationalism.

Clearly such a policy was the only one which might have
saved the Empire. The great destructive force was the

ambitions of the rival nationalities, whether dominant or subordinate, and everything which cut across the national divisions was, consciously or not, a source of strength to the Empire. The old Austria had been clerical, because the Church provided such an international loyalty, and, in the years before the war, the Socialist party, under the leadership of Viktor Adler, was one of the principal supports of the Empire, again because of its international appeal. The introduction of universal suffrage at the express wish of the Emperor in 1907 was a deliberate attempt to utilise these international forces: Socialism and Clericalism would, it was hoped, become the dominant issues, and the disruptive nationalism of the middle classes would be submerged in the struggle between the two, in the vast game of *rouge et noir*, which would take place throughout the Empire. There was no contradiction in Jews participating in such an international policy, and it is significant that it was a Jew, Joseph Redlich, whom some observers before the war regarded as one of the few men capable of saving the Austrian Empire.

The best Austrians of this school had a dispassionate and conscientious spirit similar to that of a good official of the League of Nations (which closely resembled their ideal for the Austrian Empire), and they believed that the only answer to the increasing danger of nationalism, especially the nationalism of the Southern Slavs, was a bold policy of economic and cultural well-being. They agreed with the Government that the first step must be the reassertion of Austrian power, and even the most enlightened of them welcomed the annexation of Bosnia and Herzegovina by Aehrenthal in 1908 as the opening of a new era of energy and reform in Austrian policy. But they were not content with a policy of prestige: the Southern Slavs were first to be cowed, but then they were to be won over by sweeping reforms. Austria was to free the land from the tangled and corrupt legacy of Turkish rule and was to introduce a modern system of education. The condition of the Southern Slavs inside the Austrian Empire would then be so obviously superior to that of the Serbs outside that nationalist propaganda would lose its sting and Serbia herself would welcome inclusion within the Austrian tariff system. This policy of efficient government and positive amelioration had been tried often enough in Austria (and not only in Austria) to resist nationalist movements—particularly of course in Lombardy in the days before 1848. Indeed the programme of reforms, which Baernreither, one of the leaders of this group of Austrian statesmen, outlined for Bosnia in 1910—settlement of the land, improved communications, education, and more power for the Governor—is almost word for word the programme which Ficquelmont, Metternich's second-in-command, proposed for Lombardy in 1847. Take for instance this passage of Baernreither's memorandum, change Bosnia-Herzegovina to Lombardo-Venetia, Serbia to Piedmont, and the whole thing is applicable to the days before 1848:

If we can make the material existence of the people of Bosnia and Herzegovina better than that enjoyed by their brothers in Serbia; if we can effectively promote and maintain order, justice, and popular education, while sparing religious feelings, not injuring national idiosyncrasies, and, scrupulously avoiding any sort of brandishing of the torch, intervene firmly when there is anything dangerous on foot —then we shall win even the Serbian section of the population over to our side.[1]

It is perhaps doubtful whether an alien government, however efficient and however reforming, can permanently provide any real answer to the appeal of nationalism; that self-government is better than good government is no new discovery. But it is fair to say that neither in Lombardy nor in Bosnia was the reforming policy ever really tried— in Lombardy from sheer inertia and lack of initiative, in Bosnia because the Government had no real belief in reform. Aehrenthal was ready to talk about the benefits of Austrian

[1] Baernreither, *Fragments of a Political Diary*, 81.

rule in order to please the Austrian liberals; but he was secretly convinced that the Serbs, both within and without the monarchy, would regard any concessions as weakness and that they would understand no argument but force. In any case reforms in Bosnia would immediately lead to a demand for reforms from the Croats under Hungarian rule and were therefore bitterly opposed by the Magyars; the Hungarian problem was serious enough, and a quarrel over Croatia might well lead to the break-up of the Empire. It is easy now to see that Austrian statesmen should have braved Hungarian opposition, for the conciliation of the Southern Slavs offered the one chance of preservation for the Empire; but they were perhaps right in fearing Magyar disaffection even more than Croat. The irreparable mistake in this, as in many other problems, was made not in 1908 or in 1909, but by Francis Joseph forty years before, when he had chosen the easy solution of satisfying the Magyars by giving them a free hand with the Croats.

Indeed it is no exaggeration to say that Francis Joseph did more than any other man to bring the Empire to ruin. Throughout his reign he cared only for his military power and his prestige abroad. He is reported to have said to Theodore Roosevelt: "You see in me the last monarch of the old school", and he was right; he was the last monarch who believed that it was the duty of his peoples to sacrifice themselves for the dynasty, but not the duty of the dynasty to do anything for the peoples, and the last monarch to play fast and loose with his obligations towards his subjects, because he believed that he was above all ordinary standards. Francis II, on hearing someone described as an Austrian patriot, answered, "But is he a patriot for me?" Francis Joseph never even asked such a question, because it did not occur to him that there could be such a thing as Austrian patriotism distinct from loyalty to him personally. The dynasty did indeed represent an imperial element cutting across the lines of national division; but, as Maria Theresa and Joseph II recognised, it could be a binding force only so long as it brought well-being to its subjects. Francis Joseph, by his concentration on dynastic interests and his short-sighted policy of allying himself with the dominant nationalities in order to safeguard his military power, used up the capital of imperial loyalty which he had inherited from his reforming ancestors. Francis Joseph took from his subjects and gave nothing back; it was therefore inevitable that by the end of his reign his subjects had lost interest in the Empire.

In countering nationalism with the imperial idea there was a great danger of emphasising the Emperor at the expense of the Empire, and this danger was particularly great for the Germans: their conception of the Empire had rested on domination, their domination over the other nationalities, and when they abandoned this idea it was not to turn to free co-operation, but to another domination, the domination of the Emperor. This change was the more startling in that it was the German liberals who had been most critical of the Emperor in the earlier years of the reign; their conversion did not ring true—it looked as though they were currying favour with the Emperor in order to regain under cover of his authority the supremacy which they could not attain by their own strength. The Germans were no doubt genuinely convinced that the Southern Slavs would be happier within the Austrian Empire than united with Serbia; but they hardly troubled to conceal their belief that the Southern Slavs would not be tempted by these prospects and that the Germans alone could be relied upon for unquestioning support of the Empire.

Friedjung was among the most enthusiastic supporters of Aehrenthal's policy and a staunch advocate of reform. But it was not without satisfaction that he received from Aehrenthal documents purporting to prove that the Serbo-Croat leaders were engaged in a treasonable conspiracy against the Empire; for the more disloyal the Croats were, the more the loyalty of the Germans would stand out in contrast. Aehrenthal asked Friedjung to write a series of articles based on these documents, and Friedjung, with the whole weight of his authority as an historian, did all that Aehrenthal could have wished—indeed more than Aehrenthal wished, for the articles were so violent that Aehrenthal had them stopped after the first number. Friedjung not only abandoned all attempt at impartiality, he abandoned too all sense of criticism and vouched for originals in Serbian which he had never seen and which he could not have read if he had seen. The Croat leaders brought an action, and in the ensuing "Friedjung trial" it was shown that the documents were forgeries of a particularly crude nature.

It was said at the time that the forgeries had been made in the Austrian legation at Belgrade and, although this is probably untrue, the Austro-Hungarian Foreign Office undoubtedly knew that the documents were forged; Aehrenthal himself may not have been so sure of their nature, but he certainly had some doubts of their authenticity and could have had those doubts confirmed if he had bothered to enquire. The main guilt must therefore rest with Aehrenthal and the Foreign Office, but Friedjung too must be condemned for having accepted documents as authentic merely because they were given him by the Foreign Minister of the Empire. Baernreither, who acted as mediator between Friedjung and the Croat leaders, passed a very fair judgement on the affair: "Friedjung has been shamefully used by Aehrenthal. But he laid himself open to such abuse by his fantastic loyalty, his credulousness, and his overweening conceit".[1] The contrast between Friedjung the historian and Friedjung the politician is at first sight overwhelming. Friedjung had chronicled the incapacity and folly of the Austrian Foreign Office under Buol or Mensdorff; now he acted as though a miraculous change had come over it in the interval. Friedjung had castigated severely the blind arrogance

[1] Baernreither, *Fragments of a Political Diary*, 104.

of Biegeleben or Esterhazy, when they talked of giving the Prussians a sound thrashing; but he applauded Aehrenthal, when he used exactly similar language about the Serbs. Friedjung had seen the wisdom of compromising, as Rechberg advocated, in 1863; but he was all for bullying and the mailed fist in 1909. It was not so much that Friedjung was incapable of judging contemporary events, although that is a common failing of historians; it was that for the German movement Friedjung had the key, and for the Slav he had not. Friedjung realised what the German movement was, because he was himself by sympathy a German, and his national feeling enabled him to appreciate the strength and, one might say, the sacredness of the German cause. With the Slavs he had no emotional link and therefore their nationalism appeared to him merely as a treasonable conspiracy. The one is indeed the complement of the other. *The Struggle for Supremacy* is shot through and through with emotional appreciation for both sides and it was this very emotion which prevented Friedjung from understanding the first elements of the Southern Slav question. He wrote badly and foolishly about the Croats; but that cannot lessen the greatness of what he wrote about the rise of Germany.

What the policy of prestige did not do, its outcome, the Great War, did—it raised the German Austrians once more to the first place in the Empire. The alliance with Germany was made so close by the exigencies of war that the old days of the German Confederation seemed almost to have come again. The idea of *Mittel-Europa* was revived, and there was bound to be revived with it the idea of the predominance of the German Austrians, for on them the scheme would turn. Such indeed was the basis of a political manifesto in which Friedjung joined in 1915—Germany and Austria-Hungary were to form a close confederation; Serbia was to be absorbed into the Austrian Empire, at any rate militarily and economically; and the Southern Slavs might later form a third unit within the Habsburg Empire, when they had given sufficient proof of their loyalty. The national cultures were to be tolerated and encouraged, but German was to be the official language throughout the Empire. The plan is very similar to the Linz programme of 1880, and it undoubtedly represents the permanent elements in Friedjung's political programme. There is no longer much talk of reform or of the cultural mission of the German Austrians—they were to predominate, because they had the power of Germany behind them and because they would be the link between the two empires. The old ambition of predominating in both Germany and Austria had indeed gone; but the German Austrians claimed the first place in Austria right down to the fall of the Monarchy.

The break-up of the Empire seemed to have solved the old problem of the dual nature of the German Austrians. They could never have brought themselves voluntarily to renounce all that was meant by the Empire—the predominant position and all the advantages Vienna enjoyed as the capital; but with the Empire destroyed there seemed to be nothing now to prevent the German Austrians staking all on their nationality, as the Pan-Germans had advocated. Their nationalism was indeed all they had left and it is therefore no wonder that even in the darkest hour of defeat they desired incorporation in the Reich. That unification was denied them by allied dictation; but to all German Austrians after the war it seemed only a matter of time. Almost the last words that Friedjung wrote expressed this belief:[1] "Now that Austria has fallen, our whole feeling is concentrated in affection for the race which was the kernel of the old Monarchy and so for the German nation as a whole. At present there are obstacles in the way, but in the end we shall return to the mother-country whence one of the best stocks has migrated to the south-east in the pursuance of a historic mission." It is no injustice to Friedjung to say that he was more at home with German nationalism than with

[1] In the preface to his *Historical Essays*.

the dispassionate and enlightened ideals of the best Austrians. Friedjung himself is the best illustration of why these
Austrians failed: for the Austrian Empire to survive there
had to be an abandonment of nationalism, and if Friedjung,
a cultured, intelligent man, could not bring himself to this,
small wonder that the less cultured, ordinary subjects of
the Empire clung to their nationality. On that rock—the
refusal of the nationalities to compromise or to abate their
claims—the Empire foundered.

It would be a dangerous over-simplification to believe that
the break-up of the Austrian Empire has in any way solved
the Austrian question. Despite the expectations of 1918,
the union of German Austria with Germany has not been
achieved; but there can be little doubt that, were certain
extraneous elements removed—the interference of certain
powers and the present uncivilised system of rule in Germany—the Germans of Austria would be as content within
a national German state as are the Germans of Bavaria or of
Saxony. Yet even the absorption of German Austria into
Germany would solve the problem only for the Germans
within the present Austrian state and not for the Germans
outside it, nor for the other races which once composed the
Austrian Empire. It is this, quite as much as the character
of the present rulers of Germany, which inclines some German Austrians against unification with Germany, for they
hope still to revive the international organisation once
secured by the Austrian Empire. In that empire there was
never a free co-operation of peoples, but there was at any
rate some co-operation on however coercive a basis, and to
that extent better than no co-operation at all. Before the
war the German Austrians had the opportunity of leading
the way to a system of freedom and equality among the
nationalities; that opportunity they refused to take, and
the events of the last twenty years have made the situation
infinitely more difficult. Nevertheless the opportunity is still
there, once the German Austrians make it clear that they

have abandoned all belief in their cultural superiority over the races of the other states. If, however, the German Austrians try to revive the elements which held the old Empire together—clericalism, the dynasty, and the co-operation of the upper classes against the lower—then the new system will fail as the old system failed, and a revived Habsburg Empire will produce what the old Habsburg Empire produced—a great European war. The lesson of the pre-war years and of the break-down of the Empire is plain—that only a federation based upon equality and free co-operation can be either fruitful or permanent.   That lesson was not heeded by Austrian statesmen before the war; it was not heeded by the Allied statesmen in 1919; and there is no sign that it is being heeded to-day by the politicians in Vienna. Changes there may well be, but there can be little doubt that any new settlement of the Danube valley, however different its protective colouring of professed ideas, will be based like the present settlement and the Austrian Empire upon force, and that it will be as unstable and as productive of European disturbances.

The best thing about the old Empire was that it did produce some men, however few, who saw beyond national rivalries, and who tried to make Austria something more than a machine for building up a large army. It was Friedjung's greatest defect that he had little appreciation for this element in Austria—he saw only the indifference to nationalism, he ignored what was to be substituted for it, and he confused the feudal opponents of nationalism with the military bullies who ruled Austria from 1849 to 1860 and from 1906 to 1914. This is the one great deduction from Friedjung's greatness as an historian, and once this has been said there is little to add of *The Struggle for Supremacy* except unstinted praise. It was said of Burke that he gave up to party what was meant for mankind. Of Friedjung the opposite is true. Driven from politics against his will, he set out to continue his political activity on another field, but he produced

instead a great work of history. There was no future in
politics for Friedjung's divided loyalty; but it was this
divided loyalty, which enabled him to write the best and
most impartial account of one of the most decisive and vital
struggles in the nineteenth century. The conflict of 1866
marked the beginning of an epoch in which Friedjung was
still living when he wrote this book. That epoch was closed
in 1918, but the problems with which Friedjung deals were
not solved. *The Struggle for Supremacy* is primarily great
history; but it is still what Friedjung designed it to be—an
introduction to contemporary politics—and such it will
remain so long as there is an Austrian question.

A. J. P. TAYLOR

Three Gates, Higher Disley,
      Cheshire
   January 3, 1935

CHAPTER I

THE RECOVERY AND DEFEAT OF AUSTRIA (1849–1859)

IT was a forecast of the future development of Germany, when, on April 3, 1849, the first German Parliament offered the Imperial Crown to Frederick William IV, King of Prussia. Yet Frederick William could not accept this supreme symbol of monarchic power at the hands of the revolution; for he believed that monarchy rested on divine right and was to be maintained by the sword. Thus, not for the first time in German history, a dogma barred the way to action. When one of the liberals advised him to accept the Imperial Crown, the King said: "If you could have addressed yourself to Frederick the Great, he'd have been your man; but I am not a great ruler".

In the old legend, the man who attempts to penetrate the secret of the veiled picture has to pay for his prying with something worse than death—a joyless, sterile life. Heinrich von Gagern[1] and his friends, when the King failed them, became political shadows—figures more tragic in German history than even the fallen great revolutionaries in that of France. Their political ideas proved ultimately victorious; but, through no fault of their own, they themselves were precluded from translating them into practice.

Frederick William did not want to let the great oppor-

---

[1] [Heinrich von Gagern was the leader of the moderate liberals in the Frankfort Parliament, who wished to unite Germany under the Prussian Crown.—Translator.]

1

tunity slip altogether. It was his plan to achieve the unity
of Germany, not by war or by revolution of the peoples
against their rulers—for that he regarded as a sin against
divine right—but rather by a peaceful solution, by negotiations with Austria and agreements with the German princes.
His mind was full of fantastic illusions about the future of
Germany. The prior rights of the House of Habsburg filled
him with mystical awe; to them he would have left the
throne of Imperial Germany. On the other hand, he wanted
to unite all Germany outside Austria in a closer federation
under his own leadership: he was to be put at the head of the
federal forces and would then be content with the rank of
Imperial Vicar and "Commander-in-Chief of the Germans",
or at most of King of Germany. In May 1849, he made a
proposal of this kind to Prince Schwarzenberg in Vienna,
though, on the advice of his ministers, divested of his
romantic political ideas. A German Federal State was to be
set up under the leadership of Prussia, which could then
conclude an indissoluble offensive and defensive alliance
with Austria. The details of this plan were remarkable. The
union of the two powers was to have a common representation abroad; and the ministers at the foreign courts were to
be appointed by each side in turn according to a fixed rule.
It so happened that just at that time Prussia was helping
the rulers of Saxony and Baden to suppress a rebellion which
they themselves could not master; and a number of German
states—among them Saxony and Hanover—accepted in
their panic this plan of a narrower federation; but before
long the kings began to search for a way of escape from such
distasteful commitments.

It hardly needed the genius of Prince Felix Schwarzenberg to defeat so visionary and hesitating a rival to Austria's
predominance. Schwarzenberg was unmoved by the King's
romantic plans; he had no sympathy with the idealistic
element in the German character and did not understand
the deeper forces which were to mould the future. He lived

in the present and made the most of it. Dispassionately he reckoned with the real factors in the situation—the intentions of the Tsar Nicholas, the characters of the German princes, and, above all, the military strength of the various states; and he determined, even at the risk of war, to reestablish Austrian supremacy in Germany. By making the most of Frederick William's horror of the revolution and of his subconscious dependence on Austria, he succeeded in shaking the King's belief in the policy on which he had embarked. The lesser German princes, in their distrust of Prussia, needed little encouragement to ally themselves more closely than ever to Austria and the Tsar supported Austria unhesitatingly.

Schwarzenberg left the King of Prussia no choice but to fight for the leadership of Germany or to give in. A war with Austria was contrary to all the political instincts both of the King and of his ministers, Brandenburg and Manteuffel. Austria could perhaps have been defeated by a revival of the revolution in Italy and Hungary; but Frederick William rejected such an idea with horror. Moreover his Minister of War, General Stockhausen, declared that the Prussian army was no match for Radetzky's veterans. The King preferred to give up his dreams; and at Olmütz[1] a penitent Manteuffel agreed to re-enter the German Diet. The Minister and his party, to which Bismarck still belonged, regarded the surrender as a necessary consequence of their political convictions; but in the eyes of Europe Prussia had suffered a severe diplomatic defeat.

Schwarzenberg had yet more ambitious plans; he wanted the whole Habsburg monarchy to be included in the German Confederation and in the Zollverein. In this way the armed forces of all Germany could be secured for the protection of the endangered Austrian possessions in the south and east.

[1] [By the Punctation of Olmütz, Prussia agreed to abandon her plans for a North German union under Prussian control and to return to the Diet of 1815, which Austria had revived.—Translator.]

He also intended to lessen the political power of Prussia by increasing that of the other four German kings; Germany, outside Austria and Prussia, was to be divided into four circles and each king would command the forces of his lesser neighbours. At the head of the Confederation there was to be a Directory, to control foreign affairs, commerce, and war. In this ruling committee, which was to consist of Austria, Prussia, the four kings, and, as a seventh member, the two Hesses, Schwarzenberg was confident of being able to secure a permanent majority for Austria. Representative government would be limited or abolished in all the states; the soldier was to rule.

This project took no account of the wishes of the people; and in any case the smaller kings would soon have allied themselves with Prussia to check the predominance of Austria. Schwarzenberg's plan had elements of greatness, but, like the Prussian plan, it could only be established on the battlefield. At the Dresden Conference the Austrian proposals were only half-heartedly supported by the smaller states and they were destroyed by the Prussian objections. Schwarzenberg had therefore to be content with the revival of the Diet. "Heaven knows", he wrote, "I am no admirer of the existing federal constitution; we have made a serious effort to create something real and practical; but if nothing comes of it, things must remain as they are, for a torn, threadbare coat is, at any rate, better than no coat at all. In my humble opinion, the Diet is a cumbersome, outworn instrument, totally unadapted to present circumstances; I think indeed that, at the first shock, from within or without, the shaky structure will collapse altogether."

In the Diet at Frankfort, Austria now commanded a majority, which in the following years weighed heavily on a humiliated Prussia. The Confederation, it is true, had only a shadowy existence and its decisions were usually concerned with matters of detail. But Schwarzenberg and his successors found an expression of Austrian greatness in making

Prussia conscious of her isolated position. Austria was within her rights in trying to guard her inherited powers; and it would have been a great and statesmanlike achievement to have created a lasting order in Central Europe by including Prussia in a Habsburg Empire of Germany. But, once Schwarzenberg's plan had failed, it was petty to aim at irritating and humiliating Prussia; and only Frederick William's unshakable faith in Austria could have stood it.

Prussia had dangerously revealed the objects of her ambition before she had the courage to give her full strength to their achievement. Frederick William's proposals, however timid, to form a closer German Federation under his leadership had left a feeling of apprehension in the little courts of Germany. Against this threat to their independence the less aggressive power of Austria seemed their only protection. For the German kings would never endure subordination to one of themselves; King William of Württemberg once said that he could, under compulsion, accept a Habsburg as Emperor, but never a Hohenzollern. Such was the hold Austria had over the German courts; yet how weak these bonds of mistrust and traditionalism were to prove!

Otto von Bismarck, the man who was to destroy Austria's position in Germany, was appointed Prussian Minister to the Federal Diet in August 1851, and at Frankfort, for eight years, he experienced the contempt with which Prussia was regarded. He did not come to Frankfort as an enemy of Austria. Like his fellow-nobles, he had welcomed the complete breach with the revolution of 1848 and the reconciliation with conservative Austria; he still believed that the relations between the two states could be restored to the harmony which had existed in the time of Metternich. It had then been the rule that neither of the two great powers made a proposal to the Confederation without first securing the agreement of the other. It was no part of the policy of either to canvass the votes of the small states, still less to use these votes to put the other in a minority. When Bismarck, on his entry into office, visited Prince Metternich at Johannisberg, the creator of the Confederation and the statesman who was to destroy it were agreed upon this conception. It was the sword of Prussia which protected the weak German princes against France; Bismarck, therefore, regarded it as an unseemly amusement for these princes, in peace-time, to ally themselves with Austria to outvote Prussia at the Diet. He knew that no Austrian statesman would ever allow the foreign policy of the Monarchy to be dictated in this way by a majority of the Confederation. Prussia, as an equal, ought to share with Austria the rule of Germany. The thousand-year-old Dualism of Germany, Bismarck once wrote to Manteuffel, was not to be removed by the device of majority decisions.

This policy of Bismarck's, which derived from the ideas of Frederick William and Manteuffel, was, however, faced with serious obstacles. Austria had reason to suspect that Prussia had only postponed her plans for German unity and the Austrian statesmen were therefore on the watch. Nor were they far wrong; for as early as 1851 Bismarck wrote to Manteuffel that, at the right time, Prussia must again attempt to unite Germany, in the more limited sense,[1] under her own leadership. Even the friendship of the Prussian conservatives for Austria could never be permanent so long as the German question remained unsolved.

For the Prussian representative at Frankfort this was a trying time. Even the social formalities of Count Thun, the Austrian Minister and President of the Diet, were designed to offend Bismarck, that proudest and most sensitive of men. Bismarck did indeed, as he later expressed it, manage to give the Count some social polish; but Thun, entirely in the spirit of Schwarzenberg's policy, continued to treat Prussia as an upstart. On one occasion he demanded that Prussia should abandon the tradition of Frederick the Great; whereupon Bismarck replied that, rather than advise such a policy, he

---

[1] [That is, Germany excluding Austria.—Translator.]

would recommend an appeal to the sword. "Count Thun",
Bismarck wrote, "compared Prussia to a man who had once
won a hundred thousand guelders in a lottery and now
counted on it as part of his annual income. I replied that, if
people in Vienna shared his views, I could see that Prussia
would have to try the said lottery once more; whether she
would win was in God's hands."

When Schwarzenberg died on April 5, 1852, the conservative alliance between Austria, Russia, and Prussia, that important heritage of Metternich's policy, was still in existence,
and even Bismarck had not clearly determined to destroy
it; it was on this alliance that the supremacy of Austria in
Germany and Italy rested. Metternich had not created the
Holy Alliance merely as a protection for conservatism, but
far more as the corner-stone of the power of Austria in
Europe. In this he was following the great traditions which
for centuries had dominated the policy of Austria, and which
often brought success even to her more feeble rulers. Since
the days of Maximilian I, every Emperor and minister who
determined Austrian policy had been firmly convinced that
Austria needed strong alliances to make up for the reverses
in war, which she so often encountered. The policy of
alliances was the continuation of the policy of marriages, by
which Austria had been founded.

To show the evil which sprang from leaving this path is
in fact the theme of this book; the policy which the masters
of Austrian diplomacy had laid down for their successors
must therefore be considered. For a hundred years, throughout the time of Eugene of Savoy and until the days of
Frederick the Great, Austria was in alliance with the mari-
time powers, England and Holland; with the help of this
alliance not only Belgium and Italy, but indeed the whole
inheritance of Maria Theresa was defended. It was Kaunitz's
master-stroke to raise against Frederick II a coalition of
practically the whole continent. Metternich was equally

successful when he followed the same path by cultivating
the alliance with Prussia and Russia which had been made
in 1813. When Metternich's unsound domestic policy collapsed in the revolution of 1848, it was the alliance of the
northern powers which saved the tottering Austrian Monarchy. If the King of Prussia had accepted the German
Crown, if the Tsar had not offered his army for the suppression of Hungary, the Empire could hardly have been
re-established. After a severe crisis, Schwarzenberg restored
this alliance and left it as his greatest achievement to his
successor.

The period in which Prince Eugene, Kaunitz, Thugut,
Philip Stadion, Metternich, and Schwarzenberg controlled
Austria's foreign policy, covers more than four generations;
in this century and a half no other Continental state had
such a record of diplomatic talent and tradition. This political tradition was largely responsible for Austria's great successes, even after unsuccessful wars. These statesmen (with
whom Andrássy may be counted, because of his alliance with
Germany) knew well the weak points of their state. They
knew that the lack of unity in its structure, the mediocrity
of most of the aristocrats who filled the leading places in the
administration, and the defects of the military organisation,
made it impossible for Austria to withstand an attack on
more than one front. Unlike a unified, national state, she
dared not risk a fight to the finish. Her power, indeed her
very existence, rested on treaties. In every European conflict Austria stood for the maintenance of the existing order
and sought allies among those who had the same interest.
So absolute is this rule that, after the unification of Germany
and Italy, Austria joined with her former enemies to maintain the new European system, even though it was her own
defeat that had enabled this new system to be built up on
the ruins of the old.

At the time of the Crimean War Austrian diplomacy completely abandoned this wise traditional rule and was heavily

punished by Austrian isolation in the wars of 1859 and
1866. Count Buol, Schwarzenberg's successor, overrated
Austria's strength; in the struggle between the Western
powers and Russia, to whom Prussia remained attached, he
wanted to keep complete freedom of action and become the
arbitrator of Europe. He could have chosen either to satisfy
Russia by strict neutrality or to create a new system of
alliances by uniting with the Western powers, in which case
he would have been able to check Russian preponderance.
Either policy would have its rewards, but it must be followed
unflinchingly. Instead the Habsburg monarchy hesitated.
First, in April 1854, came a treaty of neutrality with Prussia;
next, in December, an alliance with France and England,
but without the diplomatic services which they expected
being rendered by Austria until after the fall of Sebastopol.
As a result, all Europe complained that Austria was unreliable. Francis Joseph rightly felt that his ministers had
entered on a dangerous path and objected to the alliance
with the Western powers; but Buol threatened to resign and
the ill-advised ruler let himself be persuaded. The Tsar felt
deeply what he called the ingratitude of Austria. He is said
to have asked the Austrian Ambassador, George Esterhazy:
"Do you know who were the two most foolish kings of
Poland?" And as Esterhazy preserved an embarrassed
silence, the Tsar answered his own question: "Sobieski and
I". Both, said the Tsar, had saved Austria, without earning
any thanks. The German courts, too, were offended by
Buol's arrogance. "Everyone in Munich and Stuttgart",
wrote Bismarck on December 21, 1855, "is unanimous in
condemning Buol; most of all, the opponents of Russia, who
say that his direction of Austrian policy has been incredibly
bad. At any rate, he has managed to destroy all faith in
Austria and all respect for himself. Pfordten [the Bavarian
Minister] compared him to a locomotive, which doesn't
know where it is going and, on being asked, answers only
with steam and whistling."

Thus, by the end of the Crimean War, the diplomatic creation of Metternich had been destroyed. To resist the restless forces which were striving for unity in Italy and Germany, Austria must now rely solely on her own strength. Usually mistress of the art of finding allies, she could now find none to help her to defend the international system of 1815.

Throughout the war Bismarck had watched from Frankfort the Austrian mistakes and had studied the dangers, which he was to face later himself. He was one of those who urged Frederick William not to follow the wavering policy of Austria, but to remain true to Russia. It is clear from his despatches to Berlin that adherence to conservative principles was no longer with him the decisive consideration; he was thinking exclusively of Prussia's security and power. He therefore advised the King to support Austria in her eastern policy only if she would concede to Prussia a share of power in Germany. For the sake of the future Bismarck wanted to keep on good terms with Russia. His distrust of Austria he explained by saying that any Prussian with his experience must view the position from the angle of Austro-Prussian rivalry. "The fear of seeing our benevolent dispositions abused by Vienna", he wrote, "perhaps makes me prejudiced even in fundamental questions." Particularly important in the development of his ideas is the despatch of February 15, 1854, in which he uttered a warning against chaining the trim, seaworthy Prussian frigate to the old, worm-eaten Austrian galleon. But he still thought it would be possible, on the next European conflict, to persuade Austria to renounce Germany by offering the help of Prussia elsewhere. In fact nothing would have induced Austria voluntarily to surrender her primacy in Germany; every Austrian statesman was agreed on that. For a European power to give up such a position without a struggle would have been to sign its own death-warrant. In the following years, therefore, Bismarck entirely abandoned

the policy of alliance with Austria and began to seek allies
against her. In the great memorandum of May 18, 1857, he
even went so far as to suggest France as the destined ally
and argued strongly against the maxim that a legitimate
Monarchy should not ally itself with a power which rested
on revolution. He had now grown to the stature of the man
capable of remodelling Europe and stood out, head and
shoulders, above the other Prussian diplomats. If Frederick
William read Bismarck's despatches, he must have been
horrified. For till the end he remained subservient to
Austria; and he was deeply mortified that his visit to Vienna
in 1857 did not lead to better relations. But at this point his
mind became clouded, and in the autumn of the same year
his brother William had to take over affairs as Regent.

In 1859 Austria had to pay heavily for her diplomatic
mistakes. When Napoleon III combined with Cavour to free
Italy, the Cabinet of Vienna looked round for allies in vain.
The English people sympathised with the Italians and
Russia rejoiced that her faithless friend was being punished.
But the Austrians counted firmly on being able to bring not
only Prussia, but all Germany into the war against France,
the hereditary enemy. It was therefore planned to put two
armies in the field: the smaller to crush Sardinia and defend
Italy, the larger to take up its position on the Rhine and
threaten Paris. The Austrian hegemony in Germany was
about to be put to the test. Confident of a majority in the
Diet and encouraged by the rising war-feeling in southern
Germany, the Cabinet of Vienna meant to bring the strength
of the whole nation to the support of the Habsburg
Monarchy.

In Berlin opinions were divided. The memory of Olmütz
was still fresh and among both people and statesmen the
feeling predominated that Prussia should seize the opportunity to become master of Germany. Of the Council, the
Regent, Prince William, was perhaps most favourable to the

alliance with Austria; and the Prime Minister, Prince Hohenzollern, supported and encouraged him. But the Austrian attempt to force Prussia into war by a decision of the Diet offended William's sense of Prussia's dignity. That his policy should be determined by a majority of the Diet seemed to him to mean the end of the monarchy of Frederick the Great. What he was hoping for was a concession from Austria—ultimately the permanent command of the North German federal troops—in return for help against France.

But this plan was not clearly and resolutely carried out. Prussia armed against France, but then waited for an offer from Austria, instead of frankly coming forward with her own proposals. The Archduke Albrecht was sent to Berlin to persuade the Prince Regent to enter the war; but he did not bring the offers that were expected. He proposed a national war against France: that Austria and Prussia should each put 250,000 men on the Rhine under the joint command of the Emperor and the Prince Regent. This plan was coldly received in Berlin. Prussia, it was said, was to help Austria to defend her Italian possessions, without even being allowed the command on the Rhine; and yet that was the least reward which Prussia could expect for such help. But Austria, as the senior German power, was still far from making any such concession.

The day the Archduke left Berlin the Austrian Cabinet, without informing him or the Prince Regent, sent its ultimatum to Turin. The Prince Regent felt that his advice and help had been slighted, and he let events take their course. Indeed the action was so hasty that even Buol was taken by surprise. The order to deliver the ultimatum was issued from the Emperor's military chancery without consulting the Foreign Minister; and Buol, who disapproved of so premature a rupture, offered his resignation.[1] But all this

[1] [This was the story as Friedjung had it from Rechberg (see Appendix II) and Rechberg no doubt had it from Buol. The Austrian ar-

would not have been decisive if the Austrian army in Italy had been in a position to defeat the Piedmontese before the arrival of the French.

There is plenty of evidence of the shortcomings of both the French and Austrian armies in man-power, in equipment, and, above all, in generalship. Chance played a strikingly large part in the war. At the end of it France certainly counted as the first military power in Europe. But just because the Austrian army came near to winning every battle, just because a better generalship could have defeated the enemy, her army, too, won for itself a new esteem among contemporaries.

Opinion in the Austrian army unanimously desired, as commander-in-chief, Lieutenant-General Baron von Hess, Radetzky's chief of staff in 1848 and 1849, who had fought at Aspern, Wagram, and Leipzig. But the choice fell on Count Gyulai, a friend of the Emperor's Adjutant-General,

chives too seemed to confirm Buol's account, for there was no record of any Council of Ministers at which the ultimatum to Sardinia was discussed. Nevertheless the ultimatum was discussed at a Council, for the Minister of Police, Fichten von Kemphausen, made a note of it in his diary which has recently been published. Attention was first drawn to the important passage in the diary by Srbik in his *Metternich*, ii. 506. It is perfectly true that the ultimatum was advocated primarily by the military authorities, but Buol himself supported it and declared that "England and Prussia were becoming daily more favourable to the Austrian cause". The non-recording of this Council enabled Buol to pass himself off to Rechberg as a victim of the military clique.

Nor is it true that Buol resigned because of his disapproval of the ultimatum. He was dismissed by Francis Joseph, when the isolation of Austria became apparent, and when the complete bankruptcy of Buol's policy was finally revealed. Buol was in a feeble-forcible way the political heir of Schwarzenberg, and Rechberg was brought in instead as the political heir of Metternich. (It had been Rechberg who had arranged Metternich's flight from Vienna in 1848 and who had accompanied him on its most dangerous part.) It was Rechberg's task to abandon the arrogant bullying of Buol and to restore the system of European alliances with which Metternich had been able to maintain Austria.— Translator.]

Count Grünne, who was all-powerful in military matters. Equally disastrous was the effect of aristocratic influence on the choice of the subordinate generals. At the head of the seven army corps were Princes Liechtenstein and Schwarzenberg and Counts Clam-Gallas, Stadion, and Schaffgotsche; only two, Benedek and Zobel, did not belong to one of the great families.

When Gyulai crossed the Ticino with 100,000 men, it was imperative for him to engage the Piedmontese and defeat them before the French arrived; for the French divisions were only just beginning to appear at the foot of the Alpine passes and in the harbour of Genoa. But while the Piedmontese awaited what seemed an inevitable defeat and Turin trembled before the advancing enemy, Gyulai hesitated. The French seemed to him too near; and in spite of the despairing entreaties of Kuhn, the Chief of the General Staff, who insisted on the weakness of the enemy, he decided that the undertaking was too risky. For weeks he remained inactive, and the French had time to complete their inadequate armaments and appear on the Po in overwhelming force. The Austrian army was now thrown on the defensive. Still on enemy soil, Gyulai chose a strong position and awaited the attack. But Napoleon III led his army northwards, across the Austrian front, and by appearing on the Ticino before Magenta directly threatened Milan. On the news of the French diversion, Kuhn wanted to attack their columns while they were still dispersed. But Gyulai decided that, as the French had turned his flank, he was already beaten, and ordered a retreat over the Ticino; he would, indeed, have preferred to retire altogether to the Quadrilateral.

Now at last, Hess arrived to give his advice; and, at a council of war between him, Gyulai, and Kuhn, it was decided to await the enemy behind the Ticino and there offer battle. The battle was fought on June 4, at the bridges of Magenta. That evening the Austrians were undefeated

over two-thirds of the field. Gyulai and Kuhn were resolved
to continue fighting the next day. Then, however, came the
news that MacMahon, on the right wing, had occupied
Magenta; a renewal of the battle seemed, after all, impossible. It was decided to retreat and to evacuate Milan,
and the next day the undefeated army withdrew to the
Quadrilateral.

Napoleon had retired to bed knowing nothing of Mac-
Mahon's decisive stroke, and had sent to Paris an uncertain
message, which appeared the next day in the *Moniteur*, to
the effect that the French army "was reorganising" for a
fresh battle. Then came the news of the taking of Magenta.
Yet the victory was so incomplete that the Austrians were
allowed to retire unmolested; and it was not until June 8
that Napoleon made his solemn entry into Milan. This explains his own remark, that he hated war because chance
played too great a part in it.

In the Quadrilateral the Austrian army was reorganised.
Two new army corps were created and Francis Joseph,
advised by Hess and Ramming, himself took over the
command. Hess advised the Emperor to remain on the
defensive in the Quadrilateral until the army had rested.
Ramming, on the other hand, was for an immediate attack.
The Emperor could not make up his mind to follow either
policy wholeheartedly; so the army was twice sent across the
Mincio and twice, when Hess's influence again prevailed,
withdrawn. At last it was decided to advance and fight a
decisive battle on the Chiese. Half-way there, on June 24,
the two armies met at Solferino. Neither side expected the
decisive struggle until the following day; but Hess had made
his dispositions so well that the Austrians were ready for
any eventuality.

The Austrian plan was that Stadion, in the centre, should
remain on the defensive, while Benedek and Wimpffen
enveloped the enemy on the wings. But only Stadion and
Benedek did their part. Wimpffen was one of those Austrian

generals whose nature it was, in Suvaroff's phrase, to be beaten. Instead of obeying the Emperor's order to attack, he hesitated and, at two o'clock, ordered the retreat. Stadion now received the full weight of the French attack and the retreat became general. When the defeated army recrossed the Mincio, the fate of Italy had been decided.

It was at Solferino that Benedek acquired the great reputation which was to put him in command of the army in 1866. During the morning he drove back the Piedmontese opposite him. The ammunition of an infantry regiment gave out and he shouted: "Give 'em the cold steel, lads!" and when their charge was victorious he rode up to them, calling out: "I should like to kiss the lot of you!" The defeat of the centre, however, made the victory of the right wing useless; and at 3.30 came the order from the Emperor to retire. But Victor Emmanuel, on hearing of the French success, had commanded his army to advance with the words: "The King, too, must have a victory." Benedek, therefore, replied to the Imperial message: "Honour forbids me to retreat at this moment"; and, in the midst of a thunderstorm, the 18,000 Austrians completely repulsed the 27,000 Piedmontese. It was nine in the evening when Benedek withdrew with all his wounded and prisoners, leaving the Sardinians to achieve the glorious occupation of a deserted position.

During Austria's hour of need the Court of Berlin had been torn between the desire to check Napoleon's threat to the balance of power, and the dislike of helping its rival. The Prince Regent never wavered in his intention of securing for Prussia the military leadership of Germany; but he lacked advisers who would ruthlessly pursue this aim. It is true that there were politicians about him who put the interests of Prussia above the federal obligations invoked by Austria, and who were eager to seize the opportunity offered by Austria's embarrassment. Lassalle and the leading liberals were in favour of this policy; and so were many of the

diplomats, such as Usedom, Bismarck's successor at Frank-
fort, and Pourtalès, the Prussian representative at Paris.
Bismarck, too, would have supported such a policy with all
his strength; but before the outbreak of war he had been
recalled from Frankfort and sent as ambassador to St.
Petersburg. As he later remarked, he was put out in the cold.
Out of consideration for the pro-Austrian feeling in South
Germany, Prussia did not want to be represented at the
Diet by an opponent of Austria. From St. Petersburg he
strongly advised against any mobilisation, which would only
strengthen the Austrian position and threaten France. If he
had been in power, he would have attempted to establish a
new system in Germany by threatening Austria and, at the
same time, holding out the inducement of armed assistance.
For he had already formulated his policy—first the exclusion of Austria and then an alliance between the two
empires. With this in his mind, he wrote on May 12 to the
hesitating Foreign Minister, Schleinitz: "I regard the federal
relationship as an illness of which Prussia will sooner or
later have to be cured *ferro et igni*, unless we take a treatment for it immediately while the season is favourable".
And could there be a more favourable season for the treatment than when Austria was being defeated at Magenta and
Solferino?

The Prince Regent entirely agreed with Bismarck's aims,
but not with his methods. He disliked leaving the German
Habsburgs without help in their Italian struggle. He was
hoping, therefore, to increase Prussia's power in Germany,
not by threats, but by a friendly agreement with Austria;
and for a moment such an agreement seemed possible. When
Gyulai evacuated Lombardy, Austria offered to cede to
Prussia the command on the Rhine, in return for a Prussian
guarantee of the Austrian possessions in Italy. But by now
the Cabinet of Berlin was aiming higher than this; and the
Prince Regent, despite the advice of the Prime Minister,
Hohenzollern, could not bring himself to accept this offer.

After Magenta and Solferino, however, it became increasingly difficult to resist the popular clamour for assistance for Austria. Prince Windischgrätz was sent by Francis Joseph to Berlin, to work for a German national war against France. He found the Prince Regent full of personal sympathy for the Emperor; but the Habsburg was too proud, even in adversity, to offer, say, a division of the presidency of the Diet, in return for armed assistance. He would surrender none of his power in Germany; and the Hohenzollern was too scrupulous to increase the Austrian difficulties by exorbitant demands. At last, on June 25, the Prussian representative at Frankfort announced that his Government had decided to mobilise six army corps for the lower Rhine. After the war, the Prince Regent assured the Kings of Bavaria and Saxony that, if the French armies had made any further progress, he would have declared war on France. Prussia, he thought, by thus protecting Germany against France, was bound automatically to secure the leadership of Germany.

This development filled Bismarck with alarm; for he thought that Prussia would gain as little by this mobilisation against France as Russia had gained by the suppression of the Hungarian revolt in 1849. "We are not even acting as Austria's reserve," he wrote on July 1, "we are actually taking the war off her hands altogether. With the first shot on the Rhine, the German war alone will count, because Paris will be threatened. Austria will get a breathing-space; will she use it to help us to improve our position in Germany? . . . And if the war goes badly, the federal states will abandon us as ripe plums fall from a tree in a wind; and every prince on whom French troops are billeted will run for shelter to a revived Confederation of the Rhine."

It was Austria herself who got her rival out of these difficulties, by hastily and unexpectedly concluding the armistice of Villafranca. This step took the Prince Regent and Windischgrätz equally by surprise; and even serious

historical works describe it as incomprehensible, or seek for
some secret influence in Francis Joseph's counsels. It would
appear that the excellent work of the Austrian General
Staff on the War in Italy is not sufficiently well known, for
there the weakness of the Austrian army is clearly disclosed.
It had been found necessary to send one Hungarian corps
back from the front as unreliable, and to dissolve a Croat
corps as undisciplined. Moreover, there were no reinforcements. Nine of the twelve army corps were already in Italy;
one was needed to hold down Hungary; and now the last
two army corps of the empire had also to be despatched to
Italy. Far from having a second army ready for the Rhine,
as Austria had earlier proposed, she would have found it
difficult to provide the three corps (80,000 men) due under
her federal obligation. It would hardly have been possible
to give the Archduke Albrecht, who was destined for the
Rhine command, troops which had had to be sent home from
Italy. The creation of two new corps was indeed ordered;
but only untrained recruits were available and they lacked
both officers and equipment. In the army list there appeared
375,000 infantry; but 255,000 of these were untrained
recruits, for in the long years of peace it had been more
pleasant to perform parades with long-service soldiers than
laboriously to instruct raw recruits. It was disgraceful
enough to have to ask for Prussian help for the defence of
Italy. To have to confess the inability to send an army to
the Rhine was even worse. The old, much-abused Imperial
War Council had always managed to keep one army on the
Rhine and another in Italy—often a third against the Turk;
this was more than the new absolutist state could achieve.
The old privilege of defending Germany on the Rhine was
the real foundation of the primacy of the House of Austria;
it could now be no longer exercised.

Nevertheless the mobilisation of Prussia and Germany
made Napoleon feel that it was time to rest content with
what he had achieved. He invited Francis Joseph to a

meeting at Villafranca; and there the sorely tried Austrian Emperor agreed to a peace, by which Lombardy was lost, but Venice saved. Napoleon did not shrink from deceiving Francis Joseph with false information: he told him that Prussia was negotiating secretly with France and England with a view to depriving Austria of both Lombardy and Venice, and establishing Venice as an independent state under an Archduke.[1] The old distrust between the two

[1] [There were certain elements of truth in Napoleon's story. Prussia was in fact negotiating though not on the basis alleged by Napoleon. The Prince Regent was becoming increasingly anxious to go to the assistance of Austria. Schleinitz, the Foreign Minister, did not openly go against his master, but he attempted to postpone any decision as to Prussian action, and one of his temporising measures was to propose a joint mediation to England and Russia. The Prince Regent, however, insisted on laying down in advance that Prussia would only mediate on the basis of the territorial *status quo* in Italy; it was this fact (which was known to the French, but not to the Austrians) which made Napoleon anxious to conclude peace before the mediation came into being, as Austria would have become infinitely more stubborn if she had learnt of the Prussian condition. The establishment of Venice under an Archduke was not proposed by the Prussians, but by the French, who submitted it to the mediators as the French counter-proposal to the Prussian condition.

In regard to England Napoleon had more excuse. To the Prussian proposal of mediation the British Government had replied that mediation must envisage some cession of territory on the part of Austria. Moreover, Lord John Russell, the Foreign Secretary, and Lord Palmerston, the Prime Minister, both expressed their personal approval, when they were shown the terms which Napoleon was to propose at Villafranca (and which included the establishment of Venice as an independent state). Napoleon was therefore acting in good faith when he told Francis Joseph that he had English support. But the British Cabinet, strongly seconded by the Queen, refused to endorse Russell's opinion, and Russell was thus able to declare that England had never supported Napoleon's terms.

The Austrian Cabinet accepted the English and Prussian denials almost as precipitately as it had accepted the French story; and the resultant distrust was among the causes of the breakdown of the *entente* between France and Austria which had followed the convention of Villafranca.—Translator.]

German powers flared up again. Austria accused Prussia of losing the Monarchy a province by her delay; and Prussia had to dismiss her army without striking a blow. The general feeling in Germany was that Prussia, by her indecision, had led fellow Germans to disaster; and the tardy Prussian mobilisation did little to obliterate this impression.

CHAPTER II

THE FAILURE OF THE AUSTRIAN POLICY OF A GREATER GERMANY. BISMARCK AND SCHMERLING (1859–1863)

SENTIMENTAL pacifists used to believe that nothing but the militarism of monarchs prevented their peoples from settling everything peacefully. In Germany, from 1848 to 1859, it was just the other way round. The monarchs, Francis Joseph and the King and the Prince Regent of Prussia, desired and believed that the bonds between them of personal friendship, of kinship, and of common German nationality would stand any strain. Moreover, Austria and Prussia could easily co-operate as European, if not as German powers, as was shown before 1848 and after 1871: there was no question outside Germany over which they need quarrel. But they were separated against their will, often against their interest, by the aims and needs of the national movement which was the driving force in Germany.[1] After 1859 the movement for unity was inevitably strengthened by the Italian example. Everywhere popular organisations glorified the end, on which they were all agreed, although they differed as to the means. The National Association and the Greater-Germany Reform Association were driving on the ministers and princes and appealing to the ambition of both Austria

[1] [The German patriots were divided into two schools of thought, the *Grossdeutsch*, or Great-German Party, who wished to include German-Austria in a united Germany, and the *Kleindeutsch*, or Little-German Party, who desired the exclusion of Austria to render possible the unification of Germany under Prussian leadership.—Translator.]

22

and Prussia. In both countries patriots pointed to the immense political and military strength which must remain undeveloped so long as Germany was divided and urged that these forces should be used to establish the power of their own state. The penalty of failure was correspondingly great; for either, surrender on this point meant abandoning the supremacy over Central Europe to the rival power. Thus it was the newly awakened national movement that came between Austria and Prussia and revived the jealousy which had been dormant since the time of Napoleon.

Other nations have often been penalised for weakness, but Germany suffered from excessive strength. She had produced two great powers, whose rivalry now stood in the way of a concentration of German forces. Since 1871 it has become unnecessary to emphasise the political and military potentialities of Prussia. But there was a time when nationalists saw equally great potentialities in Austria. Galicia and Hungary, which, after 1849, had been brought into the German sphere of influence, were regarded as colonies, acquired for the cultural and economic expansion of Germany. The enthusiasts for a Great Germany believed themselves strong enough to use both Prussia and Austria; but neither power was ready to accept German unity, except as leader. Patriotism was strong enough in both to resist any attempt to force them into a united Germany. In German Austria only a small section of the educated classes wanted unification with Germany; and even then Austrian primacy must be assured. In Prussia the democrats and the clericals were prepared for absorption into Germany; but any such attempt would have broken on the Prussian patriotism, which centred on the dynasty. In a struggle for independence within Germany the monarchy both in Austria and Prussia could count not only on the army, but on the overwhelming majority of public opinion.

These were the circumstances in which the character of the new king of Prussia was to be displayed. William I derived from a simpler, earlier period and watched with unconcealed mistrust many of the developments going on around him. But those who jeered at his limitations failed to appreciate his strength. No one knew better how to create an army, to choose the best ministers, to superintend the administration of the state, and to advance the position of the dynasty—things which were beyond his more gifted brother. He was no sentimentalist. He embarked unwillingly on the war of 1866, but after his victory it did not perturb him that many of his royal cousins from the lesser states would have to eat the bread of exile. In the excitement of the moment it is often difficult to distinguish the essential forces at work. William had this gift in common with other founders of states and dynasties whose success was not understood by their contemporaries.

It is obvious to-day that William I was right to concentrate on his own sphere—the reform of the army. When his subjects were enthusiastically declaring that Prussia could conquer Germany by moral force, he alone recognised that what she needed was material weapons. In November 1850 the Minister for War had been forced to confess that the Prussian Army was not fit for a war with Austria; the mobilisation of 1859 had proceeded slowly and the war was over before Prussia was ready. These facts were well known, but only the King drew the right conclusion and worked ceaselessly for the reform of the Prussian army. At a time when everybody was busy talking, he recognised that the foundation of national greatness lies in the ability of a nation to defend itself.

When William succeeded to the throne the obligation of army service was universal, but only 40,000 men a year were called up. These in five annual groups constituted the field army, which should thus on complete mobilisation be 200,000 strong. The next age-classes, from 25 to 39, formed the militia (Landwehr), 400,000 strong. Such an army was suitable for a defensive war, but not for the forceful policy which even the Prussian Chamber demanded. The weakest point was that the yearly quota of conscripts had remained the same although the population had increased from 10 to 18 millions since the decree had been issued in 1816. Tens of thousands thus stayed at home, while those on whom the lot fell remained liable to be called up for nineteen years.

The King now proposed the annual conscription of 63,000 men to serve three years, and the creation of 49 new regiments to receive them. He proposed furthermore that the three youngest age-classes of the militia should be retained in the reserve of the field army. In return the older age-classes of the militia would be dismissed earlier. The change would cost the state only $9\frac{1}{2}$ million thalers a year and would provide in return an army of 370,000 men, a reserve of 126,000, and 163,000 militia.

The opposition of the Prussian Parliament to these reforms had a decisive influence on the future of representative government in Germany. The Parliament was not opposed in principle; the Chamber of 1860 granted 9 million thalers for the 49 new regiments. But a permanent grant was made to depend on a number of conditions, the most important being reduction of the period of service from three to two years—a demand rejected by the King because it would weaken the fighting strength. In 1861 the Chamber renewed the annual grant, in the hope that an agreement might still be reached. They were, however, about to refuse the grant for 1863, when the King dissolved the Parliament and ordered new elections.

The King's Government hoped to disarm popular opposition to the army reforms by a parade of activity on behalf of national unification. In 1861 Bernstorff succeeded Schleinitz as Foreign Minister. Though he disliked extreme measures, he was a genuine German patriot, and his Note to the German Courts of December 20, 1861, marked unmistakeably a return to the policy of a narrow Federation under

Prussian leadership, as initiated by Frederick William IV in 1849. At once the lesser German States took fright at Prussian ambition, though Bernstorff had merely suggested a theoretical aim and took no steps to achieve it. In consequence the majority in the Prussian Parliament found it inadequate; and when at the elections of 1862 the progressives were returned with an increased majority, the complete rejection of the army reform seemed inevitable. So at last the King resolved to follow the advice of Roon and Manteuffel—to summon Bismarck and pursue the bold policy which Bismarck had urged on him in a conversation at Baden-Baden. When, on September 23, 1862, the Chamber refused by 273 votes to 68 to provide for the 49 regiments, which had already been created, and the liberal ministers resigned, Roon once more advised the appointment of Bismarck. The King replied: "He will not do it; besides, he's not here—we cannot talk it over with him". But Manteuffel's telegram—"The pear is ripe"—had brought Bismarck back in haste from Biarritz, and Roon could answer his disheartened sovereign: "He is here and ready to answer your Majesty's summons". In the midst of the foreign complications caused by Bernstorff's Note and of apparently insuperable domestic difficulties, Bismarck was appointed Prime Minister. But he held the winning card; for in the reformed army he had a weapon without which not even he could have achieved success. At the first meeting with Bismarck at Babelsberg the King was very depressed; and the first document he gave his new minister was his abdication. But Bismarck restored his courage and assured him that he would carry through the reorganisation of the army, even in the teeth of parliamentary opposition. "The King's attitude before the interview was that of a beaten man; he left it with a firmer step, resolved and hopeful." [1]

The Emperor Francis Joseph was also in difficulties. The

---

[1] Bismarck, *Gedanke und Erinnerungen*, i. 267.

collapse of the absolutist regime made fundamental reforms essential and, in December 1860, after Count Goluchowski's short Ministry, Anton von Schmerling was appointed Minister of State. Schmerling had first come to the front in Frankfort, when the Imperial Regent, the Archduke John, had appointed him President of the first German Ministry. Despite his lack of experience, he had shown himself the equal of the leading liberals in parliamentary ability; he answered their revolutionary enthusiasm with courage and irony and, at the right moment, with armed force. Among the moderates, who favoured a constitutional monarchy, he enjoyed a high reputation, even after the growing enthusiasm for a Prussian hereditary empire had compelled him to resign. To safeguard Austrian interests he had not shrunk from an alliance with his enemies, the democrats, against a Hohenzollern empire and by so doing had wrecked the first attempt at German unity: for he could never accept a united Germany unless Austria stood at the head. On his return from Frankfort he became Minister of Justice and introduced in Austria trial by jury and publicity for proceedings in the law courts. When, in 1851, against his advice, the Constitution of 1849 was abolished, he resigned and returned to his judicial career. Unlike most of his countrymen he had a clear idea how Austria ought to be organised and governed. The Constitution which he issued on February 26, 1861, was designed, in defiance of Hungarian opposition, to unite all the Habsburg dominions. This Constitution became later the basis for the Constitution of the Austrian half of the Dual Monarchy; but nothing could force the Hungarians into a unitary state. Their consciousness of national independence was too intense and had, moreover, regained its political instrument by the revival of local self-government in the Hungarian counties—the *Comitats*. This was Goluchowski's most disastrous legacy to Schmerling. The destruction of the centralised bureaucratic government directed from Vienna should not have been the prelude to negotiations, but the result of an agreement with Hungary. There was little sense in negotiating about constitutional concessions when the German officials and teachers had already been expelled from Hungary and the administration handed over to the Magyar nobility.

Schmerling, however, was confident of victory, for he overestimated the strength of the idea of Austrian unity. He believed in the political legacy of Joseph II and was undismayed by Joseph II's failure. He combined an unshakable faith in his mission with an exaggerated idea of his own ability and often neglected to conciliate important people. This probably had a bad influence on his relations with Francis Joseph, who was in any case prejudiced against liberalism, and much preferred to compromise when faced with opposition. The Emperor did not long encourage this ruthless pursuit of imperial centralisation, and it was only for the first two years that Schmerling enjoyed his full confidence. Then he turned to other advisers and, with Schmerling still in office, introduced a new system of government. Schmerling, after the failure of his plans and his own resignation, could reasonably console himself with the thought that his projects had never been given a real chance.

The foreign policy of the Monarchy similarly lacked the unity and clarity which only firmness and resolution could give it. Rechberg, the Foreign Minister, had little sympathy with Schmerling's ideas. A man of long diplomatic experience, he had succeeded Schmerling in Frankfort in 1849. Then, after an interval during which Thun and Prokesch-Osten represented Austria at the re-established Diet, Rechberg returned and, in the years from 1855 to 1859, earned Bismarck's sincere respect. Rechberg's desire for the cooperation of the two German powers was much the same as Bismarck's had been in 1850, and it would have been fortunate for Austria if Bismarck, at the beginning of his career in Frankfort, had had to deal with a man of Rech-

berg's views; but since the Crimean War Bismarck was
determined on a conflict with Austria. Rechberg therefore
found him friendly, but unyielding; he could appreciate
Bismarck's great gifts, but he did not realise his complete
freedom from the prejudices of his fellow-nobles. When
Bismarck was appointed Ambassador at Paris, Rechberg
made to Gramont, the French Minister at Vienna, this
comment, a strange mixture of truth and error: "If Bismarck
had had a proper diplomatic training, he would be one of the
first of German statesmen, if not *the* first; he is courageous,
resolute, and ambitious, but incapable of sacrificing a prejudice or a party view to any higher consideration. He has
no real political sense; he is a party-man in the strictest
sense of the word, and, as he is able and conciliatory and,
moreover, an enemy to Austria, we regard his appointment
with distrust and alarm." Rechberg expressed himself still
more strongly at the end of the liberal era in Prussia: "If
there is a change of Ministry in Prussia, it will be Bismarck's
turn and he is capable of pulling off his coat and fighting
on the barricades". At first, when Rechberg succeeded Buol
at the beginning of the Italian War of 1859, he joined
in the complaints against Prussia's hesitation and after the
war despatched a Note bitterly denouncing her as untrustworthy. But he soon decided that it was better to work
for a reconciliation with Prussia in order to renew Austria's
strength after her losses and to return to the traditional
methods of Austrian conservatism, delay, and conciliation.
He wanted to leave the German question alone, because he
doubted Austria's creative ability in Germany. He regarded
Napoleon III as Austria's arch-enemy and believed that, to
injure her, Napoleon would reopen the national question in
Germany and Italy. Although by nature impulsive and
quick-tempered, Rechberg was cautious and conservative
in his political outlook: Austria and Prussia should remain
united, if only to check democratic tendencies in Germany.
The pivotal conceptions of his policy were a strong Monarchy

at home and the equality of the two great states within the German Confederation.

Eighteen months later Schmerling entered the Cabinet with views on the German question very different from those of his colleague. Full of patriotic confidence, he despised Rechberg's narrow outlook; and the popularity he won by the introduction of parliamentary government in Austria gave a fresh impetus to Greater-German propaganda. Schmerling was obsessed with the idea of making centralised Austria the dominating state in the German Confederation, and for this purpose he set out to appeal to German public opinion, confident he could use it for Austrian ends, or control it if it became dangerous. He remembered that this had been possible in the stormy days of 1848 and saw it was so once more in the subservient Austrian Parliament. There was from the beginning a certain coolness between Schmerling and Rechberg. Schmerling had not forgiven Rechberg for reaping the fruits of his hard work at Frankfort in 1849; it was he who had had to fight the revolution, and when opinion in Germany began to change, Rechberg had achieved an easy success. Now, when Schmerling proposed a daring, aggressive policy, Rechberg raised objections and Schmerling found himself hampered by diplomatic routine. He proposed a German policy of the most ambitious sort. Austria should give parliamentary representation to the whole of Germany. She should appeal to national feeling by creating a single Customs Union including Austria; by establishing a uniform standard of weights and measures and of money; and by introducing a uniform civil and criminal code. At any rate, the greatness and security of Austria demanded that she should take the lead in proposing reform.

At first the influence of Schmerling prevailed. The Prussian Note of December 20, 1861, reviving the proposal for a narrower federation, seemed to challenge an answer from Austria. For a time, Rechberg's hasty temper overcame even his doubts of Austria's strength in Germany; and the Ministers of the lesser states were unanimous in resisting Prussian greed. Count Bloome was therefore sent on a mission to the German courts to propose common action against Prussia, and on February 2, 1862, an Identical Note, completely rejecting the Prussian claims, was issued by Austria, the four German kingdoms, and the two Hesses. Not content, however, with a merely negative attitude, the Greater-German party in Vienna secured positive proposals from Austria; the Austrian Cabinet came forward in the Diet with the draft of a federal reform. There was to be a Federal Directory, centralising all German affairs, and side by side with it, an Assembly of delegates selected from the representative bodies of the various states. Austria further proposed that a uniform procedure of civil law and a uniform law of debt should be drafted and submitted to an assembly of delegates from the various states. The value of these proposals could not be disputed; and if Schmerling was right, they would increase the power of Austria in Germany. She seemed once more sure of a majority in the Diet, since Prussia had aroused general mistrust by her proposal of a narrower federation; and any extension of the authority of Frankfort would be virtually an extension of Habsburg power. If Prussia gave up part of the rights of the Prussian Parliament to an organisation in Frankfort controlled by the Cabinet of Vienna, Prussian sovereignty must suffer a great loss; Prussia would have surrendered her independence for the sake of Germany. Everyone knew that in similar circumstances the Emperor of Austria would refuse to make such a sacrifice; and William I, on the advice of Bernstorff, refused likewise. Once more it was shown that the German Constitution could never be reformed so long as there were two great powers in Germany. According to federal law, a unanimous vote was necessary for the Austrian proposal; and the Prussian vote was withheld. If Austria wanted to force the reforms through, she would have to appeal to the people, and in this case William I, unlike his brother, would leave the future of Germany to be settled by arms. Thus there was already sharp opposition between Austria and Prussia; and German public opinion supported Austria, because her Government was in agreement with her representative assembly, while in Prussia the domestic conflict was becoming more bitter every day. This, then, was the situation when Bismarck took office, to carry through the army reform and so become the most unpopular man in Germany.

Every Prussian, with the exception of a few republicans and clericals, was agreed that Germany must be united under Prussian leadership. But there agreement ended. Though the King was aiming at the command of all the German forces, or at least of those of North Germany, he felt that a war with Austria or the other German princes would be a national disaster. Hence his answer when King John of Saxony told him that even the street-urchins were saying that Prussia was aiming at war with Austria: "Of course street-urchins know better than I".

Public opinion took a quite different view. People were convinced that a progressive home policy was all that was needed to win the whole of Germany for the Prussian Monarchy; the Crown Prince and his wife, and his father-in-law, Prince Albert, all shared this view. The Prince Consort, who never lost his interest in Germany, always believed that it was through Parliament that Germany would be won; and he had inspired his daughter Victoria with his own idea of uniting the nation under a progressive Prussian Monarchy. To her and her husband, the quarrel with Parliament and the appointment of Bismarck seemed a disaster for both Monarchy and people.

Bismarck did not share the opinion either of the King or of the Crown Prince, but he intended to use the methods of both. He realised the importance of the Prussian army as a

factor in the situation; but he also realised the strength of
the national idea which inspired Germany. Hitherto, in fact,
he had differed from the King on practically every European
question, and it had not been easy for William to accept
him. As Prince Regent during the Italian War, when
Bismarck was already being proposed as Foreign Minister,
he is reported to have said, "That would be the last straw,
to give the Ministry to a man who would turn everything
upside down".[1]

Bismarck was one of the few who had thought out the
consequences of the rivalry between Austria and Prussia;
and it seemed to him, as he said, "a mathematical impossibility" to solve it, except by war. The moment, therefore,
that he was appointed Prime Minister, he got into touch
with the Hungarian exiles, particularly Kiss and Count von
Seherr-Toss. To Seherr-Toss, whom he met on his farewell
visit to Paris, he said: "I want to secure for Prussia the
position which is due to her in Germany as a purely German
state. I recognise the value of Hungarian help and I realise
that the Hungarians are not revolutionaries in the usual
sense of the term. In any case, Frederick the Great tried to
ally himself with the discontented Austrian nobility. If we
win, Hungary, too, will get her freedom. You may count on
that."[2] From this time on Seherr-Toss sent Bismarck regular
reports on the situation in Hungary. Moltke's Minute of
February 1860 shows that in this Bismarck was more daring
and revolutionary in his conception than the men who controlled the Prussian army. For Moltke only thought in terms
of a defensive war against Austria and dreaded an inevitable
gain for France. "If there is a breach between Austria and
Prussia", he wrote, "the struggle will produce a strong
empire under Habsburg or Hohenzollern; but Germany will
have to pay for her unification with the loss of provinces in

[1] The Prince Regent to the Duke of Coburg, according to the latter's
Denkwürdigkeiten, ii. 479.
[2] Seherr-Toss, *Erinnerungen aus meinem Leben*, 140.

the east and in the west". Thus even Moltke had to be converted to the view that a decisive struggle was necessary.

From the outset, Bismarck was faced with difficulties on all sides. Failing to secure a compromise with the Progressive Party, he broke completely with the supporters of constitutionalism and, in his speech of January 27, 1863, claimed for the King the right to enact the Budget if the two Houses of Parliament could not agree on it. Thus, in defiance of the Constitution, he deprived the representative assembly of its control of expenditure and taxation. His challenge to Austria was equally sharp. The Austrian plan of reform had just been submitted to the Diet, and Bismarck warned Karolyi, the Austrian Minister at Berlin, that Prussia would regard any attempt to override her by a majority decision as a breach of the Federal Constitution and would withdraw her representative from Frankfort. Austria could choose, he said, between co-operation with the lesser German courts or with Prussia; if she chose the former, a conflict with Prussia was inevitable. When Karolyi objected that Austria could not abandon her traditional influence with the German courts, Bismarck replied that Austria "should move her centre of gravity to Buda-Pest".

In the Note of February 28, 1863, the Cabinet of Vienna emphatically rejected this policy: "If our Monarchy refuses to sacrifice the legacy of centuries of history—a position sanctified by treaties and founded on the power and greatness of the House of Habsburg, we are to be accused of insolence to our ally, Prussia! If the Imperial Court will not help Prussia to make good claims which have no legal basis, which are indeed an infringement of the rights of other states, then it is Austria who is lacking in consideration for the other German power! . . . If Berlin makes us choose between withdrawing from Germany — moving, as the Prussian Minister suggests, our centre of gravity to Buda-Pest—and the threat of finding Prussia among our enemies in the next European conflict, we must leave such ideas to the judgement of public opinion; and it will decisively condemn them, should they ever be put into practice!"

By this candid expression of his intentions, Bismarck seemed to have raised for himself insuperable difficulties; and he increased them, in February 1863, by the treaty with Russia for the extradition of Polish political refugees, which aroused a storm of indignation, especially in Western Europe. All this seemed to strengthen Austria's position in Germany. Yet it was this very treaty with Russia which laid the foundation of Bismarck's later successes, for it won him the gratitude of the Tsar, Alexander II.

Before long the Austrian proposals for reform came before the Diet at Frankfort; there was, however, no crisis, as they did not secure a majority. Many of the German princes were unwilling to give up the least jot of their sovereignty either to Austria or Prussia, and so were ready to wreck any reform; and this time Prussia sided with them. The boasted influence of the Austrian Cabinet with the German courts was indeed largely imaginary; it tended to vanish at the decisive moment. To Schmerling, however, this seemed merely a temporary check which could be put right by a greater effort. For popular feeling even in North Germany was turning against Prussia as a result of the domestic conflict; the National Association itself declared that the Government of Bismarck was leading Prussia to ruin. Schmerling earnestly advised the Emperor to turn this feeling to account. He hoped that a reform of the German Constitution would strengthen the system of German centralisation in Austria and help him to hold the Slavs and Magyars in check. For his German policy he could count on the support both of the Democrats, who were turning more and more against Bismarck, and of Austria's old friends, the Clericals.

One of the leaders of the Clerical party was the Hereditary Prince of Thurn and Taxis, who was related by marriage to

Francis Joseph, and who was ambitious to play a big part in German affairs. He happened to see a memorandum submitted to Schmerling by Julius Fröbel, who had been condemned to death for his part in the October Revolution of 1848 in Vienna, but had afterwards been pardoned and had emigrated to America. Having learnt his lesson, Fröbel returned, hoping now to achieve his aim of German unity not by revolution, but by serving one of the great powers. Schmerling found him a post in Austria, because he saw how useful the former democrat might be in building up an Austrian party in Germany. Fröbel, in his memorandum, proposed that a meeting of German princes should be called at Frankfort under the presidency of the Emperor of Austria—a standing committee of Monarchs to rule Germany with the aid of a Chamber selected from the various Parliaments. The idea of such an array of princes fascinated the Hereditary Prince of Thurn and Taxis; and in March 1863 he sent Baron von Dörnberg, who acted as his foreign minister, to propose this plan to Francis Joseph. The Emperor was offered the prospect of taking his rightful place as successor of the Holy Roman Emperors at the head of the German princes and so determining at Frankfort the future of Germany. Francis Joseph accepted the plan enthusiastically; but it was to be his, and his alone. He did not, therefore, consult his ministers, but only Baron von Biegeleben, the expert on German affairs at the Foreign Office, who warmly agreed with him and worked out the details with Dörnberg. Rechberg, Biegeleben's chief, was completely ignored, while Schmerling only learnt from Dörnberg and Fröbel of the Emperor's intentions. The origin of the plan was thus almost more remarkable than the plan itself. For the Emperor embarked upon this great project of calling the princes together at Frankfort without consulting his ministers and intending to employ them only in its execution. Biegeleben was hoping that the possession of the Emperor's confidence might lead to permanent control of policy; and even Dörn-

berg saw a wide field opening for his ambition. Such was the
force of private intrigue in Austrian politics.

When the situation seemed to the Emperor ripe, Schmerling and Rechberg were officially consulted. Schmerling,
already initiated, needed no conversion, since he believed in
the possibility of a moral conquest of Germany. But Rechberg, deeply offended at being informed so late, used every
argument against the proposal, the most convincing being
that it had no chance of success. Such a policy, he urged,
could not be carried through without resort to arms, since
the unanimity needed for an alteration of the Federal
Constitution was unattainable; to carry through the reform
by force would split Germany into two camps and war with
Prussia would be inevitable. The Emperor, however, was
not to be moved and, when Rechberg offered his resignation,
refused to accept it, remarking indignantly that he was not
going to have his ministers dismissing him. He liked to have
in his Cabinet men of different views, and to hear their
various opinions, while reserving the final decision to himself. Rechberg, regarding himself first and foremost as the
servant of the Emperor, felt it his duty to obey his
sovereign's will and to assist in the execution of a plan which
he himself had at first opposed. But he laid down one condition when he consented to remain in office: he, and not
Schmerling, should accompany the Emperor to Frankfort;
for he could not remain Foreign Minister if he were passed
over on such an occasion. Schmerling rightly took it as a
personal defeat that he, too, was not chosen to go with the
Emperor. Indeed, in view of his reputation in Germany,
everyone was astonished at Schmerling's absence from
Frankfort; and Rechberg, who did not believe in the success of this meeting of princes, acted without energy or
enthusiasm. It was not the first time that the Emperor had
neglected Schmerling, for he was displeased at the way in
which the minister took all the credit for the new Constitution and allowed his sovereign's name to be thrust into the

background. According to Fröbel, the Emperor rejected Schmerling's request to accompany him to Frankfort with the words: "If I take you, what room will there be for me!" This can hardly be true,[1] but Schmerling's complaint to Fröbel was justified: "Where are we to find the strength and goodwill to carry through any big measure? In Austria everyone works against everyone else."[2]

The struggle in the Cabinet over the Frankfort project lasted for weeks. Rechberg made every effort to tone down Schmerling's ambitious and far-reaching proposals; it was a battle between common sense and the courage which wants to conquer the world.[3] When, during this period, the Duke of Coburg visited Vienna to work for reform, he found Schmerling still confident of victory; on July 11 he was talking proudly of his days as Imperial Minister in Frankfort and looking forward to reappearing soon in the old Imperial city. But on a later visit the Duke found him depressed and afraid that he was going to be ignored. The Archduke Rainer, one of Schmerling's loyal supporters, also expressed the fear that reactionary tendencies were predominating and that little could be expected from the plan. "Schmerling", wrote the Duke of Coburg's representative soon after, "gives the impression of a tired man who realises

---

[1] [It is quite probable that Francis Joseph did use these words; but Friedjung, writing in the Emperor's lifetime, could not say so. —Translator.]

[2] Fröbel, *Denkwürdigkeiten*, 241 and 258.

[3] [There was another reason for Austria's desire at this moment to get into closer touch with Germany, and one with which Rechberg sympathised. The Polish revolt had brought protests to Russia from France and England, and it looked as if Austria would fall between two stools, as during the Crimean War. She did not dare to act against the two Western powers, but she did not want a war with Russia. A federal reform of Germany would give Austria the military support of all the lesser states, and perhaps of Prussia as well, so that Austria could with less misgiving face a war, which Rechberg believed certain. Cf. Engel-Janosi, *Graf Rechberg; Vier Kapitel zu seiner und Oesterreichs Geschichte.*—Translator.]

that his policy is being crippled by conflicting influences."
The Emperor aimed at striking a mean between the ambitious projects of Schmerling and the pessimism of Rechberg; he hoped to conciliate the princes and yet please
popular feeling. The document which resulted was a compromise; and it was to be Austria's last chance of addressing
Germany. Compared with the strong central power and the
popular assembly elected by universal suffrage, which were
established in Germany after 1866, this proposed Constitution shows clearly how little Austria had to offer. There was
to be but the ghost of a popular assembly, elected by the
separate parliaments; control of Federal affairs was to be
left to a Directory, presided over by Austria. The authority
of the central power was to remain wretchedly small; even
the Federal army was hardly to be strengthened. Still, it
seemed a promising beginning for a Great-German union,
and everywhere outside Prussia it was received with
enthusiasm. Even supporters of the National Association,
among them the Duke of Coburg, were affected by the
popular excitement and followed the lead of Austria.

The meeting of the princes was therefore an Austrian
success, even though a temporary one. The character of the
meeting was entirely determined by the personal policy of
the Emperor Francis Joseph. For in Austria questions of
policy, both foreign and domestic, were decided by the
monarch and not, as is often thought, by his advisers. With
a quick understanding and tireless energy, Francis Joseph
had made himself master of the various problems with
which he was faced; and his comprehensive knowledge was
all the more remarkable in that no other European monarch
was faced with such a variety of questions. For his empire
was vitally affected by every Continental disturbance, and
he ruled over a number of nationalities with discordant
views as to the organisation of the state. Yet the Emperor
was usually well informed and often astonished his ministers
by his exact knowledge of the questions under discussion.

The Emperor's personality stands out clearly from many contemporary judgements. On January 25, 1852, during an official visit to Buda-Pest, Bismarck wrote: "The young ruler made a very good impression on me. He combines the enthusiasm of youth with the dignity and self-possession of maturer years; he has fine eyes and an attractive, frank expression, particularly when he smiles. If he were not Emperor, I should find him somewhat too serious for his age. The Hungarians are delighted with his excellent Hungarian accent and with his elegant horsemanship." The deep impression which the defeat of 1859 made on Francis Joseph appears in the later account of Orges, the editor of the Augsburg *Allgemeine Zeitung*, who was sent to the Emperor by the Duke of Coburg. Orges gave Francis Joseph an outline of the state of opinion in Germany. "The Emperor interrupted me several times to enquire what had gained the sympathy of South Germany for Austria and how that sympathy had been lost. . . . My audience lasted an hour and a quarter and I wasted no time on empty compliments, but said outright what I wanted to say. Once or twice, when I had to say something unpleasant to His Majesty, I asked if I could speak freely; each time the Emperor replied— certainly and without fear. . . . Everything I said to the Emperor was very *German* and very *Liberal*." When Orges remarked that nothing could stop the growth of parties and that government would have to be carried on through them, the Emperor said: "Yes, if only the parties were clearly established and distinguishable, but that is not the case; and it is even worse when they keep quiet, or pursue aims which are different from those which they profess".

Francis Joseph enjoyed the advantage of a remarkably accurate memory; but too good a memory may weaken the power of decision by confronting the mind with too many distracting considerations, while a system so complicated as the Austrian might well make the most determined man hesitate. The history of the Italian War and its aftermath shows clearly that the Emperor was often influenced by the most contradictory arguments. It was this which made Napoleon III think that Francis Joseph lacked energy. For although he insisted on making all important decisions for himself, his policy varied according as the influence of the different ministers predominated; and only in the parliamentary affairs of Hungary after 1867 did he habitually defer to his ministers' advice. It is this which explains the unexpected nature of many of the decisions in the first part of the reign. The Emperor was often on the point of abandoning an adviser at the very moment when he was following his advice. Thus the meeting of the princes at Frankfort marks both the triumph and the beginning of the decline of Schmerling's policy; the dismissal of Beust was decided on just when he had managed to overthrow the pro-Slav ministry of Hohenwart; and Andrássy left office immediately after his greatest achievement, the Austro-German alliance. The Emperor was determined never to lose control, and he preferred ministers who merely executed his own wishes. Impatience at the slow development of his plans was another cause of the constant changes of policies and ministers; but his intentions were always sincere and he was genuinely convinced of the necessity of such changes. The one characteristic which dominated his political plans was a rare sensitiveness to the fluctuations of public opinion; and the increased reputation which Austria enjoyed in the second half of his reign was largely due to the personal respect for the Emperor of both rulers and peoples. When the rashness of his early years had been checked by experience and self-control, he became one of the most influential rulers of his time.

On August 16, 1863, amidst popular enthusiasm, the Emperor was received with ceremony at Frankfort. Instead of the elaborate speech drafted for him by Biegeleben, which he rejected because he did not speak like that in real life and would not use such high-flown language to the princes, he delivered a short opening address which made a great impression; and he presided over the discussions as ably as if he had been concerned with parliamentary affairs all his life. His chief supporter was King John of Saxony, the spokesman of the pro-Austrian majority, to which the other Kings also belonged. Prussia could only count on a small minority consisting of Baden, Weimar, Mecklenburg-Schwerin, Oldenburg, and Waldeck, who rather doubtfully insisted that the solution of the German problem depended on the exclusion of Austria. Their spokesman was the Grand Duke of Baden, the son-in-law of William I. With 24 votes in its favour, the Austrian proposal was, with some amendment, accepted. But the success was only apparent; it was nullified by a clause providing that the resolutions should not come into force until Prussia had been won over to this new German Constitution.

Nevertheless, Europe was at first greatly impressed. For a long time Napoleon III feared that a great Austria-Germany was about to emerge as an insuperable barrier to French ambition; and Queen Victoria, meeting Francis Joseph shortly afterwards at Coburg, had a personal request to make. It was her maternal duty to her dear children, the Prussian Crown Prince and his wife, to express the hope that the Emperor would not interfere with their rights and position. The Emperor, obviously surprised by the request, replied reassuringly; but it showed how much his prestige had increased.

Everything now depended on the consent of Prussia; and this was refused. Before the meeting of the princes, Francis Joseph had visited the King of Prussia at Gastein and had tried to persuade him to come to Frankfort; and without waiting for his answer a formal invitation was brought to William at Baden-Baden by King John of Saxony, as the delegate of the assembled princes. It seemed impossible to refuse when, as William said, twenty princes invited him and a King came as their messenger. But Bismarck was adamant and after a stormy interview, in which he threatened to resign, he managed to persuade the King not to yield; he held him ruthlessly to the policy which he had always advised: Prussia must never let herself be bullied by a majority in the Diet. During the interview Bismarck had held himself in check, but the strain was so great that he broke the latch of the door as he went out and when he got back to his room had to smash a jug as an outlet for his feelings. But he had won and the success of Austria was an empty one. Rechberg did his best at the ensuing conference of ministers at Nuremberg to make something of the opportunity. He proposed that those states which had accepted the Frankfort resolutions should establish a Federation without Prussia, who would thus be left out of a united Germany. Apart from its inherent difficulties, such a plan was bound to fail, as the German princes had no intention of putting themselves under the House of Habsburg. The existence of two rival powers within the Federation was the guarantee of their own sovereignty; even at Frankfort George V of Hanover had been asking: "Does Austria mean to ruin us?" The ministers of the lesser states at once rejected the Austrian proposal and, as Rechberg had prophesied, Schmerling's scheme came to nothing. Rechberg felt more strongly than ever that unless Germany could be ruled by the friendly co-operation of Austria and Prussia, the sword must decide between them. This was the thought at the back of his mind when he remarked to one of the other German ministers: "If you prefer it, we can easily come to an agreement with Prussia!"[1]

Austria had shown that she had inherited all the traditions of those Holy Roman Emperors who, in medieval theory, ruled the world, but whom, in practice, any powerful prince could defy with impunity. Her moral authority, depending only on custom and tradition, was valueless in any real conflict, unless supported by material strength.

[1] Beust, *Aus drei Vierteljahrhunderten*, i. 336.

Yet Bismarck was not quite sincere when he dismissed the Austrian achievement as a mere reception of the Emperor in Frankfort by "a lot of princes in their best uniforms". He knew well that his own King respected the existing order in Germany; and the Crown Prince had openly condemned the absence of the King from Frankfort: Prussia, he thought, ought to have taken part in order to show her sympathy for the cause of German unity. At every step the Minister, already engaged in fighting both Austria and the Prussian Chamber, found the Crown Prince opposed to him. There was only one man who supported Bismarck, and that with some hesitation; but that one man was the King.

Bismarck had now surmounted his initial difficulties. His view of the future was very different from that of the King; in a phrase that horrified his contemporaries he pointed to "blood and iron" as the means of uniting Germany. Not that he underrated the dominant ideas of his time; it was his ruthless use of them which shocked the world. The various parties were at one moment attracted by him and at the next repelled; but always they were left breathless. His sensitiveness to new ideas was only equalled by the freedom with which he rose above such ideas; with the confidence of genius he had no patience with those who could not follow his thought. It was his constant change of methods that gave his enemies their text; for he used in turn every party and every European state to assist in founding the German Empire. Napoleon III, Russia, Austria—all were at one time his allies and at another his enemies; all the German parties were to denounce him as untrustworthy. For long they nursed their wounds and they openly rejoiced at his fall. But posterity will not condemn him for that; deeds, not fidelity to party, make a statesman. Bismarck was a good hater; he fought uncompromisingly, especially in his three internal conflicts with the Progressives, the Clericals, and the Socialists. But he respected strength and eventually compromised with a section of the Liberals, and later with the Clericals. He has been accused of checking the spread of humanitarianism, of deepening national hatreds, and of discouraging the love of freedom. But the idealistic German of the era of Schiller was already disappearing when Bismarck came to power; Germany was in danger of losing herself in a desert of phrases and sentiment, and Bismarck awoke her from her dreams. The world has roughened and coarsened since Bismarck's day. Other nations may lay the blame on him; but he gave the Germans a fatherland sooner than they dared to hope, and they, at least, must be grateful.

The Austrian hatred of Bismarck after 1866 did not endure for long. He was able to convince Francis Joseph that even while preparing for war he had never lost sight of the idea of recreating the old alliance between the two states. The arch-enemy of Austria became the founder of the new German alliance and exchanged the reputation of a selfish, deceitful statesman for that of the pillar of European peace. In fact, people always thought of Bismarck what he wanted them to think. Later historians even tried to depict his policy between 1861 and 1866 as pacific—Prussia was represented as having been attacked by Austria despite the efforts of Bismarck. His character needs no such embellishments; he can stand the truth, warts and all.

CHAPTER III

THE CONQUEST OF SCHLESWIG-HOLSTEIN. BISMARCK AND RECHBERG

BISMARCK'S run of ill-luck was now at an end. King Frederick VII of Denmark, the last of his line, died on November 15, 1863, leaving the succession to Schleswig-Holstein doubtful, and Bismarck saw his opportunity of influencing the destiny of Germany. The rising of the Duchies against Denmark in 1849 had failed, and Prussia and Austria, in their hatred of popular movements, had vied with each other in disarming them and handing them back to Denmark. The Protocol of London,[1] which was signed and guaranteed by Denmark and the great powers, recognised the Danish possession of the Duchies and the indivisibility of the Danish Monarchy; in return Denmark promised to observe the autonomy of the Duchies and not to interfere with the German national rights, either in Holstein, which belonged to the German Confederation, or in Schleswig, which was never to be separated from Holstein. To ensure the unity of Denmark in the future, Duke Christian of Augustenburg, who had some more or less doubtful claims to Schleswig-Holstein, was persuaded to abandon these claims for a payment of $2\frac{1}{2}$ million thalers. Unfortunately this settlement was not as final as it seemed. Augustenburg's sons had not renounced their claims; and the German Confederation had not been made a party to the treaty.

[1] May 8, 1852.

46

The most decisive factor, however, was the determination of the Danes to evade the conditions on which the Duchies had been returned to them. The Great-Denmark party was in control; they denied Germany's claim to Schleswig, since it was not in the Confederation, and they demanded that a Constitution should be issued, incorporating Schleswig with Denmark, and leaving Holstein with a separate administration. In 1863 a unitary Constitution was drafted on these lines. The protests of the Confederation and of the two German powers were ignored and a Federal execution was therefore decided on; but since Schleswig was not in the Confederation it was decided to occupy only Holstein with German troops. The dying Frederick VII refused to take the responsibility of signing the unitary Constitution. "I will not sign it," he said, "Christian can do it!" and Christian IX,[1] seeing the danger of war, hesitated. But his minister, Hall, pointing to the excited crowds round the palace, declared that he could not on any other terms guarantee the security of the Monarchy. Full of doubt the King gave way.

At this challenge an immense storm of indignation swept over Germany and Duke Frederick of Augustenburg took advantage of it to put forward a claim to the Duchies on the ground that he had never recognised his father's renunciation. In Schleswig-Holstein everyone had waited patiently for the King's death, in the hope of getting a Duke of their own in the person of Augustenburg. Many even of the German princes enthusiastically embraced the Duke's cause. The Grand Duke of Baden instructed his Minister at Frankfort to undertake the representation of Augustenburg in the Diet; the Crown Prince of Prussia offered his support; and the Prussian Chamber resolved by 261 votes to 63 that the honour and interest of Germany demanded the recognition of the Duke.

Everything now depended on the two great German

---

[1] [The new King was a distant cousin of Frederick VII and was married to his niece.—Translator.]

powers, who could alone enforce the will of Germany. But they were bound by their signatures to the Treaty of London; they had recognised the indivisibility of the Danish Monarchy, even if the Gottorp line should die out. It was particularly difficult for conservative Austria to ignore one of the treaties on which the state of Europe, and therefore her position in Germany, depended. Certainly the new right of nationality claimed to be a higher law than that of treaties; but could Austria accept such a claim without involving herself in endless conflict at home? When the Municipal Council of Vienna petitioned the Emperor to intervene on behalf of the Germans of Schleswig-Holstein, it was sharply told to confine itself to civic affairs.

The Prussian Prime Minister was determined to profit by the situation; it would be a great advantage for him to turn the attention of Germany from his domestic conflict to a national cause. Since the day of his appointment he had nursed the idea of solving part of the German confusion by intervention in Schleswig-Holstein. On December 22, 1862, when Frederick VII was still alive, Bismarck had written: "A solution of the Danish question in our favour can only be achieved by war; and it will be easy to find the excuse for a war as soon as the European situation is favourable". The breach of the Treaty of London by the Danes provided sufficient grounds for intervention. Bismarck could not foretell whether this would open up the whole German problem, but he was not deterred by the possibility. He had no intention of going to war with Denmark just for an ideal; there must be an increase of power for Prussia, if possible by the direct incorporation of the Duchies.

The claims of the Duke of Augustenburg were therefore sharply rejected by the Prussian Cabinet, for two reasons. Firstly, Bismarck did not want to be thrown into direct opposition to the great powers who had signed the Treaty of London. Secondly, it was not in the interests of Prussia to be committed to any claimant, when there was a chance of her getting the Duchies for herself. The war was to be the means of discrediting the forces of liberalism in Germany and re-establishing the shaken authority of the Monarchy. Little of all this could be made public: it was only announced that Prussia was mobilising in order to make Denmark recognise the Treaty of London. But this was equivalent to acknowledging the Danish right to the Duchies, on condition that their autonomy was respected. All Germany was indignant that a German power should rest content with the personal union of the Duchies with Denmark, when there was a chance of freeing them altogether. The opportunity was going to be lost—the Danish promises were worthless and to abandon fellow-countrymen to them would be treachery. Even William once exclaimed to Bismarck, "Aren't you a German at all?"

Austria could not ignore a question which concerned all Germany. Francis Joseph regarded himself as the leading German prince, and felt it his duty to watch over the rights of Schleswig-Holstein. Austria, while recognising Christian IX as heir to the Duchies as well as to Denmark, demanded from him the grant of an autonomous Constitution for the Duchies, in fulfilment of the Treaty of London. Further than this Rechberg hesitated to go; he was concerned more with the enforcement of treaties than with national rights. In fact, the Court of Vienna was very much offended that the German princes had allowed themselves to be so carried away by popular enthusiasm as to propose in the Diet the complete emancipation of the Duchies. Rechberg had no patience with the Augustenburg claim: "This agitation really cannot be tolerated", he exclaimed, on receiving one of the Duke's harmless proclamations.

Thus, after years of opposition, the Prussian and the Austrian policies seemed, but only seemed, to coincide. In reality Rechberg was mistaken; for he looked to the general recognition of the Treaty of London as the end of the whole drama, whereas Bismarck regarded a joint war against

Denmark as merely the prelude. Rechberg was delighted that Austria and Prussia were at last co-operating, and Francis Joseph, disappointed with his experiences at Frankfort, was ready to abandon the policy of Schmerling. Schmerling found himself disregarded and powerless to oppose a policy which was based on respect for treaties. His only advice was not to break with Augustenburg altogether and not to separate from the lesser German states. These, however, Rechberg despised, and he managed to deprive his rival of practically all influence in German affairs.

After many vicissitudes the policy of co-operation, with which Bismarck had begun his career, seemed once more possible. For Bismarck had nothing of the doctrinaire in his composition and he gladly took what the occasion offered: the alliance of Prussia and Austria at any rate guaranteed a successful issue in the diplomatic struggle against the non-German powers, who grudged Schleswig-Holstein to Germany. "We learnt in 1849", he said, "that it is bad to fight one against four; two against three is better." At a stroke Prussia had ceased to be isolated and what was to happen later could be decided later; if Austria would voluntarily surrender the Duchies to Prussia, so much the better. From now on Bismarck was all friendliness and frankness to the Austrians; for two years his relations with the Hungarian exiles were broken off. It was natural for Francis Joseph to sympathise with a Monarch who was struggling against parliamentary claims; and he too was delighted with the new turn in German affairs. Both in Vienna and Berlin Bismarck made great play with the dangers of the democratic movement in Germany, or, as conservative circles expressed it, of the European revolution, and he urged the need for a strong foreign policy in order to check it. He had long been ready, as the needs of the moment might dictate, either to resist popular opinion or to ally himself with the forces of the revolution. For the moment he used the fear of a new revolution to separate the Cabinet of Vienna from the liberal German states. Schwarzenberg had gathered the German princes round Austria; Bismarck was beginning to divide them.

Bismarck had all along determined only to respect the agreement of London until the obstinacy of the Danes provoked a war. The Treaty would be observed and the great powers would not be challenged. But according to international law, war dissolves the treaties between the conflicting states and the Duchies would then fall to Prussia by right of conquest. When, after the War of 1866, Bismarck was reproached with having at first recognised the rights of Denmark, he replied in the Prussian Parliament (December 20, 1866), that he had never advocated the retention of the Duchies by Denmark. "I always held firmly to the principle that personal union with Denmark was better than what existed; that an independent prince was better than personal union; and that union with Prussia was better than an independent prince." He was interrupted by a burst of applause and then continued: "Which was attainable, events alone could show. If personal union had been the maximum obtainable, I should not have been justified, in view of the situation in Germany, in rejecting this *payment on account.*"

In his Reminiscences Bismarck explains his original intentions. Here he tells how, at the first Council after the death of Frederick VII, he urged William to follow the example of his ancestors and increase the greatness of Prussia by seizing the Duchies. The King indicated to the secretary that these remarks should be omitted from the official minutes. "The King", Bismarck writes, "seemed to think that I had spoken under the bacchic influence of a good lunch and would be glad to have my words consigned to oblivion. But I insisted that they should be placed on record, which was done. While I was speaking, the Crown Prince threw up his hands, as though he doubted my soundness of mind; my colleagues sat in dead silence."

Austria was afraid of being taken unawares. On January 10,

1864, a Council of Ministers under the presidency of the Emperor discussed the conditions of the alliance with Prussia and especially the fate of the Duchies after the war. It was proposed that they should be completely separated from Denmark only with the consent of both German powers. By accepting this clause Prussia would have identified herself with the policy of Rechberg: the outcome would hardly have been honourable for Germany, but at any rate there could have been no quarrel between Austria and Prussia over the spoils. Bismarck, however, rejected this solution. Both German national feeling and Prussian interest demanded the complete separation of the Duchies and the treaty with Austria must at least not rule out this solution. Bismarck therefore made a counter-proposal to the Cabinet of Vienna: nothing should be arranged by the two powers concerning the future of the Duchies; Austria and Prussia should merely agree to settle the question in friendly co-operation after their conquest.[1]

The Cabinet of Vienna realised that this proposal left the way clear for a future war: Austria would certainly have the right to protest against the incorporation of the Duchies into Prussia, but she would not be able to insist on the solution she required. Rechberg later explained what led him to accept this dangerous clause. Bismarck was threatening to act alone against the Danes—Prussia need not then pay any attention to Austria at all and Austria would be left exposed to the contempt of Germany. Austria might, of course, outbid Prussia by denouncing the Treaty of London and establishing the Duke of Augustenburg in Schleswig-Holstein with the support of German public opinion.

[1] The negotiations between Austria and Prussia over Schleswig-Holstein were first described in detail by Sybel, *Die Begründung des Deutschen Reichs*, which is based on the Prussian archives and which is the chief source for these diplomatic events. [Later investigation, and particularly the publication of Prussian documents, has shown that Sybel often garbled his sources in order to present Prussian policy in a favourable light.—Translator.]

Schwarzenberg could have risked such a plan, but Rechberg was not made of such stern stuff. He was, however, unwilling to let Prussia have the honour of emancipating Schleswig-Holstein alone, and so agreed to Bismarck's proposal. It was always Rechberg's weakness to see the right course, but to allow himself to be diverted from it.

The Cabinet of Vienna, therefore, accepted the Prussian draft and on January 16, 1864, a joint war against Denmark was agreed upon.[1] Schmerling, already pushed into the background, made no attempt to oppose it. Just before the War of 1866 he attempted to clear himself from responsibility for the disastrous policy that had taken Austria to Schleswig-Holstein by explaining that he had not been consulted: the decisive Council had been held, accidentally or intentionally, while he was absent on a visit to his daughter in Venice. The truth is that he refrained from interfering in foreign politics in the hope of being left in peace to carry out his internal policy of creating a unitary state. Public opinion in Austria was practically unanimous in condemning the breach with the Confederation and the co-operation with Prussia, and demanded that Austria should put into execution the resolution of the German Diet.

In the Austrian Parliament the debate on the war against Denmark, from January 28 to 30, produced fierce attacks on Rechberg's policy. The ministers pointed in vain to the dangers of quarrelling with all the great powers for the sake of the Federal Diet, which could dispose of Holstein only and not of Schleswig. Nearly all the speakers criticised the

[1] The future of the Duchies was determined by Article V of the Treaty as follows:

"In case of hostilities against Denmark and the consequent lapse of the treaties between Denmark and the German powers, the Courts of Austria and Prussia reserve to themselves the establishment of the future condition of the Duchies only by mutual agreement. They will, if necessary, make the relevant agreements for reaching an understanding. In any case they will not make any decision as to the question of the succession except by common agreement."

co-operation of constitutional Austria with a state whose
chief minister had violated the Constitution and was hated
by the people. Schmerling had to come to the rescue of a
policy of which he disapproved. He gave the assurance that
the alliance with Prussia would have no effect upon internal
conditions in Austria; "this gentleman", Bismarck, had
quite enough to do in Prussia without interfering in Austrian
affairs; and he loyally supported Rechberg's defence of
treaty rights, though he struck a note out of sympathy with
his colleagues when he said that Austria would soon re-
establish good relations with the Diet. The proposals of the
opposition were often foolhardy, as usually happens in
inexperienced parliaments, but some of the speeches had a
prophetic sound. "Why are we acting with Prussia?" cried
Schindler, the best of the speakers—"Is Prussia our friend
anywhere? Is not Austria denounced as the arch-enemy of
Prussia? Prussia has scarcely digested Silesia and now she
is getting her claws into the Duchies, while we are leading her
into them with drum and trumpet. *But what music will get
her out again?*"

The campaign against Denmark naturally ended in the
victory of the allies. The most significant thing was that the
Prussian troops were given no opportunity to display their
military superiority. The aged Field Marshal Wrangel was
in command and he took little notice of the advice which
Moltke sent him from Berlin; as a result the campaign was
not a model of strategy, and the Austrians were given little
reason to be dissatisfied with their antiquated shock tactics.
After the Danes had been expelled from the Duchies, the
Prussians wished to seize Jutland as hostage for the islands
belonging to Schleswig, but Austria hesitated. She feared
to go too far and perhaps bring England into the war.
General Manteuffel was sent to Vienna to persuade the
Austrian Cabinet, and he succeeded, but only when Rechberg
had exacted from Berlin the definite promise that at the
end of the war Schleswig-Holstein, though receiving an

independent government, should not be separated from the Danish Crown.

After the war Prussia at first fulfilled her promise. At a conference of the powers in London, Prussia and Austria jointly proposed that Schleswig-Holstein should be organised as a separate state with the King of Denmark as Duke. But Bismarck was soon freed from his unwelcome engagement. In the first place, the Danes did him the invaluable service of rejecting the proposed compromise, foolishly relying on the half-promises of the English ministers. In the second place, the indignant public opinion of Germany hardly needed the encouragement of his press and his agents to come to his assistance; he wanted to be forced, and still more he wanted Rechberg to be forced, to give up the policy of the personal union with Denmark. Now he could not have too many mass meetings in Schleswig-Holstein and in the rest of Germany. He wrote to Zedlitz, the Prussian Commisar in Schleswig: "We must let the whole pack howl". And they howled. At Rendsburg, in Holstein, forty thousand men swore to give their last drop of blood for the independence of their country. The Prussian petition, praying the King for the complete emancipation of the Duchies, had thirty thousand signatures.

There was still one way in which Prussia could get control of the Duchies without provoking opposition by a formal annexation. The Duke of Augustenburg, feeling that his fate depended upon Prussia, approached the Crown Prince, with whom he had been friendly for many years, and offered to enter into a close alliance if Prussia would support his claims. The Crown Prince warmly supported this idea, and his wife was even more enthusiastic, for it seemed to them scandalous that Schleswig-Holstein should remain under Danish control; even King William welcomed the suggestion. Bismarck, however, was not so eager. He strongly resisted the Duke's claims, because he recognised that they would be the chief obstacle to the complete absorption of the Duchies by

Prussia. The Duke, moreover, had surrounded himself with
liberal advisers and relied for support on that very democratic party which Bismarck was then engaged in fighting.
Bismarck, therefore, practically told the Duke's representative, Ahlefeldt, that he did not trust the Duke's promises:
princes, he remarked, usually thought that their actions
could be judged by a standard different from that used for
ordinary mortals, and the action of the Duke's father in
letting his son advance the family claims which he had
already sold to Denmark did not encourage confidence in
the honour of the House of Augustenburg. Nevertheless, the
Duke might be useful for Prussian policy, and Bismarck
encouraged William to write a letter to the Crown Prince,
in which he accepted the Duke's proposals. But if Prussia
were to support him, the Duke must promise certain concessions to William "as prince to prince": Prussia must be
given a naval station in the Duchies; Rendsburg must
become a federal fortress garrisoned by Prussian troops;
Schleswig-Holstein must enter the Zollverein; and, most
important of all, a military convention must put the army
of the Duchies under the command of Prussia. At this time
the Duke's prospects seemed cheerless, and he therefore
welcomed the Prussian offer; in a letter to the King on
April 29 he unconditionally accepted the Prussian terms.

When the situation was sufficiently advanced, Bismarck
sent a despatch to Vienna in which he proposed a new
programme. Schleswig-Holstein was to be taken from the
Danes and handed over to the Duke of Augustenburg, on
condition that he dismissed his liberal advisers and respected
the interests of Prussia; these interests were only vaguely
indicated, but, in fact, Augustenburg was to place his army
under Prussian control, as all the German princes did in
1871.

Rechberg found himself outmanœuvred; Danish obstinacy
and German national feeling made it impossible to leave the
Duchies in the possession of Denmark, and he was being

forced to abandon the firm ground of treaties. In Austria he was ever more loudly accused of only having helped Prussia by his policy, and, what was worse, Schmerling, who had never forgiven his defeat over the meeting of the princes, supported the accusation. Prussia was aiming at seizing the Duchies, as Rechberg's opponents, Schmerling and Biegeleben, had prophesied, and they no longer made any secret of their disagreement. Public opinion demanded that Austria should support Augustenburg unreservedly, even at the cost of a breach with Prussia, and should act in conjunction with the lesser states, as in the time of Schwarzenberg. Rechberg had not the strength to resist. He feared to quarrel with Prussia, but, since the Constitution of 1815 was based upon the equal sovereignty of all the federal princes, he could not consent to limit the rights of a German prince in favour of Prussia. He therefore resorted to a little diplomatic trick, which only made the situation worse. He sent for Wydenbrugk, Augustenburg's representative in Vienna, and told him that Austria had decided to support the Duke's claims, but only on condition that the Duke did not under any conditions conclude a separate treaty with Prussia infringing any of his sovereign rights. Wydenbrugk hastened with the joyful news to his despairing master in Kiel, and the Duke of Augustenburg, when he was summoned to Berlin, obstinately opposed the Prussian demands. "You must not try", he said, "to trap me with paragraphs; you must trust my goodwill!" Relying on the Austrian promises, he rejected a treaty with Prussia, which would undoubtedly have given him possession of the Duchies, and thus fell between two stools.

Meanwhile the war against Denmark was renewed. The Danes hoped to exhaust the patience of Germany by retiring to their islands, but the conquest of Alsen finally convinced them that the sea was no protection against the newly awakened energy of Germany. On October 30, 1864, peace was concluded and Schleswig-Holstein was surrendered to the two German powers without any reference to the claims of the Duke of Augustenburg. At first Austria and Prussia remained on good terms. The two rulers were personally friendly and believed that they were strong enough to control the bickerings of their Cabinets. The King looked upon Bismarck's aim of annexing the Duchies as completely unattainable; the establishment of Augustenburg still seemed to him the best solution, but, since he did not intend the campaign to be completely fruitless, the army and navy must be added to the military power of Prussia. With this in mind, William, in company with Bismarck, visited Francis Joseph at Schönbrunn on August 22, 1864, to seek a friendly settlement of the question of the Duchies.

Bismarck and Rechberg also thought an understanding possible. Certainly during the past year they had disagreed, but their quarrel had remained within friendly limits. Bismarck, though he did not shrink from war if it were necessary, would have been content, at any rate for the moment, with a division of power in Germany, provided that Schleswig-Holstein came under the control of Prussia. Austria was ready for an agreement, but wanted an increase of territory for herself, and indicated that she would surrender her share of the Duchies in return for the county of Glatz; but it seemed too much to William to hand over his own subjects in exchange for new acquisitions. On June 13, 1890, Bismarck gave the author the following account of the conversations:

The four of us—His Austrian Majesty, my Royal Master, Rechberg, and I—sat in a room at Schönbrunn. Rechberg declared that the Duchies could be handed over to Prussia only if Austria received the county of Glatz in order to preserve the balance of power in Germany. This the King would not agree to: the inhabitants had no desire to be transferred to Austria; indeed, petitions and addresses were being sent, begging the King not to separate them from Prussia. I put it to the Emperor that it would be in accordance with the spirit of our alliance if Prussia received the Duchies without giving any compensation; our alliance was not *a trading company*, dividing its profits in a fixed percentage, but rather a hunt, in which each party took its own spoils home. If, in continuance of our alliance, we waged war against France and Italy and recovered Milan, Prussia would not demand territorial compensation, but would be content with a contribution towards the cost of the war. This argument had an effect on the Emperor, as was shown by his asking if Prussia then regarded annexation as the most desirable solution of the question of the Duchies. I was very pleased to have the question so directly put in the presence of the King, for I had never been able to get a definite answer from him. I therefore turned to him and said I was not empowered to answer this question. But the King hesitated and replied that he was not exactly thinking of the absorption of Schleswig-Holstein. I therefore had to drop the subject.[1]

No agreement was therefore possible and Rechberg had to listen to the growing complaints that he had let himself be tricked by Bismarck. To save his policy he now proposed an enlargement of the alliance in an anti-French sense; the Austrian Monarchy would get no compensation, but it would get a guarantee for Venice, Trieste, and Dalmatia, and could then leave Schleswig-Holstein to Prussia. Bismarck seemed prepared to consider this and late into the night discussed with Rechberg the conditions of an alliance against France. But Rechberg was now to learn how shaken his ministerial position was. He sent for Biegeleben and told him to draft a treaty on these lines. Biegeleben refused; he reproached Rechberg with heading for a war with France, in spite of the complete unreliability of Prussia, and told him he must draft the treaty himself. Rechberg's draft was approved by the two rulers and they parted full of friendly assurances. But the agreement was only useful in case of a French aggression and really did not alter the situation at all. The failure of Rechberg's policy was complete.[2]

[1] In his *Erinnerungen* (i. 344) Bismarck gives substantially the same account. He says, however, that William replied to Bismarck's question about the Duchies that he had no right to them and could therefore put forward no claim.

[2] [It is impossible to ascertain exactly what took place during these

This was clearly shown in the negotiations for a commercial treaty between Austria and Prussia; once more Rechberg failed to secure any concessions. In the commercial treaty of 1853, which had been concluded for twelve years, Prussia promised to negotiate for the admission of Austria into the Zollverein on its expiration. Austria wanted this clause repeated on the renewal of the treaty in 1865, so that it should come into force in twelve years' time. Great importance was attached in Austria to this clause which seemed to preserve her right of entry into the Zollverein. For it appeared that Prussia alone had benefited from the Danish campaign, and, if Rechberg's policy were to be defended in the coming meeting of the Austrian Parliament, it was essential that he should be able to point to this one small success.

The correspondence of Rechberg and Bismarck at this time reads like the swan-song of the Prussian alliance.[1] Rechberg implored Bismarck not to refuse him this token of Prussian friendship. Bismarck in reply emphasised the illusory nature of the promise and declared that he could not understand how Austria could attach so much importance to so worthless a formality. In the end, however, he

conversations at Schönbrunn. But apparently on the last night Bismarck and Rechberg came to an agreement by which the Duchies were to be partitioned—Schleswig to Prussia and Holstein to Austria—the two countries were to form a defensive alliance, and Austria was to cede Holstein to Prussia if she recovered Lombardy. This was the treaty which Biegeleben refused to draft. What Friedjung does not make clear is that the two monarchs also refused to sign it; William because the price for his assistance against France was not high enough—he wanted a better position in Germany, not merely territory; and Francis Joseph, because he was not willing to commit himself definitely to the Prussian side, thus alienating both France and the lesser German states. The two ministers then drew up a vague declaration that they were resolved to settle German affairs in a spirit of friendly co-operation; it was this declaration which was approved by the monarchs. See Engel-Janosi, *Rechberg*, 149.—Translator.]

[1] Sybel, iii. 393.

advised the King to yield in order to strengthen Rechberg's
threatened position. But while Bismarck was on holiday in
France, the other Prussian ministers, anxious lest Prussia's
secure control of the Zollverein be weakened, resolutely
opposed any concession; and it is significant that William
decided against Bismarck. His answer was that the friendship of Austria was not likely to last long if it could be
endangered by such trivialities. Bismarck was genuinely
anxious to help Rechberg, as his letter to Roon of October 16
shows: he complained that Bodelschwingh, the Minister of
Finance, Delbrück, and others were working against him.
"If they succeed," he wrote, "it will be obvious in Vienna
that we attach no value to their alliance; they will act
accordingly, and first of all in the Danish question, in which,
led by Schmerling, they will go over to Beust and Pfordten.[1]
But a breach with Austria would be ill-timed from every
point of view and I disclaim all responsibility for the effects
of such a mistake on our foreign policy." Bismarck, however,
was far away in France and the King followed the advice of
the ministers on the spot. The Austrian demand was refused.

This provoked a ministerial crisis in Austria. Schmerling
declared to the Emperor that his position in Parliament
would be gravely endangered if, after such a failure, Rechberg remained in the Ministry. At the next Council of
Ministers, which was to discuss the Commercial Treaty with
Prussia, Rechberg was astonished to see his subordinate,
Biegeleben, appear, uninvited by him; and Biegeleben supported Schmerling's suspicions of Prussian friendship.
Against Rechberg's advice, the Council decided to send a
sharp note to Berlin concerning the Commercial Treaty.
Immediately afterwards both Rechberg and Schmerling
offered their resignations on the ground that it was im-
possible for them to work together. The Emperor, needing
Schmerling to lead Parliament, decided against Rechberg,

[1] [The Prime Ministers of Saxony and Bavaria, who were the leading
representatives of the lesser states.—Translator.]

who left office on October 27, 1864, declaring that if Austria pursued this policy she must prepare for an open conflict with Prussia.[1]

Rechberg's policy was undoubtedly based on a sounder understanding of the real strength of the Austrian Empire. The idea of letting Schleswig-Holstein go and receiving in return a Prussian guarantee of Venice and Dalmatia was worth serious consideration. But it was unanimously condemned by Austrian public opinion as a cowardly surrender to a weaker opponent. Prince Metternich, the Ambassador in Paris, even announced that he would resign if Austria left Schleswig-Holstein in the lurch. Rechberg tried to avoid directly opposing this feeling by a compromise. Hence his acceptance of the meeting of the princes and later his half-hearted support of Augustenburg; before long, however, he had withdrawn, as the Duke's friends said, "all but the little finger of his proffered hand". This made his policy appear uncertain and even confused. The statesman's most important task is to influence others, and Rechberg lacked the ability to do this; he was not even able to gain the support of King William for his pro-Prussian policy, and Francis Joseph, who agreed with him in essentials, let him go when he realised that the opposition was universal. Rechberg during his ministry and afterwards was often

[1] [Rechberg actually resigned on October 18 before the meeting of the Council; his account to Friedjung is therefore not quite accurate. Biegeleben's opposition to Rechberg was, however, expressed in a minute which he submitted to the Emperor on October 19. Biegeleben argued that the Prussian alliance was useless, as Austria would never pay the Prussian price. Austria should therefore make a frank *entente* with Napoleon, as it was in the interests of both that Italy and Germany should be kept divided; at the back of his mind Biegeleben may have had the idea of exchanging Venetia for Silesia. Rechberg in reply argued against any exclusive alliance with either France or Prussia and urged that Austria must keep in with all the powers. See Engel-Janosi, *Rechberg*, 125-8. Francis Joseph, Esterhazy, and Mensdorff all favoured Rechberg's policy as a continuation of the "conservative" alliance against the Revolution.—Translator.]

under-estimated; later he came to be valued at his true
worth and Bismarck always spoke with respect of his
insight and honesty. If Rechberg had entered office some
years earlier, at the time of the Crimean War, he might have
been able to confirm the alliance with Prussia; but by the
time he was appointed the schism between the two states
could no longer be healed. In attempting to cure the disease
he became its first victim.

CHAPTER IV

THE endless fluctuations of Austrian policy astonished all Europe, and inspired Palmerston to make the scathing remark that it took Francis Joseph all his time to keep the peace between his ministers. Austria veered between the opposing policies bequeathed to her by her two outstanding statesmen of the nineteenth century, Metternich and Schwarzenberg. Metternich made possible a lasting understanding between Austria and Prussia when he persuaded Francis I to refuse the title of German Emperor, offered to him by twenty-eight German princes in 1815. Schwarzenberg, provoked by the Frankfort Parliament's offer of the empire to the House of Hohenzollern, had reversed this policy. He set out to humiliate Prussia; and in the years following Olmütz the anti-Prussian policy found increasing support, both among the aristocracy and among the liberals.

Ludwig Maximilian von Biegeleben, Counsellor for German Affairs in the Austrian Foreign Office, was the man who inherited Schwarzenberg's political tradition. A Catholic, born in Darmstadt in 1812, he had been sent to Vienna in 1840 as Chargé d'Affaires for the Grand Duchy of Hesse, and in 1848 Gagern had made him Under-Secretary in Archduke John's Ministry. He had been an uncompromising supporter of the Great-German policy, and in 1850 had been appointed Under-Secretary in the Austrian Foreign Office.

Radowitz[1] had tried to tempt him to Berlin, but his sympathies lay with Vienna. By 1852 he was Counsellor for German Affairs, and he remained responsible for all the correspondence on Germany until his resignation in 1872. There had been a long series of Germans employed in the Austrian Foreign Office to manage German affairs. The most influential had been Bartenstein, a professor from Strassburg, who controlled foreign policy under Charles VI and until the rise of Kaunitz. During the Napoleonic Wars, first Johannes Müller and then Gentz determined Austria's German policy. Biegeleben was the last in this tradition. Before long his learning and his enormous industry had given him a dominant influence in the Foreign Office; a Catholic and an aristocrat, he saw in Austria the embodiment of conservatism. At a time when Europe was increasingly dominated by new forces, Biegeleben placed all his faith in European treaties as Austria's only bulwark against her enemies in Germany and Italy. His faith in Austria's moral superiority and unshakable position survived every crisis and was largely responsible for the final disaster; for his dogmas were never modified by experience and he completely lacked political judgement. But his literary ability and his brilliant style distracted attention from these shortcomings. Francis Joseph, himself a conscientious worker, appreciated his thoroughness and was inspired by his enthusiasm. "Biegeleben", he said at the time of the Frankfort meeting, "is the only man in the Foreign Office who can get anything done."[2] Biegeleben fully sympathised with Schmerling's ambition to dominate Germany and, in consequence, accused Rechberg of timidity in refusing to challenge Prussia while the empire was in difficulties in Hungary and Italy. Rechberg, for his part, had a poor opinion of Biegeleben, realising that his passionate conservatism was driving Austria into war with Prussia. But

---

[1] [Prussian Foreign Minister in 1850.—Translator.]
[2] Fröbel, *Mein Lebenslauf*, ii. 246.

Rechberg was isolated in his own Foreign Office. Biegeleben's enthusiasm for the Great-German policy was shared by both Meysenbug, the Director of the Foreign Office since 1862, and Max von Gagern, Hans von Gagern's youngest son; and this hostility within the Ministry was one of the causes of Rechberg's downfall.

Rechberg himself suggested Mensdorff as his successor, and his advice was accepted. Francis Joseph was anxious to maintain the friendship with Prussia; and Schmerling welcomed a colleague who approved of his domestic policy of centralisation. There were, moreover, many people who hoped to take advantage of Mensdorff's weakness to influence foreign policy. Of these, the most important was Count Maurice Esterhazy, the Minister without Portfolio, who was working to overthrow Schmerling, and now hoped to control foreign affairs without being held responsible for them. Esterhazy, like Rechberg, wanted to maintain the Prussian alliance. He believed that the lesser German states were rotten with democracy and that Austria and Prussia must unite against this danger to monarchy and aristocracy.

Alexander, Count of Mensdorff-Pouilly, belonged to that fortunate class who reached the highest offices in Austria without any effort. Baron Pouilly, his grandfather, was a French *émigré*, who sent his sons into the Austrian army. Emmanuel, the elder, distinguished himself in the wars against France, was made a Count, and took the name of Mensdorff from one of the family estates. Finally he married a Princess of Coburg. His family was thus related to most of the ruling houses of Europe, and Alexander Mensdorff, Rechberg's successor, was cousin to the Queen of England. Mensdorff had fought with distinction in 1848 and 1849, and in 1859 commanded a cavalry division; he had the reputation of a sound soldier, but that was all. Yet, whenever there was a difficult political task to be performed, Mensdorff seemed destined to be chosen. In 1852, at the age of 38, he became Ambassador at St. Petersburg, where he stayed until relations between Austria and Russia became strained. On the outbreak of the Polish revolt in 1863 he was appointed Governor of Galicia, in spite of his lack of political experience. And now that difficulties had arisen with Prussia, it was once more Mensdorff who was called upon to solve them as Foreign Minister. Even this was not to be the end; for after the war of 1866, when there was trouble between the Germans and Czechs in Bohemia, Mensdorff became Governor of Bohemia; and he died, as Governor of Bohemia, on February 12, 1871. He had neither the striking ability nor the ruthless ambition necessary to sustain such a career. He was a gentleman, considerate and understanding, more fitted for a life of meditation than for action and administration. "There is not in the world", wrote the historian Motley, in 1866, when he was American Minister in Vienna, "a more honest, straightforward, or chivalrous man than Count Mensdorff; but I fear the enemy has been able to take advantage of this honesty." Mensdorff won everybody by his politeness and charm; but there was no strong personality behind his charm. He was sensible but weak, distrusted his own abilities, and was easily persuaded to change his opinions. Having no confidence in himself, he was always unwilling to accept responsibility; but—and this was the reason for his appointment to so many important posts—he always made a favourable impression. Francis Joseph trusted him completely, and Mensdorff served him in return with a feudal devotion. That it might sometimes be his duty to oppose the Emperor's will never occurred to him; so, under the influence of others, he embarked on a policy with which he himself fundamentally disagreed.

This was the man who was called upon to oppose Bismarck. His reply to the Duke of Coburg's letter of congratulation shows how helpless and uncertain he felt on taking up office. Like his predecessor he was anxious to avoid a struggle with Prussia which might—for he knew Austria's military shortcomings—prove disastrous for the

Monarchy. His views on the political situation and the future of Germany were cautious and sensible. But he felt too inexperienced to rely on his own judgement, and in consequence became wholly dependent on the permanent officials in the Foreign Office; he consulted Biegeleben on everything and allowed himself to be pushed further than he wanted to go. There was nothing to restrain Biegeleben's impetuosity; he could force a quarrel on Prussia, while Mensdorff had to bear the responsibility.

The result was that Mensdorff's appointment brought about a complete change in the tone and content of the Austrian despatches. Three despatches in the new manner were sent to Prussia on November 12: Austria definitely named Augustenburg as the future ruler of Schleswig-Holstein, but sharply insisted that the Duchies were not to become a Prussian vassal state; and Prussia was accused of deliberately prolonging the affair with a view to annexation. Werther, the Prussian Minister in Vienna, complained of this unfriendly tone, and Mensdorff's answer showed how extraordinary the situation was: the Emperor himself, he said, regretted that Biegeleben often wrote so sharply. Mensdorff seemed to have forgotten that he was responsible for the despatches which Biegeleben submitted to him for signature. In the personal negotiations, however, Mensdorff was his own master; and in them he returned repeatedly to the idea of abandoning Schleswig-Holstein to Prussia in exchange for part of Silesia.

Biegeleben had been right to suspect Prussian evasiveness; for Austria's refusal voluntarily to surrender the Duchies was forcing Bismarck to change his policy. The more, in his own words, the storm "of rage and hatred" rose against him, the more determined he was to bring his foreign policy to a successful conclusion. There could be no turning back; for his enemies at Court, in the royal family, and in Parliament were watching eagerly for his failure. Yet already he had given them furiously to think, for Prussia was well on the way to securing the Duchies. Everyone, from the King down, wanted the incorporation of the Duchies, either directly or by means of the military and commercial treaty advocated by the Crown Prince; the Opposition complained that Bismarck's constitutional conflict had made the moral conquest of Germany impossible and that his alliance with Austria prevented the annexation of the Duchies. Bismarck, however, had already made up his mind to deprive Austria of her share of the spoils of the Danish war. He still did not think it would be necessary to resort to force; in view of Austria's weakness in Hungary and Italy, the mere threat ought to suffice. The problem was to overcome her unwillingness to part with her rightful gains. Austria was still a friendly power; as late as January 1865, William's speech from the throne spoke of the alliance's "firm and enduring foundation in My German patriotism and that of My ally". First of all, the patience of the Cabinet of Vienna must be exhausted; perhaps, while Prussia was making herself at home in the north, Austria would lose interest in her distant, useless possession. Bismarck could wait as well as act; and in spite of Austrian complaints, he left the proposals of November virtually unanswered.

December passed, and January, and still there was no news from Berlin. Francis Joseph told the Prussian Minister that he was getting desperate. Meanwhile a Prussian party was founded in Holstein; and the financial deficit of the Duchies, a legacy of the war, was cleverly exploited to discourage Augustenburg's supporters: a Duke, as Bismarck told them, would cost them 50 million thalers. Bismarck had many irons in the fire. He would support Augustenburg if Prussia's military and financial supremacy were assured; but he also suggested to Austria that the Duke of Oldenburg had claims worth considering. He was quite frankly trying to make Austria heartily sick of the Duchies. On February 8 Karolyi, the Austrian Ambassador, urged him to come to a final settlement. "Why?" said Bismarck. "Why cannot our joint possession be a final settlement? However, do not disturb yourself," he added, as Karolyi protested, "we shall keep faith and submit our conditions. . . . You see, we stand before the question of the Duchies like two men at a well-spread table; one of them has no appetite and therefore energetically forbids the other, whose mouth is watering, to sit down and eat. Well, we can wait; we are quite comfortable as we are and we shall not move until we are offered satisfactory terms."

Behind the careless confidence of these words there was a deep-laid policy. These were only threats, but he believed that threats would be enough. When Count Goltz reported from Paris that Napoleon III seemed inclined to come to an agreement with King William in case of an Austro-Prussian war, Bismarck firmly declined the suggestion. "It seems to me better for the time being to stick to the marriage with Austria in spite of a few family quarrels and not to do anything until a divorce becomes necessary; to sever the tie now would invite all the disadvantages of infidelity." So Bismarck wrote on February 20; the next day he despatched his counter-proposals to Vienna. Prussia agreed to the establishment of the Duke of Augustenburg, but only on certain conditions; the military forces were to be under the command of the King of Prussia and were to take an oath to him; the port of Kiel and the fortress of Rendsburg were to become Prussian arsenals.

The gravity of the situation was not fully appreciated in Vienna; only Biegeleben saw the growing danger of war. He took his stand on the principle that Austria could not break the Federal Constitution by allowing a German prince to become a Prussian vassal; rather let Prussia buy the Duchies outright for a sum of money. "You would hardly believe", Mensdorff said to the Saxon Minister,[1] "how many people support the idea of monetary compensation. Plener (the

[1] Friesen, *Erinnerungen*, ii. 117.

Minister of Finance) is always pointing out to the Emperor
that it would balance the budget for years to come." But
Mensdorff's opinion was comparatively unimportant; it was
Biegeleben who determined Austrian policy. Biegeleben
showed at once that he welcomed the opportunity for a
conflict offered by the Prussian proposals by his message
to the Duke of Augustenburg: "I would rather grow
potatoes than rule under such conditions". Rechberg was
no longer there to advocate a division of power with Prussia;
and the Emperor was coming more and more to agree with
Biegeleben that Prussian ambition needed a lesson. In this
spirit the Austrian answer to the Prussian proposals was
drawn up. It accepted everything that did not affect the
Federal Constitution or the sovereign rights of princes; Kiel
and Rendsburg could go to Prussia and the Duchies might
enter the Zollverein. But firmly and unanswerably, on
constitutional grounds, the Note refused even to negotiate
on a basis of Prussian military and financial supremacy in
Schleswig-Holstein.[1]

On February 27, the day on which the Prussian proposals
were rejected, Roon, the Prussian Minister for War, asked
Moltke for a report on Austria's military strength. Clearly,
Bismarck had warned his colleague of the dangers of the
situation. Ever since his Frankfort days he had felt that war
with Austria was the ultimate solution. Now, hard-pressed
by his difficulties at home, and convinced of Austria's weakness, he began to prepare for it.

The Austrian recognition of Augustenburg greatly

---

[1] A few weeks later, Mensdorff hinted to Augustenburg through the
Duke of Coburg that the Prussian demands might form the basis for
an agreement. When Biegeleben heard of this (*Denkwürdigkeiten des
Herzogs von Koburg*, iii. 479) he said to the representative of the Duke of
Augustenburg: "The Minister's letters and casual remarks may have a
certain significance, but the Duke should base his policy only on the
public Notes and acts of the Government of Austria". Biegeleben thus
regarded himself as the real controller of Austrian policy, and did not
hesitate to dismiss the remarks of his official superior as unimportant.

strengthened his party in the Duchies. The native officials, through whom the Government of the two powers administered the country, regarded the Duke as their lawful chief, and received instructions from him; and 50,000 people signed a petition demanding his establishment. But Prussia had no intention of being ousted by a democratic movement supported by her enemies throughout Germany. William regarded the agitation as being directed against him personally; in April 1865, to assert his rights, he moved the Prussian naval station from Danzig to Kiel. Prussia was thus treating the Duchies as her own property, and Austria was told, when she complained, that she was at liberty to do the same. Prussia claimed the right to make the way easy for her solution — the annexation of the Duchies — but accused Austria of bad faith when she tried to do the same for her candidate—the Duke of Augustenburg. By taking her stand on this principle, Prussia could treat every attack on her authority and every manifesto in favour of Duke Frederick VIII as an offence against the legal sovereign—the Crowns of Austria and Prussia as joint owners.

These joint Dukes of Schleswig-Holstein formed a curious partnership. Under the treaty with Denmark, each possessed a half right over the "eternally inseparable Duchies"; and each was striving to enforce this indivisibility, Prussia by getting it all for herself, and Austria by transferring both her own share and Prussia's to Augustenburg. Patriotic historians try to show that their country has always fought on the side of right. Bismarck would have had no patience with such a conception; he frankly described the question as one, not of right, but of might. "If Austria wants to remain our friend, she must make room for us." The Prussian Council of May 29, 1865, was therefore not concerned with legal rights, but with the expedience of securing unrestricted control of the Duchies by war. Bismarck explained that, except for the oath demanded by the King from the Schleswig-Holstein army, the conditions proposed

to Austria in February could be obtained without war; but
he thought it was time to annex the Duchies, even though
it meant a war with Austria. "Sooner or later", he continued,
"we shall have to fight Austria, now that the Cabinet of
Vienna has revived the policy of humiliating Prussia. But
we cannot advise His Majesty to go to war; that decision
His Majesty must make for himself. If the decision were in
favour of war, the whole Prussian people would joyfully
endorse it." The truth of this was doubtful; but all Bismarck's colleagues, except the Minister of Finance, supported him. Moltke spoke decisively in favour of annexation
and, if necessary, war; the Crown Prince, equally decisively,
opposed it and voted for the establishment of the Duke of
Augustenburg.[1]

The King hesitated to follow the advice of Bismarck and
Moltke. But he objected strongly to the agitation conducted
by Augustenburg, ordered him out of the Duchies, and,
when the Duke refused to go, wrote a personal letter to
Francis Joseph demanding his expulsion. The breaking
point was near. Bismarck warned the Prussian representatives in Paris and Florence, Goltz and Usedom, of the
approach of war, and instructed them to find out whether
Italy would give military help, and if France would remain
neutral. At the end of July he delivered an ultimatum to
Austria: Prussia could not continue negotiations, unless the
agitation in the Duchies in Augustenburg's favour were
stopped. The King did indeed pay his annual visit to
Gastein; but on the way he held a Council at Ratisbon, to
discuss ways and means in case of war. Francis Joseph was
also convinced that war was inevitable, and said so to his
newly appointed Prime Minister, Belcredi, on July 27.

The crisis was again avoided. Austria had no wish to
fight; and William realised that war would be unpopular in
Prussia, where the people wanted the annexation of the
Duchies, but not at such a price. The whole royal family,

[1] Sybel, iv. 121-4.

moreover, led by the Crown Prince, were on the side of the Duke of Augustenburg. The Crown Princess was a strong supporter of the progressive party and was convinced that it would one day be her husband's mission to unite Germany on a liberal basis. When the Decree of June 1, 1863, was published, limiting the freedom of the press, the Crown Prince condemned it as illegal in a speech at Danzig. Queen Victoria feared a revolution in Prussia and was anxious that her children should separate themselves from the cause of the King and his Minister. The Danzig speech did not seem to her to go far enough, but in a letter to Bismarck on June 30, 1863, the Crown Prince went further: "What result", he wrote, "do you expect from such a policy? Do you imagine that continued defiance of law and justice will soothe public opinion? I regard those who are leading His Majesty, my gracious father, along this path as the most dangerous advisers for Crown and country." The Crown Prince announced that he would absent himself from the Council until Bismarck resigned; and he kept his resolve for two years. At the time of the Ratisbon Council, he wrote to Duncker, one of his liberal advisers: "If the Duke really gave way and accepted even worse conditions new complications would soon be found to produce a war". The Crown Princess's uncle, Duke Ernest of Coburg, shared her enthusiasm for Augustenburg's cause and all her sympathies lay with her cousin, Mensdorff, the Foreign Minister of Austria.

In such an atmosphere William could not stand firm, and he agreed with Francis Joseph that the Duchies were not worth bloodshed. The Austrian Minister at Munich, Count Blome, prepared the way for a compromise. In July 1865 the Ministry of Schmerling fell and Austria ceased her appeals to liberal opinion in Germany. Belcredi and the conservatives had no wish for an alliance with the liberal German states against Prussia and Blome strongly urged on William the necessity of co-operation between Prussia and Austria to resist liberalism and democracy. Blome feared Biegeleben's disapproval and he made it a condition that the negotiations should be kept secret: Biegeleben did not learn of the Treaty of Gastein until it had already been signed on August 14, 1865. Both sides made concessions; Lauenburg was surrendered to Prussia in return for a payment of 2½ million thalers; the fate of the Duchies was left undecided, but the joint rule was ended, and in future Prussia was to govern Schleswig and Austria Holstein; Prussia received the harbour of Kiel in Holstein and the necessary military roads to the northern Duchy.

Bismarck was not particularly pleased with the treaty, which he himself described as "a papering over of the cracks". It was a compromise, not only between Austria and Prussia, but between William and his Prime Minister. Bismarck accepted it, because, even if he wanted war, it was his fixed principle that the breach with Austria must not expose Prussia to the charge of breaking faith. He was content to have established the doctrine that the Duchies must not be lost. Even liberals were beginning to admit that he was paving the way for Prussia's greatness, and the idea of annexation was gaining ground. The liberal opposition in the Prussian Chamber, hitherto enthusiastic on behalf of Augustenburg, was silent and embarrassed when Bismarck, in his speech of June 13, 1865, demanded their opinion on the Schleswig-Holstein question. "I cannot deny", he exclaimed, "the painful impression it makes on me to find that this assembly, which is acclaimed throughout Europe as comprising all the intelligence and patriotism in Prussia, can contribute nothing to this great national question, which has been agitating public opinion for twenty years."

The Austrian Government signed the treaty without enthusiasm. Public opinion throughout the Empire condemned the concessions to Prussia and regarded the treaty as an act of unpardonable weakness. Everywhere in Germany, the abandonment of the Duke of Augustenburg was denounced as treachery, in view of Austria's promises during the past year, and it convinced the lesser states that Austrian friendship was not to be relied on. The Treaty of Gastein was almost as great a blow for the Great-German party as the collapse of the policy of centralisation in Austria which followed the dismissal of Schmerling.

For a long time the Austrian Court had been determined on the dismissal of Schmerling. He had tried to hold the disruptive forces within the Empire in check by a strong centralised administration, thinly disguised under parliamentary forms. But in return for their support the German Austrians demanded genuine parliamentary government, freedom of the press, and above all an end of the Concordat with Rome, and these the Emperor had no intention of granting. Schmerling needed the help of the Crown to carry through his unitary system against Hungarian opposition; to secure it he had to oppose the liberal demands and thus destroy his own popularity. As a matter of fact he had little sympathy with liberalism. "I have no real interest in politics," he said once, "I am a soldier by nature and have got involved in politics against my will. I can't stand this perpetual turmoil. In the evenings I like to read a good book or go to the theatre, but these political fellows live in a state of constant excitement; something has to be happening all the time."

At Easter 1865, Francis Deák came forward with proposals for an agreement between Austria and Hungary. He gave up the demand made in his famous speech of 1861, that the two nations should only be united by the person of the same ruler, and accepted the idea of a joint army and a common foreign policy; he proposed that delegates from the two Parliaments should meet "from time to time" to make the necessary arrangements. Here was a way out of Schmerling's difficulties. He could enter into negotiations

with Deák and could then claim with justice that his firm
government had forced the Magyars to reconsider their
absolute refusal to co-operate; or he could try, by firmness,
to drive the Hungarians to further concessions. He chose
the second course, in the spirit of his well-known saying,
"We can wait!" and firmly rejected Deák's overtures. He
counted on the Emperor's willingness to pursue a waiting
policy to the bitter end, but his position was already shaken.
The Emperor wanted results and, to keep his support,
Schmerling had to oppose the liberal demands in Parliament.
But all that he achieved was the accusation of treachery
from the liberals and a complaint from the Emperor that
too many concessions had already been made in the Constitution, in consequence of which it was impossible to get
the army estimates accepted.

Seeing the Schmerling Government shaken, the conservative Hungarian nobility determined to destroy it altogether.
They had originally recommended Schmerling for the purpose of restoring order in Hungary, but he had not acted as
their instrument for long. He had drawn up the centralised
constitution against the advice of the Hungarian ministers,
Vay and Szecsen. When they resigned Schmerling had
nominated Maurice Esterhazy as Minister without Portfolio
and Forgach, who was succeeded by Hermann Zichy in 1864,
as Hungarian Chamberlain. Zichy remained loyal to Schmerling, but Esterhazy kept in touch with his Hungarian friends
and shared their hostility to the German bureaucratic state.
Esterhazy had no sympathy with the claims of the Parliament to have a share in the government of the country. He
lived still in the world of Metternich, out of all touch with
present reality. He had forgotten his mother tongue,
Hungarian, and had never mastered German: even with
his ministerial colleagues he preferred to speak French.
Esterhazy fostered the Emperor's dislike of parliamentary
methods and liberal demands; he advised him to abolish the
Constitution of 1861 and to restore the absolute power of

the Crown. This would achieve two things. The German middle-classes, who were becoming ever more arrogant, would be thrust back into obscurity, and the Hungarians, who hated the unitary state, would be delighted by the disappearance of the Imperial Parliament. Esterhazy regarded the Revolution of 1848 as an episode which could not interrupt historical development, and he wanted to restore the Hungarian Constitution as it had been before the Revolution. Once more Church and aristocracy, protected by a limited suffrage, would combine to resist the forces of liberalism; provincial assemblies, similar to the Hungarian Diet, would perform the same function in the other provinces of the Monarchy, while above them all the Crown would have complete control over Imperial affairs. Esterhazy hoped that such an offer of provincial autonomy would win over the Hungarians; above all it would destroy the hated German bureaucracy.

This plan appealed to the Emperor, for it would free him from parliamentary interference with the army estimates. Esterhazy's influence was strengthened by his personal charm, which was felt even by the leaders of the Hungarian liberals. No one had greater influence over Francis Joseph, and Mensdorff was completely at his disposal. Beust has described his visits to Mensdorff during the War of 1866: "When I had sat down opposite his desk, little Count Esterhazy would walk in, pull up a chair beside the Minister and would sit by him, just like a music master beside his pupil at the piano". But with his penetration Esterhazy combined an extraordinary indecision; he saw so many sides of a question that he could never arrive at a conclusion, and he had the same effect upon those who came under his influence. One of his subordinates once said of him: "No one has a quicker or clearer understanding; he can see in a glass of water all the microbes, which anyone else could only discover with a microscope—but the Lord didn't make such creatures to be seen with the naked eye". Esterhazy there-

fore preferred to let things ripen of themselves; his strength
lay in patience and secrecy. In the Schmerling Cabinet he
hardly uttered a word and Schmerling never knew how
Esterhazy was working against him. Already in 1864 Esterhazy had joined with Rechberg to overthrow Schmerling.
The plan had failed and Rechberg had fallen; but Esterhazy
had remained and his time was coming.

During the winter of 1864–65 Schmerling had come
sharply into conflict with the German Left. The liberals
wanted the establishment of ministerial responsibility; but
this and other demands—among them the demand for a
parliamentary enquiry into the state of siege in Galicia—
were sharply rejected. The liberal leaders denied any intention of overthrowing the Ministry, but in criticising it by the
standards of a parliamentary state they were really condemning it to death. The chief struggle came over § 13 of
the Constitution, which allowed the Government to enact
laws without the consent of Parliament during an adjournment. Schmerling opposed the demand that laws so enacted
should be submitted for parliamentary approval on its
reassembly, because he knew that he would never get the
consent of the Crown to such an alteration of the Constitution. Moreover he found it impossible to reach an agreement
over the Budget. To cover the deficit the assembly reduced
the army estimates from $105\frac{1}{2}$ to 90 million guelders,[1]
although the Minister of War declared that he could not
accept a reduction of more than 11 millions. Attacked by the
liberals in Parliament, and by the conservatives in the
Cabinet, Schmerling found himself deserted on all sides.

The time had come to strike, and Esterhazy approached
Deák, the leader of the Hungarian liberals. Deák had little
sympathy with Esterhazy's obscurantism, but he realised
that the co-operation of the conservatives was necessary
for the destruction of the unitary state, and he threw his

[1] [The Austrian guelder, or florin, was worth at par 2 gold francs,
or 1s. 8d.—Translator.]

influence for the moment on Esterhazy's side. When, on
Esterhazy's advice, the Emperor visited Hungary in June,
he was greeted everywhere with wild enthusiasm, and returned home convinced that his German ministers had completely misrepresented the loyalty of the Hungarian people.
Esterhazy now achieved his first victory; Zichy, Schmerling's right-hand man, was dismissed and his place taken by
George von Majlath, and Schmerling was not informed of
the change until after it had taken place. This proof that he
no longer enjoyed the Emperor's confidence left Schmerling
no choice but to resign. The Ministry only remained in
office long enough to carry the Budget. To make the way
easier for its successor, the Emperor ordered that the reduc-
tions demanded by Parliament should be accepted, and on
July 30 the ministers were relieved of their posts. Esterhazy was now master of the situation. He remained Minister
without Portfolio, in order to escape the burden of ad-
ministrative detail; but the new Cabinet, with Belcredi as
Prime Minister, was entirely his creation.

Count Richard Belcredi was an excellent advertisement
for the aristocratic government which was to replace the
German bureaucracy. Honest, cultured, and with a wide if
academic knowledge of politics, he had earned a high reputation as a lawyer, and had risen at a comparatively early
age to be Governor of Bohemia. He shared Esterhazy's
belief in aristocratic and patriarchal government, but
wished to give it a more modern appearance. He relaxed
Schmerling's press restrictions and secured an amnesty for
most of the political prisoners of the various nationalities.
Representative government was not to be destroyed, but
legislation was to be left mostly to provincial assemblies,
in order to check the growth of a strong central parliament;
to the liberal unitary state he opposed the state of tradition
and local autonomy. The Slavs might be won over to
aristocratic government, but never to German middle-
class bureaucracy. Both the absolutism of the fifties and

the system of Schmerling had elevated the bureaucracy at
the expense of the nobility; Belcredi hoped to supersede
the bureaucracy by granting local self-government and so
return to the state of things before 1848.

These were the principles of the new Government. But
Belcredi was not the man to carry through a clear and
determined scheme in the face of Austria's financial and
political difficulties. At the Emperor's request, Mensdorff,
in spite of his belief in Schmerling's policy, remained
Foreign Minister in the new Cabinet; and he told the Saxon
Minister, Könneritz, shortly after the creation of the new
Ministry: "Financially and from the military point of view,
Austria is in a most difficult position, and the political
situation is not much better. Certainly *the names are there
for the new Ministry, but there is no Programme for it.* On
'certain questions' the Ministry must stand together! But
the differences of opinion are so great that it will be impossible to create a homogeneous administration." Even
worse than this lack of agreement was the way the revived
aristocratic Government exploited the state. Esterhazy
had owed the state death duties to the amount of 230,000
florins ever since 1856 and Plener, the Minister of Finance
in Schmerling's Government, had put in an execution
against his colleague. Larisch, the new Minister of Finance,
was not so conscientious; all interest on the debt and 90,000
florins of the debt itself were remitted, and Esterhazy was
allowed to pay in nine annual instalments. This sort of
thing could only be done by abandoning the principles of
Plener's administration and dismissing all his chief advisers.
The new officials stopped at nothing and they received a
profit on every financial operation undertaken by the
Government. Larisch cannot be excused on the grounds
that he knew nothing of these transactions. He was one
of the largest landowners and mineowners in Austria, and,
as an experienced business man, he must have known
what was going on. But the Ministry of Counts, as it was

popularly called, acted throughout on the principle that the
state and the aristocracy were synonymous, as the new
finance laws showed. The sugar and spirit taxes were
amended for the benefit of large-scale manufacture, which
was almost entirely concentrated in the great estates; and
private investors in the Francis Joseph and the Crown
Prince Rudolph Railways were guaranteed a high rate of
interest by the Government, and yet retained exclusive
control of the Companies.

Belcredi's good name was used to cover these corrupt
transactions and he was not observant or experienced
enough to check them. The domestic problems of the Empire were more than enough for one man. On September 20,
1865, an Imperial decree announced that the Constitution
was "suspended"; it was a better word than "abolished".
It was hoped, by destroying the unitary state, to secure
agreement among the different nationalities. The Slavs at
once rejoiced, but the Magyars waited unmoved to see
whether they were to benefit by the *coup d'état*. The Old
Conservatives were once more in power in Hungary. They
were strong patriots and moreover constitutionalists.
Esterhazy had to work through them, because in Hungary
there was no absolutist party in his sense of the word at all.
Under the pressure of public opinion the Old Conservatives
returned to the policy of 1860, of concentrating power in
the hands of the Magyars; they had however learnt something from experience, for they preserved Schmerling's
administration, and did not revive the local self-government of the *Comitats*. They secured important concessions
for Hungary. On September 1 the Transylvanian Diet, set
up by Schmerling, which had sent representatives to the
Viennese Parliament, was dissolved, and the new Diet was
instructed to unite with the Buda-Pest Parliament. It
met in the Magyar town of Klausenburg, and surrounded
by a mob crying "Union or death", voted for the complete
absorption of Transylvania into Hungary. New elections

were then ordered in Hungary also, at which the liberal
followers of Deák were once more successful—the Old
Conservatives had but a few dozen supporters.

Majlath and Sennyey, the Old Conservative leaders, disliked the Constitution of 1848, but as sensible politicians they
recognised that nothing could shake the nation's belief in
its legality, since it had been regularly passed by the King
and the Parliament. They advised the Emperor formally to
recognise the Constitution, as a step towards reconciliation
between Crown and people, but only on condition that it
should be revised before it was put into force. From the
standpoint of Belcredi and Esterhazy this step had grave
disadvantages. How could the legality of the Hungarian
Constitution be recognised at the very moment when the
Austrian Constitution of 1861 was being abolished? Were
the laws of 1848 more valid than those of 1861? Was it not
indeed dangerous to establish the greatest creation of the
Revolution as a fundamental act of state? But such objections had to be ignored when there was the chance of an
agreement. At the opening of the Hungarian Parliament on
December 14, the speech from the throne declared that
there was no obstacle to the "formal validity" of the laws
of 1848, but then demanded that the Parliament should
remove from the Constitution everything which encroached
too closely upon the royal prerogative, and should more
clearly define the affairs common to the whole empire,
especially the unity of the army, which the revolutionary
laws had completely ignored; until this was done, the
government of Hungary would remain in the hands of the
Emperor. Deák replied that Hungary could not be satisfied
with a formal recognition of her Constitution: an independent Ministry, responsible to Parliament, must first be
established; then only could a revision of the laws of 1848 be
discussed.

This was not a merely formal question. Both sides, the
Government and the national party, knew how important

it was to be in possession of power during the negotiations, and for some time no agreement could be reached. There were two fundamental problems to be settled: the scope of the affairs common to both nations, and the limits of royal and parliamentary power. Agreement over the first was relatively easy; if the crown remained powerful, it could employ the strength even of an independent Hungary for the benefit of the whole empire. The real problem lay in the division of power. Men like Esterhazy and Belcredi could not bring themselves to accept the complete victory of the parliamentarians; they feared that such a victory might destroy the power of the aristocracy and Church in the western half of the Monarchy as well. Nevertheless in the early months of 1866 there was a growing desire for a settle-ment. The Emperor was sincerely anxious to put an end to the conflict with the Magyar nation. Moreover the growing danger of war made it desirable to appease Hungarian pride. It was for this reason that the Imperial Court took up its residence at Buda-Pest from January 29 to March 5. All the ministerial councils were held there and it looked as if the centre of gravity of the whole empire had been transferred. The German Austrians were being swamped by Slav majori-ties in the Diets and the central Parliament was still dis-solved. The reconciliation with Hungary was one of the signs that portended war.

CHAPTER V

BISMARCK's success in the summer of 1865 had been incomplete. He now began to seek new and more effective weapons to supplement the traditional methods of orthodox diplomacy. He had not yet made any use of the growing forces of German nationalism, and few people realised that he had already determined to make Prussia the leader of the new Germany. His rare allusions to this ambition were laughed to scorn by his opponents: whoever united Germany it would not be Bismarck, the reactionary enemy of all popular causes.

It is part of Bismarck's greatness that in his autobiography he frankly admits responsibility for the war against Austria.[1] In this he shows himself much greater than admirers such as Sybel, who think to do him a service by distorting the truth and throwing the blame on Austria. He himself says that he became convinced that a war was necessary in his first days at Frankfort when he read Schwarzenberg's arrogant despatches announcing to the German courts the humiliation of Prussia at Olmütz: his "youthful illusions" concerning the friendship between Prussia and Austria were immediately destroyed. "The Gordian knot of German relations", he writes, "could not be untied by a friendly dualism; it had to be cut by war.

[1] See *Gedanken und Erinnerungen*, i. 127, 289, 327; ii. 194, 268.

85

Both from the standpoint of the Prussian patriot, anxious that Prussia should take the lead, and from that of the nationalist who desired German unification, the conscious or unconscious support of the King of Prussia, and through him of the Prussian army, had to be secured for the national cause."

With great skill Bismarck made the King "consciously or unconsciously" the executor of his plans, but only after a bitter struggle with almost the entire court. That is why his Recollections deal so shortly with this period. He did not care to show in detail how the case against Austria was built up, until the peace-loving King was convinced that she was threatening his hereditary rights and power, and that he must fight in self-defence. Bismarck himself says that even if the Austrian Court had adopted Rechberg's policy, a dualistic system in Germany could only have been a temporary expedient. The idea of a conflict with Austria so obsessed him that he used even to dream about the battlefields of Bohemia. In 1881, when William recounted a remarkable dream to him, he answered: "Your Majesty's story encourages me to describe a dream which I had in the spring of 1863, when there seemed no way out of our difficulties. I dreamt I was riding along a narrow mountain path, with a precipice on my right and on the left sheer rock; gradually the path narrowed until my horse refused to go on and there was no room to turn round or dismount. Then I struck the rocks with my whip and called on God. The rock-face fell like a piece of stage-property and revealed a broad road leading down to the Bohemian plain; and everywhere there were Prussian troops and colours. I awoke strengthened and joyful."

Before Bismarck went any further, he had to be sure that none of the European powers would interfere in case of a war with Austria. The benevolent neutrality of Russia would be his reward for the Polish treaty of 1863; he was sure of Italian support; and England always held aloof from Continental affairs. But it was vitally important that France should not turn the Prussian flank by invading the Rhineland. Immediately after the Treaty of Gastein, therefore, Bismarck began to sound Napoleon III as to his intentions in the event of an Austro-Prussian war. Napoleon shrouded his plans in secrecy. He would not say which side he favoured or what France hoped to gain from the conflict; but Bismarck could make a shrewd guess at the Emperor's intentions.

Napoleon III has a better claim than any other statesman of the nineteenth century to the title of modern politician. Firmly convinced that he must never oppose the prevailing ideas of the time, he constantly endeavoured to co-operate with them and exploit them for the benefit of his dynasty and of France. The Bonaparte family believed that Napoleon I had fallen because he had disregarded the national feelings and just claims of France's neighbours, particularly the Germans. Napoleon III felt that the demand for national unity was everywhere irresistible and that the unification of Germany, of Italy, and even of Poland, was only a question of time. But on the other hand, he counted on the popular love of peace and desire for international co-operation to make it possible to settle all European disputes peacefully at a regular series of Congresses, with France — and therefore Napoleon — acting as arbitrator. For he was convinced that France, since she was already a national state, was bound to profit by a remodelling of the map of Europe on national lines, especially with regard to Belgium. He would have advanced his Polish plans at the time of the Crimean War had not Austria and Prussia refused to support him. And although, as Emperor of the French, he could not desire the unification of Germany, he was ready to tolerate a strengthening of the German Confederation, but was resolved to seize the opportunity offered by the almost inevitable civil war to extend his frontier, perhaps even to the Rhine. If Austria and Prussia quarrelled he could use the promise of French support to make himself arbitrator of Europe. An Austro-Prussian understanding was the only thing which could spoil his plans.

He himself once wrote: "A Government can safely break the law, and even suppress liberty, but it will soon perish if it does not take the lead in the great causes of civilisation; and, until this simple philosophical reason for its downfall is understood, it is called fate". True to this principle, Napoleon set out to support the cause of progress everywhere. He established Free Trade in the teeth of the French industrialists, because he regarded it as the economic system of the future; without his support the Suez Canal could not have been built; he was interested in World Exhibitions and railways, in attempts at social reform, in profit-sharing, and in old-age pension schemes. No French Government since Colbert has done so much to benefit the country economically. Elsewhere he put his guiding principle even more clearly: "The Cæsar", he writes,[1] "can trample law and liberty underfoot with impunity, so long as he cares for the interests of civilisation". Here is the fundamental fallacy on which his ideas were based; for law is the foundation of all that is meant by that resounding word—civilisation. Napoleon III tried to dispense with everything that holds political passions in check and yet, dominate those passions himself. He had become Emperor by perjury and violence, and the streets of Paris had been strewn with the dead bodies of harmless spectators in order to inaugurate the new régime with a wholesome dread. His foster-sister said of him: "He is gentle and friendly, anxious to make his friends happy, and caring for mankind as a gardener cares for his flowers. But there is one spot where he must not be touched—the power and rights of his dynasty. If they are challenged his passion breaks all bounds and he becomes a tiger."[2] He

---

[1] In his *Idées Napoléoniennes*.   [2] Sybel, *Napoleon III*, 6.

thought nothing of ruling by corruption and violence or of using stock-exchange speculation as a source of income for himself and as a means of paying his supporters. Even Persigny, certainly not a man of high morals, could not refrain from remarking, when he retired from the Ministry of the Interior in 1863, "I may be ruining France by my weakness, but at least I am not selling her!" Moreover, the Napoleonic tyranny lacked greatness, especially in its later years, when the Emperor's physical weakness caused him to attempt a feeble compromise between autocracy and constitutionalism. The Mexican expedition showed most clearly the deceit and political adventurism which were part of his character; and in spite of his attempts to keep up the style of a representative of one of the old European ruling houses, he remained an upstart. Napoleon was neither the monster depicted by his enemies nor the benefactor of France described by his flatterers; had he been a legitimate prince he might have become a great benefactor of his people; but he was doomed to have to put his own selfish interests before all other motives.

He had long been preoccupied with the German problem. Regarding the Germans as the race of the future, he had no wish to provoke a conflict with them, and he was only driven to war later by the irresistible pressure of public opinion. His half-brother Morny once told Malmesbury[1] that he had

[1] Malmesbury, *Memoirs of an Ex-Minister*, i. 290. [The passage in Malmesbury reads: "Morny was a recognised natural son of Count Flahaut by Queen Hortense, and therefore the Emperor's half-brother. He was his right-hand man and generally gave him good advice, as he possessed great intelligence and tact, and was a man of the world. Morny told me that at the first period of Louis Napoleon's Presidency he was eager to fight for the Rhine, but that he had told him roughly that, if he did, 'les Allemands le flanqueraient dans le Rhin', an opinion verified in 1870." Malmesbury's style is so confused that it is impossible to be sure of his meaning, but it seems probable that Friedjung misunderstood this reference, and that what Malmesbury was trying to say was that Louis Napoleon had desired to advance on the Rhine and that Morny had advised him against it.—Translator.]

advised Napoleon at the beginning of his Presidency to march on the Rhine, and Napoleon had answered: "If I did that the Germans would throw me into the Rhine!" Of all the powers he disliked conservative Austria the most. Everywhere, but especially in Italy, she blocked his plans for tearing up the treaties and remaking the map of Europe; the very existence of Austria was a protest against the principle of nationality and a denial of all the Napoleonic ideas. Regarding the rise of Prussia as inevitable, he at once set himself to stimulate her ambition and secure her as an ally. At the time of the Crimean War, and still more urgently before his campaign in Italy, he sought Prussian support with offers of territory in Northern Germany; and the first German prince to visit him, Duke Ernest of Coburg, was eagerly sounded as to the Prussian ambitions. This was in 1854, when he wanted a Prussian alliance against Russia, and he said to the Duke: "The Prussians are not so stupid as to go to war without getting some territorial compensation. But what exactly does Prussia want? Hanover? Saxony?" And soon afterwards he remarked to the Prussian minister, Heydt, who happened to be in Paris: "I always feel that Prussia is a little too slender in the waist".

The beginning of the decline of the Second Empire in 1863 had a far-reaching effect on German history. For twelve years Napoleon had prospered, and now his star began to set. One of the main causes of this was the failure of the Emperor's health and his constant physical suffering. His plans had always been fantastic and far-flung, but until 1863 they had at least been carried out with energy. The *coup d'état*, the Crimean War, the establishment of a national Rumania, the War in Lombardy, and the acquisition of Savoy and Nice, had been a record of uninterrupted success; but there the record ended. A new generation was growing up in France; the middle classes had forgotten their fright of 1848 and no longer regarded Napoleon as the

saviour of society. Everything began to go wrong. The
elections of 1863 went against him. He encouraged the
Poles to revolt in 1863, but his co-operation with Palmerston
only exposed him to a diplomatic snub from the Tsar, and
he had to leave the Poles to their fate. The German powers
settled Schleswig-Holstein without consulting him, and, as
the patron of nationalism, he could raise no objection.
Finally there was the disaster in Mexico. Henceforth he tried
to shroud in secrecy plans which were often little more than
a mixture of fantasy and indecision. He was still full of
ideas, but he lacked the strength to carry them out.

Bismarck had closely studied the character and career of
Napoleon, and he had learnt how to win his approval. He
was already in touch with Lefèbre, Napoleon's agent in
Berlin, and was anxious to know the price of French support. Lefèbre had hinted unofficially at Belgium; and the
discussions had been carried further by Bleichröder and
Baron Rothschild in Paris.[1] But Bismarck wanted a personal
agreement with the Emperor, and therefore in October 1865
visited him at Biarritz.

At Plombières, eight years before, Napoleon and Cavour
had agreed to fight Austria and together they had studied
the map to discover the best *casus belli*. The position now
was different: Bismarck did not want French help, but
merely French neutrality. Napoleon was delighted. Encouraged by Bismarck's rosy but indefinite promises, he had
visions of an empire rounded off on the north-east and
bounded by the Rhine. But he himself was evasive and
undecided. Bismarck, hampered by not knowing how far
King William would back him, failed entirely to discover
the Emperor's real intentions.[2] Each of them hoped to
outwit the other; and since neither wished to bind himself—

[1] Keudell, *Fürst und Fürstin Bismarck*, 194.
[2] So Bismarck told Persigny in 1867, according to the latter's
Mémoires, 376.

Bismarck especially because Austria might still give way—
they eventually arrived at this highly philosophical conclusion: "We must not make events, we must let them
happen; and when they happen they will show that Prussia
and France are the European states who have most interests
in common".[1] They parted without any more definite
agreement, except that if an understanding should become
necessary the King of Prussia would write personally to
the Emperor. Dazzled by the prospect of territorial gains
Napoleon was ready to ignore the possibility that a more
powerful neighbour might arise beyond the Rhine. Some
of his advisers, among them Drouyn de Lhuys, the Foreign
Minister, and Walewski, the natural son of Napoleon I,
stood by the traditional French doctrine that it was best
for France that Germany should remain divided among
thirty-six princes, and disapproved of Napoleon's support of Bismarck.[2] Napoleon tried to reassure Walewski:
"Believe me," he said, "war between Austria and Prussia
is one of those unexpected chances which apparently should
never happen; it is not for us to prevent a war from which
we may hope to benefit so considerably". Many Germans
took the same view. Even Moltke wrote in 1860: "The
German nation of seventy million people which would
emerge from the struggle (between Austria and Prussia)
would certainly be an unwelcome result for France; but she
can count on tremendous gains—the annexation of Belgium,
the Rhine provinces, and perhaps Holland — while the
Prussian forces are engaged on the Elbe and the Oder".
Even Russian help, Moltke declared, would not make any
difference, as it had the twofold disadvantage "of being
too powerful and coming too late" Since 1860 Prussia had

---

[1] Sybel, iv. 215 *et seq.*

[2] Drouyn later asserted that he had urged on Napoleon that he need
only say: "I won't have a war in Germany", but that Napoleon could
not be persuaded to oppose Bismarck. Oskar Meding, *Memoiren zur
Zeitgeschichte*, ii. 57.

been strengthened by the army reforms and Moltke had been long converted to the war. Nevertheless, Napoleon's hopes were not entirely unfounded.

On his return Bismarck made a final attempt to persuade Austria to the voluntary surrender of Schleswig-Holstein. In November 1865 Prussia proposed for the last time that Austria should content herself with a pecuniary compensation. The offer was refused along with an Italian proposal to buy Venetia for 1000 million lire. Events in Schleswig-Holstein now took the course which was to be expected. At first Gablenz, the Austrian Governor of Holstein, was on the best of terms with Manteuffel, who ruled Schleswig for Prussia. Public support of the Duke of Augustenburg and attacks on Prussia in the press or at public meetings were alike forbidden by the Austrian authorities. But Bismarck's mysterious visit to Biarritz, the conclusion of a commercial treaty between Prussia and Italy (December 31, 1865), and the award of the Black Eagle to King Victor Emmanuel (January 29, 1866), all combined to reawaken Austrian suspicions. This state of affairs was reflected in Holstein and Prussia was able to find constant grounds for complaint. Gablenz, for instance, though he had forbidden the newspapers to call Augustenburg Duke Frederick VIII, actually allowed "His Highness the Duke". Then, worse still, Augustenburg's wife, on a journey from Altona to Kiel, was received everywhere by girls dressed in white, who strewed flowers in her path. Little girls in white, and the prayers of a few pious priests for Duke Frederick VIII, do not seem adequate evidence of a tremendous popular movement, but they served Bismarck's purpose; they made the conservative party in Prussia, the army, and finally the King, believe that Austria was tolerating dangerous attacks on Prussia's rights. Bismarck was waiting for a chance of putting Austria in the wrong and he saw it when Gablenz gave permission for a mass meeting at Altona. The meeting was forbidden to pass any resolutions, and the speeches were in consequence even more bitter against Prussia; it ended with three cheers for "our lawful, beloved prince, Duke Frederick". William was deeply offended by this performance, and on January 26 a Prussian Note was despatched to Vienna, accusing the Austrian Government of conducting "seditious agitation" against Prussia. Europe was astonished and alarmed; for the denunciation of Belcredi and Esterhazy, the disciples of Metternich, as revolutionaries, could only mean a deliberate intention to provoke a conflict. At the end of the despatch came the important announcement that, if Austria took no heed of the Prussian complaints, Prussia would claim "complete freedom of action". This despatch marks the end of the Austro-Prussian alliance. Prussia announced threateningly that she must take active steps to maintain her position in Schleswig-Holstein; and on March 13 the King issued a decree that any attempt to disturb the joint rule of Austria and Prussia in the Duchies would be punished by imprisonment. Thus in Schleswig the main objective of Austrian policy was to be punishable as treason.

Bismarck thus made Austria provide him with his strongest arguments for converting the King to the idea of war. He said to the French Ambassador, Benedetti: "If the King is to be persuaded to demand his rights he must first be convinced that someone is disputing them. But once he believes that his authority is being challenged or treated with contempt, he will agree to the most energetic measures." Bismarck told Benedetti quite openly of the struggle he had had to shake the King's faith in Austria. William agreed with Bismarck's fundamental object, the creation of a strong federation under Prussian leadership; but he still shrank from a war with Austria. He could remember how, in 1813, his father and the Prussian generals had pinned all their hopes on Austria joining the league against Napoleon; and Frederick William III had bequeathed the Austrian alliance as a precious legacy to his sons. Moreover for William, an appeal to German national feeling was a revolutionary measure. He was convinced that monarchy had been given to the Germans for their own good; a king ruled by divine right and must resist all strivings after parliamentary sovereignty on the English model. It was his belief that democrats, whatever their intentions, fostered anarchy and regicide. His escape, disguised as a servant, from the threats of the mob in March 1848 was his most painful memory; and now his minister was advising him practically to throw himself into the arms of the democrats. For Bismarck counted greatly on the German Parliament and on universal suffrage, recognising that they were not incompatible with a conservative monarchy. When the Ministerial Council met on February 28, the King, though still undecided, was already following the path which Bismarck had so carefully smoothed for him. Besides the ministers and the Crown Prince, there were present Moltke and Manteuffel, and Goltz, the Prussian representative in Paris. Bodelschwingh, the Minister of Finance, was the only minister who favoured a compromise; all the others, led by Bismarck and supported by Moltke and Manteuffel, declared that war was unavoidable unless Austria voluntarily surrendered the Duchies. Against them the Crown Prince repeated the arguments in favour of peace: war with Austria was civil war and foreign intervention was certain. But passionate opposition was not in his nature. He merely satisfied his conscience by explaining his point of view. The King's decision was remarkable: the Duchies were worth a war; but war must not be deliberately provoked and a peaceful solution, if possible, was still desirable. He added that he wanted peace, but was ready for war, since God had shown him that it was just. These words were a contradiction in terms. If a war to secure the Duchies was just, the desire for peace was meaningless; for Austria, as William well knew, would fight for her share of Schleswig-Holstein unless she received territorial compensation. The King had consulted his God in prayer and believed that the decision

of the Council was the expression of His will; but the will of
God coincided rather too well with the King's own unconscious wishes.

Immediately after the Council, negotiations with France
and Italy were set on foot. In accordance with the arrangement made at Biarritz, the King despatched Goltz with a
letter for the French Emperor, saying that the moment had
arrived for a more definite understanding. Goltz was to
ascertain the price of Napoleon's neutrality. At the same
time Moltke was ordered to go to Florence to conclude an
alliance with Italy. Moltke had already worked out his plans
for a sudden attack on Austria in the manner of Frederick
the Great in the Seven Years' War. The Prussian troops
were to surprise the Saxons and rout or disarm them while
they were still in their barracks. At the same time the
Prussian garrison in Mainz, having been secretly reinforced,
was to overpower the Austrian and other Federal troops
and take possession of the fortress. To achieve this surprise,
war must be declared on the first day of mobilisation and
the Prussian divisions must attack in their peace strength.
A rapid mobilisation would follow—one corps operating
before Mainz, while the main army of 193,000 men concentrated between Dresden and Görlitz, and only two corps,
54,000 strong, covered Silesia. Since Austria could not
mobilise so quickly, the war would be opened with a decisive
blow and the main enemy could perhaps be defeated at his
centres of mobilisation. Prussia, of course, would have to
ride roughshod over all international law; and Moltke himself must have realised that his scheme represented a
military ideal scarcely attainable among civilised nations.
William would have been the last to endanger his honour
in such an enterprise; though he discussed the plan with
Moltke, he would make no decision until he was sure of the
Italian alliance and it was to this end that Bismarck and
Moltke had now to direct their attention.

In embarking on negotiations with Italy, the King

quietened his conscience with the assurance that they committed him to nothing, so long as he remained open to a
compromise and did not present an ultimatum to Austria.
Bismarck did not contradict his master; for he too would
have preferred a voluntary surrender by Austria of supremacy in Northern Germany. But he was certain that
Habsburg pride would prefer defeat to a voluntary surrender, and, more clear-sighted than the King, saw that the
Italian alliance was a first step which would inevitably lead
to war. Peace could only be maintained if the King moderated his claims, or gave way, as his brother Frederick
William IV had done in 1850. But in 1850 William I
too had preferred Olmütz to a war; and in consequence
Bismarck's opponents at court fully expected the King to
draw back at the last moment.

The result of the Prussian Council of February 28 remained for the moment secret; had Austria known that
William was negotiating with Italy and France to secure
the overlordship of North Germany, she would at once have
prepared to meet the threat. But a good deal was learnt of
the Prussian plans through the personal relationships which
connected the Prussian and Austrian Courts and from
Bismarck himself, who made no secret of his intentions or
of the King's opposition; but Austria had isolated herself
during the Crimean War, and she seemed to have lost the
art of winning allies. Buol had left a grievous inheritance;
and after his fall Austrian policy had changed almost every
six months under the influence of first one minister and then
another. Since the Meeting of the Princes at Frankfort
Austrian policy had passed through every gradation from
a proud assertion of supremacy to a close alliance with
Prussia, and was now back again on the verge of a quarrel.
None of the leading men had been given time to carry a
policy through to a finish. Schmerling's plans had been
upset by Rechberg; and the influence of Schmerling and of
Biegeleben had brought Rechberg down when he had almost

succeeded in restoring the alliance with Prussia. Now Esterhazy was supreme; but he, unlike Schmerling and Rechberg,
had no definite plan and could never pursue any one policy
for long. The Cabinet of Vienna thus continued to be
swayed to and fro by contradictory hopes and fears.

Those who relied on the traditional good luck of Austria
—on one of those miracles which, according to Louis XIV,
continually saved the Emperor Leopold from apparently
certain disaster—could look forward undaunted to a war on
two fronts. Patriotic pride rebelled against the idea of giving
way an inch to Prussia in Germany, and still more against
surrendering a province to the King of Italy without
striking a blow. The younger officers, above all, clamoured
for war whatever the risk, and public opinion supported
them, ready, as always, to accuse statesmen of weakness and
even treachery, because of their inability to maintain the
former power and prestige of the empire. At the bottom of
his heart Francis Joseph felt the same. It is small wonder
that, with such powerful support, this view triumphed in the
end.

Others however, and among them the Foreign Minister,
were ready to make concessions to Prussia in the matter of
the Duchies. Mensdorff was first and foremost a soldier, but
he did not share the view that the Austrian army could
fight successfully on two fronts. He was in favour of ex-
ploiting the sympathies of King William to obtain a compromise over the Duchies and so postpone to a more favourable moment the perhaps unavoidable conflict with Prussia.
He set comparatively little store by the spoils of the Danish
War and on March 23 wrote to his cousin, the Duke of
Coburg: "I did not invent the stupid Schleswig-Holstein
question and am suffering for the sins of past years.
Whether we shall get out of this most tedious of tedious
questions without a conflict I cannot yet say. . . ." Mensdorff
would have let Schleswig-Holstein go, in order to keep
Venice; but he was incapable of insisting on this policy.

In these circumstances the final decision rested with the man who had the Emperor's ear, Count Esterhazy. Esterhazy saw the possibilities of the situation clearly—too clearly, indeed; for Austria needed a man of decision, and not one who was torn by doubts. Esterhazy rightly recognised that an agreement with Hungary, or at any rate with the Hungarian nobility, was an essential preliminary to war, but he got no further than asking for proposals and minutes from all sides, which—if he read them at all—plunged him into new doubts and delays. He regarded the period of the Holy Alliance as the happiest in European history and therefore disliked the thought of a war between two of the conservative powers. He would rather have come to some agreement with Prussia regarding the supremacy in Germany; and he toyed with the idea of selling her the Austrian rights over Schleswig-Holstein for 60-70 million guelders. It never occurred to him to envisage a reform of the German Confederation in accordance with national ideas; for he despised nationalism as one of the modern enthusiasms which, especially in Germany, had little real depth. He did not, therefore, expect a war to make much difference to the existing order in Germany. An extension of territory in the old style—perhaps a bit of Silesia—was the most he hoped for; and if the war went badly, he was ready to agree to a division of Germany, in which Prussia would receive the North, and the game would go on between the two states, as it had gone on since the time of Frederick the Great. The system created by the Congress of Vienna seemed to him, in the nature of things, the best: it was to the interest of all monarchs, including the King of Prussia, to preserve it. Thus, while Bismarck was drafting a new German Constitution which allowed for the active co-operation of the German people, Esterhazy made no appeal to enlightened opinion in Germany. He himself had no ideas on Germany's future, for his ideal lay in the past; and Austria therefore embarked on the War of 1866 without a German programme.

In fact, Esterhazy was afraid of too decisive an Austrian victory, because he could not visualise any European system except that of the Congress of Vienna. He said himself: "The stakes are too high for me; for whether we win or whether we lose, the result of the war will be a different Austria from the one we know".

The war party in Vienna had no such doubts. Belcredi, completely inexperienced in state affairs, was particularly loud in his demand for a resort to arms; he found it intolerable that the leading German and Catholic power should hesitate under Bismarck's diplomatic provocations. He urged that "the system of Metternich must be abandoned in favour of a policy better adapted to the times". He believed that King William was all along as determined on war as Bismarck, and the fact that he stuck to this opinion in his memoranda of 1869 says little for his psychological insight. In the same notes he heaps reproaches on Mensdorff, declaring that his colleague opposed war only because he opposed any kind of decision. This judgement was unfair; for Mensdorff really wanted peace, while Belcredi agreed entirely with Biegeleben that Austria, in alliance with the lesser German states, should challenge Prussia to give way or fight. By sheer determination Biegeleben carried Mensdorff and Esterhazy along this path. At the beginning of March, Karolyi was instructed to inform Bismarck that Austria would not be bullied into accepting any settlement in Schleswig-Holstein contrary to her interests and position in Germany. Similar declarations were made in Paris and London. The British Government was informed that Prussia had resumed the negotiations of the previous summer with Italy, that Austria would risk a war on two fronts rather than abandon her position in Germany and Italy, and that the Emperor would rely on the justice of his cause and the loyalty of his subjects rather than on German support.

These were proud words, but they only concealed the

irresolution of Esterhazy, who was still wavering between Mensdorff and the anti-Prussian party. Biegeleben, with a more than Austrian faith in the historic rights of the Habsburgs in Germany, was preaching the necessity of "breaking Prussia into her component parts". He and Belcredi were convinced that Prussia was meditating a sudden attack on Saxony and Bohemia, and reports from Berlin seemed to confirm their warnings. The Saxon Court was especially alarmed by a warning from no less a person than Bleichröder, Bismarck's banker, who told Hohenthal, the Saxon minister in Berlin, that at the Council of February 28 a surprise attack on Saxony had been seriously discussed and had only been postponed until a war should become inevitable. It is true that Moltke at any rate had seriously considered such a plan, but it is impossible to know whether in informing the Saxon minister, Bleichröder was acting on his own initiative, in order to stand well with both sides, or whether he had been put up to it by Bismarck to increase the tension between Austria and Prussia. Certainly Bismarck in conversation with Benedetti and Pfordten, the Bavarian minister, made no secret of his belief that war was inevitable. Hohenthal could not ask Bismarck himself about Bleichröder's report; he therefore invited him to dinner, seated him next to his wife, and left it to her to ask Bismarck innocently whether he really intended to overrun Saxony and attack Austria. Bismarck answered unhesitatingly: "Believe me, dear Countess, I have thought of nothing else and I have been busy with it ever since my entry into the Ministry. The moment is approaching: our cannon are already cast and you will soon have the chance of convincing yourself that our improved artillery is vastly superior to the Austrian." And when the Countess asked whether she ought to retire to her estates near Leipzig or to Bohemia, Bismarck earnestly advised her to stay near Leipzig, as her Bohemian castle was too near the spot where the Austrians would be met and defeated. Bismarck himself later assured enquiring diplomats that he had only been joking, but no one in Vienna could decide whether anything more lay behind his remarks.

All this was mere trifling compared to the news of the arrival of the Italian general Govone in Berlin on March 14, in order, it was announced, to study the organisation of the Prussian army. The very openness with which the negotiations between Italy and Prussia were being conducted was a threat in itself. Benedetti relates that the old Field Marshal Wrangel was told that an Italian general was coming, and by March 12 the news was all over Berlin. "If Prussia has not burnt her boats yet," Bismarck said to Benedetti, "they are at any rate smouldering." And soon afterwards Govone told La Marmora that several diplomats, who had not been afraid of war so long as the quarrel was confined to Prussia and Austria, became seriously alarmed the moment Italy took a hand in it.

It was in this atmosphere that the first military councils were held in Vienna on March 7 and 14. Owing to the illness of Franck, the Minister of War, the chief part was played by Henikstein, the Chief of the General Staff. Henikstein had an orderly and business-like mind, and his friend Benedek had recommended his appointment in the hope that he would remedy some of the defects in the Austrian army organisation. But he himself admitted that he had no strategical knowledge or ability, and he therefore asked Neuber, Professor of Strategy at the Military Academy at Vienna, to draw up for him a plan of campaign. Neuber, in view of the unreadiness of the Austrian army, was in favour of a concentration in a defensive position under the protection of the fortress of Olmütz. The Archduke Albrecht strongly disagreed, maintaining that, as in 1850, Austria should make use of the natural bastion of the Bohemian mountains. But Henikstein and the majority of the Austrian generals stood by Neuber's plan; and the Emperor, fearing a sudden Prussian

attack, decided in favour of the defensive policy. A Director
of Operations was now needed to co-ordinate the concentration on Olmütz; and Henikstein declared that he was completely unfit for the post. It was the Archduke Albrecht who
suggested Major-General Krismanič.[1] Krismanič had a great
reputation as a theoretical strategist; he had also some
knowledge of the field of operations in Bohemia, whereas the
attention of all the other Austrian generals had been concentrated on Italy. Above all, he had the self-confidence
which so many of the leading men in Austria lacked, and
was not afraid of shouldering responsibility; he always gave
the impression of being equal to any situation. A defensive
campaign fitted in with all his theories and he was delighted
to find both the Emperor and Henikstein already on his
side.

The military council was not, of course, concerned with the
question of peace or war; but it had enough cares of its own.
There were distressing accounts of the efficiency of the new
Prussian needle gun; above all, there was the problem of
mobilisation. In Prussia every army corps lay in the province from which its men were drawn, so that the army
could be rapidly and easily mobilised. Austria, unable to
trust her subject nationalities, never on principle stationed
troops near their homes; in consequence, men on leave and
in reserve had great distances to travel, from Transylvania
to Bohemia or from Italy to Galicia, and mobilisation
would take at least two months. The first essential was to
strengthen Bohemia against the surprise attack which was
the constant nightmare of the Austrian generals. Apart
from troops in garrison, a whole army corps—that is, eight
regiments of the line, four battalions of light infantry, and
the usual complement of cavalry and artillery—was supposed to be stationed in Bohemia. Actually there were only
five regiments, two of them Italian, and therefore unreliable;
and it was decided to reinforce them with ten battalions of

[1] [Pronounced Krismanitch.]

infantry and ten squadrons of cavalry, in all roughly 6700 men.

At once Mensdorff protested. Premature measures would give Prussia the chance of accusing Austria of arming for an offensive war without really increasing Austria's military security, for a well-prepared attack would make short work of the handful of fresh troops in Bohemia. But Mensdorff's opposition was brushed aside. There was no higher authority to co-ordinate military and political affairs. The General Staff behaved as though its activities could have no effect on the foreign situation, and Mensdorff's protests were too timid. Although he regarded these military preparations as the first mistake that led to war, he allowed himself to be overruled, and Austrian policy continued on its haphazard course. There was no aggressive intention behind the precautions taken by the generals. They were driven by anxiety to provocative measures; and in the Imperial counsels the obligations of honour and the traditions of the Monarchy outweighed all other arguments.

Austria now tried to show how pure and peaceful her intentions were. Francis Joseph could honestly say that he was only seeking to defend his empire. It seemed best to present to Prussia the direct question which the Emperor might expect from King William. Karolyi was therefore instructed to ask Bismarck: "Whether the Court of Berlin really intended to tear up the Treaty of Gastein and to break the peace, sanctified by law, between the German federal states?" At the same time Austria tried to get into touch with the lesser German states and re-establish the friendships broken by her direct negotiations with Prussia over the fate of Schleswig-Holstein. A Circular Note was despatched to the German Courts to the effect that Austria would place the Schleswig-Holstein question in the hands of the German Diet, if the Prussian reply to Karolyi's question was unsatisfactory. Austria was thus falling back on Frankfort, and was hoping to persuade the Diet to take active steps in defence of the threatened Federal Constitution.

Bismarck at once made the most of his enemy's mistake. He was finding it difficult to provoke the King to any decisive step, for Prussia was as anxious as Austria to avoid appearing as the aggressor in the eyes of Europe; now Austria had saved him any further trouble. Beust, when he saw the Austrian Circular, at once declared it to be useless; Prussia could easily deny aggressive intentions without altering her plans. When on March 16 Karolyi asked his question, with the polite assurance that it was not meant as a challenge, Bismarck answered short and sharp, "No!"[1] In a certain sense this was true, for the question and answer were not concerned with Bismarck's plans, but with the will of the King; and William certainly did not intend to attack Austria. The situation was not so desperate as that which had driven Frederick II to invade Saxony in 1756, and William, in any case, was not the man for such bold decisions. Bismarck's answer cut short any further discussion and the whole Frankfort plan came to nothing. But at least Austria had let the lesser states know that she was ready to abandon her Schleswig-Holstein treaty with Prussia and return to the Diet.

Bismarck set himself all the more eagerly to exploit the mistakes of the Austrian Cabinet. He passed on to the press reports of the movements of troops in Bohemia and encouraged exaggerated accounts of Austrian armaments. Prussia, it was emphasised, remained in the depths of peace, but beyond her frontiers there were active preparations for war. When the Austrian Government forbade the press to publish the movements of troops within the empire, Prussia replied by instructing her officials to issue the fullest reports concerning Prussian armaments. And the Austrian

---

[1] According to private information Bismarck added: he would give the same answer, if he were already drafting a declaration of war.

Secret Circular was followed on March 24 by an Open Note from Prussia to the German Courts. Austria was roundly accused of concentrating troops in Bohemia solely in order to recreate the situation of 1850, when her army had been assembled on the frontier before Prussia could arm and Prussia had had to accept the humiliation of Olmütz. This time, therefore, Prussia must arm in self-defence, and she wished to know what the other federal states proposed to do in the event of an Austrian attack. Finally, the Circular announced that Prussia was about to submit a plan for the reform of the German Constitution, as it had proved inadequate to protect her interests and those of her fellow-members in the Confederation.

If the alarmist reports of the Prussian press were to be believed, Austria was already one vast armed camp. It was calculated that if the troops in Bohemia, Moravia, and West Galicia were at full war strength, Austria had already an army of 80,000 men, ready to attack Silesia from three sides. In fact, there were as many troops in Silesia and Brandenburg as in the three Austrian provinces, and it would be much easier to put them on a war footing. Of the regiments in an Austrian army corps in Bohemia, two drew their reserves from Italy, two from Hungary, and one from East Galicia; only four could be mobilised on the spot. The Prussian army, on the other hand, was organised with a view to rapid mobilisation. In the Prussian Council on March 28 Moltke reported on the military situation. He declared that twenty-two battalions (actually it was only ten) had been transferred to Bohemia, so that the Austrians now mustered fifty-three battalions. "We must anticipate", he concluded, "that at the beginning of April there will be 70,000 men in Bohemia and, if more troops are transferred from Galicia, 22,000 in Moravia"; and although this force was not sufficient for an offensive, it could cause Prussia serious embarrassment. The information of the Prussian General Staff, based on reports from officials in Silesia, was very inaccurate, but in any case Moltke wanted to present as black a picture as possible, in order to provoke the Council to strong counter-measures. He was partially successful. As Silesia with only 25,000 men seemed to lie at the mercy of a triple attack from Bohemia, Moravia, and Galicia, it was decided to put the Silesian fortresses on a war footing. Still more important—the relatively weak Prussian artillery was to receive its full war complement of horses. But the most striking step of all was the increase of the peace establishment of the five divisions in Southern Silesia: each battalion was to add another 155 to its ordinary strength of 530 men. William only sanctioned these measures after long hesitation. Bismarck and Roon managed to get him to sign the orders on March 29, immediately before Easter, for they were afraid that he would use the holiday for a fresh delay. In fact, that evening, the King wrote to Roon: "I had quite forgotten Easter; would it be possible to postpone the despatch of the orders until Saturday? Ask Bismarck and let me know". But this was just what Roon had feared and the orders had already been hastily despatched. Mensdorff had been right in his prophecy that the Austrian armaments would drive William to decisive steps. But even this was no real preparation for a war of aggression. It was at most a flash of lightning, and the clouds might still disperse.

Moltke, believing his reports from Silesia, was seriously considering the possibility of a sudden Austrian advance through Saxony on Berlin. But obviously such an undertaking with a handful of troops—even if there were really 80,000–100,000—would be madness and could only end in the destruction or the inglorious retirement of the Austrian advanced detachment. Moltke, therefore, concluded that he only need fear a slight interruption of his mobilisation in the frontier districts. Otherwise "an Austrian offensive must put us in a favourable strategical position, because it will enable us to bring our full strength into the field before Austria can assemble her forces". Moltke added that even this temporary disadvantage could be avoided if Prussia took the initiative and attacked first. A few days later he received more accurate information of the Austrian movements and that only ten battalions had been transferred to Bohemia, as the Austrian Government had declared. He would not, however, admit that his Intelligence Department had been at fault, and wrote to Roon on April 7: "The contradiction can be explained if we assume that the order had been given for a large concentration of troops and the movements countermanded at the last moment". At any rate the reports from Breslau had done their work in the Prussian Council and William probably never learnt that they were unfounded.

The negotiations between Prussia and Italy were conducted in this atmosphere of threatening notes, marches and counter-marches, and general European alarm. The Italians were eager for a war to give them Venice, and they rejoiced at the news of Austrian and Prussian armaments. For if the two German powers fought, there would be an end of German rule in Italy.

The alliance between Italy and Prussia was hanging fire. The mutual distrust of the two Governments was well founded, for each was trying to use the other merely to frighten the common enemy. William would have liked to use the threat of war on two fronts to induce Austria to give up Schleswig-Holstein; and the Italians hoped that Austria would buy their neutrality with Venice, in order to secure her supremacy in Germany. Bismarck alone realised that the Austrian attitude made war inevitable, and worked unceasingly for a defensive and offensive alliance. The Italian Government gave him little encouragement and La Marmora, the Prime Minister, whatever his qualities as a soldier, was an irresolute, timid, and suspicious politician. He could not rid himself of the fear that Prussia was only using the Italian alliance as a scarecrow; and he was all the more suspicious because he was doing his best to dupe Bismarck in exactly the same way. He wanted Venice, if possible, without having to fight for it. When, on February 24, the expulsion of Prince Couza left the Roumanians without a ruler, La Marmora offered Austria Roumania in exchange for Venice; but the Austrians were not interested, and he had to fall back on direct negotiations with Prussia. On March 14 General Govone arrived in Berlin, with instructions from La Marmora not to enter into an alliance unless Prussia was ready for an immediate declaration of war; Govone was empowered to conclude a defensive and offensive alliance and nothing else.[1]

In Berlin, however, things had not got as far as that. William absolutely refused to launch an attack on Austria; Bismarck, whatever his own feelings, had to follow the lines laid down by the Council of February 28. Actually he himself was not yet ready to commit himself to the Italian alliance; for a compromise with Austria was still a possibility. There was another consideration: he would not be justified in plunging Germany into civil war merely over the question of Schleswig-Holstein; there must be an object of more genuinely national importance at stake. Bismarck made no secret of his intentions to Govone. In three or four months, he said, he proposed to raise the question of constitutional reform in Germany on the basis of a German Parliament, and his proposals would bring Prussia out into the open against Austria. Until then, he suggested, the two states should content themselves with a treaty of peace and friendship; when the time came, they could have an aggressive alliance based on the condition that, war once begun, it should not end until Italy was in possession of Venice.

Govone did not care for these proposals. The unity of

---

[1] The chief source for these negotiations is La Marmora's *Un po' piu di luce*, published in 1873, and here cited from the German edition, *Etwas mehr Licht*.

Germany and a German Parliament were no concern of Italy's. The Italians would have to wait on Prussia's pleasure, and meanwhile might lose the chance of negotiating a peaceful cession of Venice. Moreover, Govone was not favourably impressed with the situation in Berlin. Bismarck frankly confessed to him that the King would not be persuaded to energetic measures in Germany until the alliance with Italy was concluded, and Govone also saw that there was a strong party at Court working against Bismarck. Twice his promised audience with the King was postponed; it was not till March 22 that Bismarck secured it for him, and begged him to hold out to the King some hope of an Italian alliance. In these circumstances Govone thought a war between Austria and Prussia improbable, and he advised La Marmora not to conclude an alliance on Bismarck's terms. Nevertheless, though the negotiations were at a standstill, he remained in Berlin in the hope that his presence there would exercise pressure on Austria; and Bismarck was satisfied, because it left him an opportunity of reopening the negotiations.

Govone saw Bismarck often and gradually came under his influence; his despatches to La Marmora show his gradual conversion to the Prussian alliance. At first he had practically dismissed Bismarck as a charlatan, but soon their frank discussions had their effect. Bismarck said to him one day: "I hope to drag the King to war, but I can't absolutely promise it", and Govone watched the struggle at Court with ever-increasing excitement. To add to Bismarck's cares, the Prussian Minister at Florence reported the rumour that Italy was negotiating with Austria for the cession of Venice, and it was therefore essential to commit Italy at any rate to a treaty of friendship, in order to make the approach to Austria more difficult. The King distrusted the Italians and the Crown Prince believed that they only wanted to use the Prussians as a dupe. To silence these doubts Bismarck needed a definite treaty.

Govone himself thus became the advocate of the Prussian alliance. He wrote to La Marmora as early as March 22 that Italy might be tricked, but it was equally possible that Bismarck would fall, if he was not given means of influencing the King; and the new Cabinet would consist of pro-Austrians. Govone therefore proposed a compromise; a treaty should be made with Prussia on the lines suggested by Bismarck, but only binding Italy for three months. Prussia would thus be given time to open the German question and William would have three months in which to declare war. Moltke had already pointed out to Bismarck that he would not get anything from Florence unless he fixed a time-limit for the outbreak of war; otherwise Italy would get no advantage from the treaty. Govone's proposal would overcome this difficulty. But La Marmora had not fallen under the influence of Bismarck; he saw snares everywhere and no way out of his difficulties. He belonged to the school of Italian politicians who gratefully remembered Napoleon III's services to Italy and hoped that his friendship would still stand her in good stead. He decided to consult Napoleon.

It was Napoleon who now did Bismarck an invaluable service by reviving the flagging negotiations between Prussia and Italy. He did so for two reasons. In the first place, he desired the dissolution of the alliance between Austria and Prussia which formed so uncomfortable a bulwark against France. A civil war between the two German powers might mean for Napoleon the Rhine frontier. His genuine sympathy with the cause of Italian unification was his secondary motive for encouraging the alliance between William and Victor Emmanuel. He regarded the still incomplete kingdom of Italy as his own work and he was anxious to see it completed before he died. Moreover, the acquisition of Venice might distract Italian attention from the French garrison in Rome and soften Italian resentment of the Convention by which Rome was secured to the Pope and Florence became the capital of the young kingdom. For, however much Napoleon tried to rule in accordance with modern ideas, he needed the support of the French clergy for his dynasty, and so had to maintain the remnants of the Temporal Power of the Papacy.

This was Napoleon's frame of mind when, on March 3, he received King William's letter, announcing that the time for a definite agreement, foreseen at Biarritz, had now arrived. Goltz was empowered frankly to state the aims of Prussian policy; now was the moment for Napoleon to state his price for consenting to a revision of the German Federal Treaties in Prussia's favour. It was a unique opportunity; it seemed that he need only express his wishes and they would be granted. Yet when Goltz explained to him that Prussia was aiming at Schleswig-Holstein and the political and military supremacy of Northern Germany— including the annexation of certain of the most obstinate of the lesser states—Napoleon hesitated. He could not formulate his demands for several contradictory reasons. In the first place, he dared not demand Belgium, protected as it was by European treaties; and to annex the Rhineland or the Palatinate would be contrary to the principles of nationality. As he remarked to Nigra, the Italian Minister: "I have no wish to make a French Venice for myself". But there was a more important reason for Napoleon's reserve. He wanted Prussia to realise that he was casting covetous eyes on Belgian and German territory, but he did not want to reveal how exorbitant his ambition really was. He was afraid of tying himself down by expressing himself too clearly. During the crisis he might be able to achieve the limit of his desires—perhaps even the Rhine frontier; but at the very least he expected the coal-fields of the Saar, and it would be madness to reveal this to King William now. The Rhine was too high a price for Prussia to pay for Schleswig-Holstein and no King of Prussia could negotiate on such a basis. Rather than this, William would

be reconciled with Austria; and that was just what
Napoleon feared. He therefore merely remarked meaningly
to Goltz that he had heard that there were strong pro-
French sympathies in the Rhenish Palatinate and that in
the opinion of his Minister of War the frontiers of 1814
were desirable for the military security of France; thereby
indicating Saarlouis, which was Prussian, and Landau,
which belonged to Bavaria, as the lowest price of his
neutrality. He was equally reserved about Belgium; but
here agreement seemed more likely and Goltz and the
Emperor discussed the possibility of dividing it between
Prussia and France, perhaps along the Meuse.

Napoleon's evasiveness and reserve were very disturbing
to the Prussians: there was nothing to prevent a French
army appearing on the Rhine the moment all the forces of
Prussia were engaged in Bohemia. Goltz was instructed to
avoid any further discussion of the surrender of German
territory, as the King would never consent; any French
hints were to be rejected on the grounds of German national
feeling. The negotiations between France and Prussia had
reached this point when La Marmora sent Arese as special
envoy to consult the Imperial oracle about Govone's proposed alliance. Napoleon had been long decided on his
answer. He would encourage the Italians to ignore the
warnings of Drouyn de Lhuys, his own Foreign Minister.
Nigra, the Italian Minister in Paris, argued that it did not
matter to Italy whether she got Venice from Prussia or
Austria. Napoleon, however, advised a Prussian alliance in
order to balance (*égaliser*) the forces in Germany and give
the Cabinet of Berlin a fair chance of success. "In this way",
Napoleon continued, "Italy will get Venice, and France will
benefit by the conflict of the two powers whose alliance
hems her in. Once the struggle has begun France can throw
her weight into the balance and must obviously become
arbitrator and master of the situation. By occupying the
Rhineland with 100,000 men I shall be able to dictate the

terms of peace."[1] Finally, to give the Italians complete confidence, Napoleon promised to protect Italy in the event of an Austrian victory; Milan should not fall into the hands of the Austrians again. The Emperor demanded only that Prussia, and not Italy, should provoke the struggle with Austria. But whatever happened, the alliance was to be concluded as it was the only means of inducing King William to take decisive action.[2] La Marmora was now completely reassured and grateful to France for giving her permission, as his colleague Berti later expressed it, for the Prussian alliance. Napoleon, without the knowledge and against the policy of his Foreign Minister, had brought Prussia and Italy together with the intention of setting Central Europe ablaze and so securing Venice for Italy and the Rhine for France.

Napoleon's advice convinced the Italian diplomats that there was a secret treaty between France and Prussia; even Nigra thought so. But they were wrong: Bismarck indeed saw through Napoleon and was troubled by his eagerness to help. But what could he do? It would not be wise to wake the Emperor too soon from his dreams. He would certainly have liked to know what Napoleon hoped to get from the war and he was trying to find out through his Italian friends. In his conversations with Govone he continually made flattering remarks about the Emperor with the knowledge that they would be transmitted to Paris. So things stood for the next few months. Goltz could promise nothing; but, through the Italians, Bismarck dangled the most dazzling possibilities before Napoleon.

[1] Nigra, later ambassador in Vienna, recounted this conversation to the author. In his book La Marmora omits the reports which show Napoleon's policy in its true light. For he displays a tendency to contrast the magnanimity of Napoleon with the selfishness of Bismarck.

[2] Napoleon's words were (according to La Marmora): "Sign a treaty with Prussia, however vague and non-committal it may be, for it is very desirable to furnish M. de Bismarck with the necessary means to push the King into war".

Everything now went smoothly. Within a week of Arese's mission to Paris, Bismarck had the treaty with Italy in his pocket. Seldom has such a one-sided agreement been concluded except as the result of war. In this treaty of April 8 Prussia bound herself to nothing at all, while Italy was completely committed to Prussia, though only for three months. Prussia merely promised to propose a German Parliament to the German states and to pursue an ambitious national policy. If King William, the treaty declared, attacked Austria in fulfilment of this policy, Italy must put all her forces into the field. But the treaty did *not* commit Prussia to war if Italy quarrelled with Austria. For three months, then, Italy was pledged to war. If it came to war the allies promised that peace should not be concluded until Italy received Venice and Prussia an equivalent territorial acquisition in Austria.[1]

However much he desired peace, William would have been very foolish to reject such a treaty, for it left him entirely free to decide on peace or war. Italy could not involve Prussia in war against her will. But Prussia could provoke the war by proposing a German Parliament; or she could, if she preferred it, come to an agreement with Austria without infringing the treaty with Italy. If King William gave the word, 200,000 Italians must cross the Mincio. What more could Bismarck's opponents offer Prussia? The King determined to stand fast by such a minister.

---

[1] Prussia added the verbal declaration (according to Sybel, iv. 312) that instead of territorial acquisitions she would be satisfied with concessions in relation to Germany.

CHAPTER VI

THE PRUSSIAN REFORM PLAN. GENERAL MOBILISATION

WHILE Bismarck spun his net round Austria the Cabinet of Vienna lost itself in hopeless irresolution. Mensdorff was advising a direct understanding with the King of Prussia over Bismarck's head, at the price of concessions in Germany. Esterhazy would neither follow this very sensible advice nor make up his mind to war. But if the Austrian Cabinet did nothing it wrote the more. An endless stream of complaints against Prussia flowed from Biegeleben's pen; and every Note made it easier for Bismarck to convince the King that Austria was aiming at a second "Humiliation of Olmütz". He could point out that it was Mensdorff, the most peace-loving of the Austrian ministers, who was using this arrogant language. It did not matter that Mensdorff only signed the Notes very unwillingly; that was his own affair.

The Austrian Note of March 31 showed how deeply the Prussian Circular had offended the Cabinet of Vienna; it spoke of the "subversive activities" of the Prussian Government; and it closed with the assurance that Francis Joseph had no thought of attacking Prussia and demanded a similar declaration from King William. This only irritated the King; and the Italian minister reported on April 10 that the Austrians seemed to be doing their best to provoke the war, which up till then had seemed improbable. Bismarck coldly replied on April 5 that it was Austrian armaments which had caused all the alarm and added that the King was not thinking of attacking Austria.

Yet Austria had committed no act of hostility comparable to the treaty between Italy and Prussia. The new allies, fearful of appearing as aggressors in the eyes of Europe, kept their secret well; but Prussia gave Italy immediate proof that her plans for German reform were serious. On April 9, the day after the treaty had been signed, Prussia proposed to the Diet the calling of a German Parliament. Hitherto Bismarck had ruthlessly ignored public opinion in Germany; now he set out to placate it, by showing that he aimed at German unification and not merely at some small territorial acquisition for Prussia. He had to move quickly. Italy was only committed for three months; after that she could disarm and might renew direct negotiations for the purchase of Venice. Within three months, therefore, he must settle with Austria one way or another. The Prussian proposal to the Diet sketched only the outlines of German reform. The Diet was to summon a German Parliament, directly elected—and here was the most significant point—by universal suffrage. It was also to fix the day for the meeting of the National Assembly. Meanwhile the Governments were to draft a Constitution to be submitted to the Parliament. The reasons for the proposal were developed at length; the essential sentence read: "If Germany has to face a European crisis with her present Constitution, she will succumb either to revolution or to foreign domination".

The most remarkable of these proposals is that of universal suffrage. Bismarck was in the middle of his struggle with the Prussian Parliament, which, as the representative of the middle classes, was demanding not a mere share of power, but complete parliamentary supremacy as in England. The middle classes were genuinely convinced that they represented the whole nation, and believed that the capitulation of the Monarchy and nobility to an assembly based on a limited suffrage would be sufficient to secure democracy. Bismarck was now falling back on the lower classes to help him to resist the claims of the Third Estate. All the nineteenth-century statesmen who came into conflict with the liberal middle classes adopted this policy. Bismarck had been particularly impressed with Napoleon III's successful use of universal suffrage for his plebiscites and his subservient Parliament, and was confirmed in his view by Lothar Bucher, who, from being a democrat, had become a supporter of enlightened and reforming despotism.[1] Lassalle also seems to have known of Bismarck's plans; for during his case before the State Court on March 12, 1864, he declared: "The greatest games, gentlemen, can be played with the cards on the table! Great diplomacy does not need to conceal its intentions, because they rest on iron necessity. And therefore I announce to you that, perhaps before the year is out, Herr von Bismarck will have played the part of Robert Peel and introduced direct and universal suffrage!"[2] The liberals were staggered by the new trend of Bismarck's policy; and many of the conservatives were deeply distressed. Gerlach called the grant of universal suffrage "the bankruptcy of all the respectable political forces in Germany— of nobility, rank, authority, and every established institution". Now, he added, "there is no organisation left except the organisation of party warfare and it is to this noble patriotic work that we must turn". In fact Bismarck miscalculated; beyond the middle classes another class was developing, whose revolutionary force was far more dangerous and fundamental than anything seen in the Prussian Parliament. But he expressed the opinion that he would be able to manage the German Parliament provided that it had a conservative or radical, but not a liberal, majority.[3] In any

[1] Keudell, *Fürst und Fürstin Bismarck*, 253, doubts whether Bucher really had this influence on Bismarck's political resolutions.

[2] [See also Gustave Meyer, *Bismarck und Lassalle.*—Translator.]

[3] Benedetti, 103.

case the suffrage was not Bismarck's primary concern. "In a life-and-death struggle", he wrote later in his Reminiscences, "one does not examine the weapons one employs or the damage caused by their use; the important thing is the success of the struggle and the preservation of independence abroad; the damage must be put right after the peace." Bismarck only wanted to strike a blow at Austria and the lesser states; if he could convince public opinion of the honesty of his intentions, Prussia could more safely risk an appeal to the sword.

It is not surprising that Bismarck's new policy excited general mistrust. It was not likely that he had suddenly become a parliamentarian, and the German press was loud in its suspicions. The *Nationalzeitung*, for example, wrote: "Universal and equal suffrage, direct election, and a German Parliament are fine words, but what have they to do with Count Bismarck or the Diet? Suppose a real German Assembly were to meet, where are the constitutional ministers who would represent Prussia? If the Prussian gentry are so enthusiastic, let them try the experiment in their own country—there a Parliament is already in existence. . . . Prussia's internal situation justifies the coolness with which her proposals have been received throughout Germany. The same proposal by a popular Prussian Government would electrify not only Germany, but all Europe." Few in Germany judged Bismarck's proposal without prejudice. The liberals were astonished when a convinced democrat like Ziegler, the former mayor of Brandenburg, came out on Bismarck's side in a remarkable speech on April 17. "I regard the proposal", he said, "as a brilliant victory after so many defeats. . . . Even if the Prime Minister is not serious about the Parliament, which I deny, I think it wise to support him; for then he will be hoist with his own petard." Ziegler was, however, isolated in his own party. Certainly a section of the progressives desired the aggrandisement of Prussia and attacked Austria as fiercely as they attacked the Prussian Prime Minister; but one of the democrats declared that Prussia must be put where she belonged—under their feet.

Opinion abroad was ironical on the subject of Prussia's attempt to distract attention from her domestic difficulties by provoking a war. But the best judges still regarded a war as unlikely. The English in particular would not believe that after writing and talking for so long the Germans would ever actually do anything. *The Times* wrote arrogantly: "The inference from these proceedings is that there is a fair chance the peace of Europe will not be violated. As for the precise degree in which the honour of the two antagonists is preserved, we profess very little anxiety indeed. The truth is the nature of the transaction leaves very little honour to be divided between these two great monarchies, for the quarrel is most vulgar, commonplace, and discreditable. . . . The question is like most German quarrels; it rises into some degree of interest as soon as there is a chance of either party coming to blows, and subsides into tameness and insipidity as soon as the crisis has passed away."[1]

Bismarck's luck had held ever since the Schleswig-Holstein War. The patronage of Russia, Napoleon's influence over Italy, and the incompetent policy of the Austrian Cabinet had all played into his hands; the difficulties, so far, had come from the Prussian Court and public opinion. As he remarked confidently to the French Minister: "I have succeeded in persuading a King of Prussia to break off the intimate relations of his House with the Imperial House of Austria; to make an alliance with revolutionary Italy; to make arrangements, for a possible emergency, with the French Empire; and to propose at Frankfort the revision of the Federal Act by a popular parliament. I am proud of my success; I do not know whether I shall be allowed to reap where I have sown; but even if the King deserts me, I have

[1] *The Times*, April 9, 1866.

prepared the way by deepening the rift between Prussia and Austria, and the liberals, if they come to power, will complete my work".

But now for a moment Bismarck's luck failed. He had counted on a change in public opinion and on convincing the liberals that he was the man to realise their hopes. But that old spell—a German Parliament—had lost its power. His struggle with the Prussian Assembly made it look as if he was only using his opponents' weapons under compulsion and without serious intentions. Moreover a closer inspection revealed flaws in the Prussian Reform plan. The future Constitution was to be the result of an agreement between the German states. But suppose they could not agree? Again, liberal opinion strongly favoured a limitation of the sovereignty of the princes in favour of Parliament, which was certainly far from Bismarck's intentions.

The obstinate refusal of public opinion to turn in Prussia's favour was not the only disappointment. When the Reform plan was launched Bismarck had made a confident bid to detach Bavaria from Austria by offering her the supreme command of the military forces of the Southern states in the reorganised Confederation. Had Bavaria, the third greatest of the German states, joined Prussia in voting for the exclusion of Austria from Germany, the others would have fallen into line. But Bavaria unhesitatingly refused. At the Council of February 28 Bismarck had still been confident that she would accept; Moltke had disagreed with him and was now shown to be right. The Bavarian Government reflected that without Austria they would have no protection against Prussian predominance and the military command in Southern Germany would then be of little use. The present situation, with Austria and Prussia balancing one another, perfectly satisfied the House of Wittelsbach. The command in Southern Germany was refused, and a great benefit was thereby conferred on Germany; for experience was to show that the nation needed a single commander, controlling all the forces of North and South.

Bismarck had wanted to secure the important military forces of Bavaria, and at the same time to calm the suspicions of Napoleon. Prussian ambition, he said to Govone, intending it to be passed on to Napoleon, was limited strictly to Northern Germany. He described the Bavarians as the Calabrians of Germany, who could not be squeezed into a Prussian German state. The elevation of Bavaria to equality with Prussia and Austria was to be Napoleon's guarantee that the Hohenzollerns would not upset the European balance of power.

The appeal to German nationalism had not been expected to bring any accession of material strength; it had been a bid for moral support. Bismarck had hoped to prove to the King that his foreign policy could overcome Prussia's internal difficulties. This attempt had failed, the kings and princes of Germany were merely more frightened than ever of Prussian ambition and of a Prussian minister who was prepared to ally himself with the Revolution in order to humble them. The King was shaken and doubtful; and the Crown Prince, convinced that Bismarck did not take the German Parliament seriously, was fighting him more resolutely than ever. "Bismarck", he wrote to his uncle, the Duke of Coburg, on March 26, "ignores me completely. Since the autumn manœuvres in Saxony he has not vouchsafed me a single word on the burning questions of the moment. . . . His foolhardiness is absolutely inexplicable to me. . . . We are handing ourselves over to blind fate with our hands tied! For my part I shall leave no stone unturned to warn against and ward off disaster. But you know how powerless I am." The Crown Princess was even more bitter, and the Crown Prince wrote of her to the Duke on May 15: "Vicky is beside herself, for indeed a wife and mother cannot stand placidly by while everything is staked on a single throw". The Crown Prince, who longed to see the

Monarchy reconciled with liberalism, described Bismarck's policy as a "wanton gamble with the most sacred ideas", and he declared that Germany could be united under Prussian leadership only by a definitely liberal government in sympathy with the needs of the time. The King for his part was just as deeply affected by the conservative opposition to the revolutionary aspect of Bismarck's policy. The conservatives had supported the King unconditionally in his struggle with the Parliament, but now their ranks were split. Many of their leaders adhered to the principle that the good of the Monarchy and of the nobility, the cause of conservatism itself, rested on the alliance with Austria: war with Austria and flirtation with democracy must bring disaster. Wagener remained faithful to the policy of Bismarck, but Gerlach became the centre of a conservative opposition to war with Austria. As late as May 7 Gerlach wrote in the *Kreuzzeitung* in his remarkable style: "The Prussian demand for an expansion of power in Germany is justified; but so also is the Austrian appeal for the preservation of her power in Germany. This dualism is the vital basis, the real foundation, of the German Constitution. Germany ceases to be Germany without Prussia or without Austria. Prussia's honour and power are therefore the pride of Germany, and Austria's honour and power are the pride of Prussia. To injure Prussia is to injure Austria, and to injure Austria is to injure Prussia." Such appeals to tradition and to the days of the Holy Alliance were bound to have their effect on the King; and in the army, too, voices were raised against war with Austria, the old comrade-in-arms.

In the last few years, however, the King had got used to disregarding public opinion and following the advice of his minister. It was more serious when the Prussian representatives abroad began to oppose Bismarck's policy and send pessimistic reports of Prussia's diplomatic position. This was only to be expected from Bernstorff, the minister in London; he was a convinced liberal, and had given Bismarck cause to complain bitterly of his opposition during the Italian negotiations. But even Usedom in Florence was doubtful, suspecting secret negotiations between Austria and Italy which would lead to the complete isolation of Prussia;[1] and Savigny, the Prussian representative at the Diet, though he conscientiously carried out his instructions, was a keen Catholic and a pro-Austrian, and disliked the whole of Bismarck's policy. Bismarck was more isolated than ever.

The last few years had accustomed Bismarck to difficulties of this kind; but he had now to face an even graver danger from Paris. It was true that Loë, the Prussian military attaché at Paris, was sending confident reports of French military weakness. The expedition to Mexico had emptied the arsenals, and the strengthening of the garrisons in Algiers after the rebellion of 1864 had left only 100,000 soldiers in France, while 37 batteries had been disbanded during the winter of 1865–66 for reasons of economy. Loë assured the King that the French system of mobilisation was so defective that France would only be able to muster 150,000 men for an offensive war, and that only after a delay of some weeks. Against France alone, Prussia would be superior in numbers, training, and equipment.[2] But the situation was more dangerous than that; Austria and Prussia were on the brink of war and everything depended on Napoleon's neutrality.

At this moment there was a change for the worse in both French opinion and Napoleon's own views. Prussia's proposal to the Diet showed that she was planning a European upheaval and would not shrink from war; obviously it was not Austria but Bismarck who was disturbing the peace of Europe. The price of stocks fell, business was at a

[1] La Marmora, 147, 148.

[2] Loë, 'Erinnerungen aus meinem Berufsleben', *Deutsche Revue*, i. 157, 294.

standstill, and violent criticism of Prussia was heard in the French press, and before long in the French Chamber. Worse still, Goltz observed with alarm that Napoleon himself was less friendly towards Prussia; he was beginning to realise that she did not intend to make him a definite offer of territory before going to war. The Emperor had no platonic love for Prussia and he needed some tangible success to impress his restless subjects. He was disappointed in Bismarck and in Prussia; he began, in consequence, to listen more readily to the warnings of Drouyn de Lhuys against too great a Prussian predominance in Germany. Goltz reported all this to Berlin and drew the conclusion that Prussia must adopt a more pacific policy. His continual warnings against the danger from France, and his confession that he could do nothing to meet it, did more than anything else to compromise the bold policy which Bismarck was striving to carry through.

For the King began seriously to consider whether he ought not to listen to these warnings. The hostility of public opinion in the lesser states, the Bavarian support of Austria, and the obstinate desire of the Prussian people for peace might all be ignored; but the silence of Napoleon was really alarming. In vain Moltke attempted to strengthen William's confidence. He rehearsed the advantages Prussia would secure from an early offensive. She could transport her troops to the field of operations by five railway lines, while Austria had only the one from Vienna to Prague. Therefore, if both states mobilised simultaneously, the 285,000 men which Prussia would have assembled by the twenty-seventh day would outnumber the Austrians by 110,000—hence the military precautions to which Austria already felt herself compelled. This Prussian superiority would be maintained until the forty-second day and in these fifteen days Saxony and Bohemia must be invaded. Only a Bavarian alliance could neutralise this disadvantage for Austria; not that the Bavarian forces mattered, but because the Bavarian railway lines running between Western Austria and Bohemia would enable the Austrians to shorten their mobilisation in Bohemia by a fortnight.

William was not convinced by these arguments. He was already alarmed by the fact that the Austrians would equal the Prussian numbers by the forty-second day; and, when Bavaria, too, became hostile, he wrote in the margin of Moltke's minute of April 3: "I am very upset by the Bavarian defection, for with the addition of Württemberg alone they will put nearly 100,000 men into the field against us". The King estimated that they would have to weaken the army against Austria by diverting 60,000 men against the Southern states. The Minister of War sent this comment to Moltke with the significant remark: "A reassuring reply to be sent direct to His Majesty". Moltke practically refused: "It cannot be the intention of anyone to argue the King into a war, but only to simplify his decision by a clear and accurate statement of the situation". He repeated his arguments, however, in a report to the King on April 14; he emphasised once more the decisive advantage of Prussia's quicker mobilisation, and concluded: "Once we mobilise we must not shrink from the reproach of aggression. Every delay will definitely injure our position."

In this state of mind the Cabinet of Berlin was taken almost unawares by the Austrian Note of April 7, which, though no milder in tone than earlier ones, made a genuine peace offer. It did indeed repeat that Austria had made no preparations for war, while Prussia had even admitted a certain measure of armament. Francis Joseph, however, stated once again that he had no intention of attacking Prussia, and declared that peace would be secured if Prussia would cancel her war preparations of March 29. William, perhaps under the influence of the reports of the Prussian ministers abroad, was in favour of a pacific answer, so that Europe would cease to regard him and his ministers as disturbers of the peace. Just at this time Bismarck fell ill and consequently lost influence with the King. William is said to have twice returned Bismarck's draft answer to be toned down. The final version, despatched on April 15, was of a conciliatory nature; Prussia agreed to cancel her armaments if Austria would do the same.

This was Prussia's first peaceful gesture for many months, and Mensdorff exerted all his influence to secure a friendly reply. He was helped by the Emperor's genuine determination to fight only in self-defence. On April 18 Austria formally declared that she was ready to cancel all the movements of troops which gave Prussia cause for alarm, and indicated April 25 as the day on which the Emperor proposed to start disarming; naturally the Austrian Government demanded a binding promise from the King of Prussia that he would dismiss his troops on the same or the following day. Bismarck's policy had never been in such danger. Only with the greatest difficulty had the King been persuaded to ally himself with Italy and prepare for war; it looked now as if the three months for which Italy was committed would run out without anything having been achieved. Barral reported on April 19: "Bismarck is very dissatisfied with the peaceful turn events seem to have taken. . . . The essence of the question has not changed, but for the moment there is definitely no prospect of war. It is said that England and even France have exercised pressure in Vienna to achieve this result, which has also been assisted by the obstinate illness of Bismarck." But Bismarck was not going to admit himself beaten so easily. It would be difficult, he told Barral, to reject the Austrian offer; but if the King followed his advice, Prussia would at any rate keep the horses she had bought for the artillery, giving as her excuse the military preparations of the lesser states. "Both General Govone and myself", the Italian Minister added, "think that Bismarck is definitely discouraged by the Austrian proposal and the peaceful turn of the crisis." Bismarck told the French minister that he was trying to get the answer to the Austrian

Note postponed. But he failed; the Council which met on April 20 insisted on answering Austria immediately.[1] The only thing which Bismarck achieved was that instead of a fixed date—April 25, as Austria had proposed—Prussia gave a general acceptance to the idea of a simultaneous disarmament. The news of this friendly Note, which was sent from Berlin on April 21, was received with relief in all Europe north of the Alps. But in Italy there was general disappointment. Nigra reported to La Marmora on April 23 that the French were confident peace would be preserved and added: "Would to God that Austria would attack us, but that we cannot hope for". Bismarck regarded it as a grave error to dismiss the men who had been called up and to put the southern divisions on a peace establishment without having secured even a diplomatic success. The history of 1850 and of the summer of 1859 was being repeated; Prussia had strengthened her army and then done nothing. The world was getting used to empty threats from Berlin. But the King looked at it from a different point of view. He was responsible for the lives of his soldiers and would only send them to war if his conscience was clear. Everything now depended on the ability of the Austrian Government to manage William and separate him from Bismarck.

Throughout April feeling in Austria had been growing more bitter. With Prussia in alliance with Italy and demanding the exclusion of Austria from Germany war seemed inevitable. Peace could be had at a price; but Austria was too proud to surrender Schleswig-Holstein and acknowledge Prussian supremacy in North Germany. The Germans in Austria were doubly embittered by this unjustifiable aggression; for if Bismarck succeeded they would

---

[1] Benedetti, 112, according to information derived from Bismarck. Bodelschwingh, the Minister of Finance, was urging the cancelling of the purchase of horses as a pacific gesture as late as May 2. See his letter in Roon, *Denkwürdigkeiten*, ii. 267.

be excluded from their German Fatherland. They would be the hardest hit by a German civil war, and all, liberals and clericals alike, hated the Prussian minister. The Slavs added to the hatred of Prussia their general hatred of everything German. The Magyars alone remained detached; but they too desired a war, because they hoped that it would compel the Monarchy to grant them their ancient liberties in return for their help. Not a voice in Austria was raised in favour of surrendering the leadership of Germany without a struggle; not even the Slavs, who would gain by a separation from Germany, dared to advance this policy, and even peace-loving men like Mensdorff rejected such a solution. The General Staff pressed for more armaments to avoid being surprised by the enemy. On April 8 it was decided to call up another 85,000 men, but the actual step was postponed for fear of appearing aggressive. As Prussia, however, had already prepared the frontier fortresses on March 29, Austria did the same; and the field artillery was put on a war footing. These were all defensive measures; but just when the news from Berlin was improving, the Austrian General Staff discovered fresh danger on the Italian side.

Italy had been waiting for years for an opportunity to attack Austria. The difficult financial position—there was a deficit of 211 million lire for the current year—had forced Italy to drastic economies in her military budget. The men liable for service in January 1866 were not to be called up and the trained soldiers were to be kept a year longer with the colours; the economy would become effective in 1867, when the contingent of 1866 would not have to be kept and the peace establishment would be lessened by 140,000 men. Then came the Prussian alliance and the measures of economy were at once reversed. A decree was issued on March 25 calling up the contingent which had been passed over in January, but at the same time the trained soldiers were not dismissed; the Austrian General Staff calculated

that the Italians, in one way and another, had added an
extra 100,000 men to their army. Besides this increase of
numbers there began an energetic transfer of troops northwards; the Italian generals calculated that there were
sixteen Austrian brigades in Italy, and that they needed
twice as many, that is, sixteen divisions, for an aggressive
war. As the whole army only totalled twenty divisions
and even these were not yet completely formed, practically
all the troops in Italy were moving north. Even regiments
which had been sent to suppress Neapolitan brigands were
moved towards the ports and railway stations in readiness
for transportation. This was armament on a very different
scale from anything which had taken place north of the
Alps. The neutral powers all expressed extreme disapproval
of the Italian activities and the English minister, Lord
Bloomfield, in particular, warned La Marmora not to make
himself responsible for the outbreak of war. La Marmora
flatly denied that Italy was arming for war and explained
that the only troops moving north were two regiments of
cavalry, which had been found useless against the brigands
in the mountains of Southern Italy. Since this was true of
the two cavalry regiments of Piacenza and Monferrato and
La Marmora told the story well, it carried some conviction
and served to mask the much larger concentration of
infantry.[1]

Austria had friends and spies throughout Italy. In the
south there were signs of a rising of the Bourbon party and
from this source there came a report that Garibaldi's officers
were recruiting volunteers for a crusade against Austria,
while Garibaldi himself, to lull suspicions, remained in

---

[1] It is striking that Sybel (iv. 345) accepts La Marmora's assurances
and says: "It can be said here that all the rumours were baseless". The
work of the Italian General Staff, published in 1875, which Sybel ignores,
shows the contrary. Moreover, La Marmora himself says, 188: "In fact our
mobilisation, during the negotiations for disarmament, upset the work
of the diplomats and led to the military preparations of Austria, which
in turn provoked those of Prussia".

Capri. It did not need the false rumour that a troop of Garibaldians had crossed the Po to provoke the Austrian General Staff to counter-measures. Mensdorff was right when he said to the Prussian minister that armaments were dangerous, because each step provoked the next. The Austrian General Staff had never had much faith in the proposal of a simultaneous disarmament. Now the news from Italy led Henikstein to submit a memorandum to the Emperor on April 20, advising the immediate mobilisation of the Austrian army; the distance of the regiments from their recruiting centres already gave Prussia an advantage of four weeks; with Italy taking measures on a large scale Austria must move at once if she was to come with honour out of a war on two fronts.

The acceptance of this proposal would obviously be decisive. So far no one had seriously suspected Austria of aggression; but if she mobilised she would put herself in the wrong. Italy alone was no danger to Austria and Prussian participation was becoming increasingly doubtful as King William hesitated. Now, if ever, Esterhazy's usual irresolution might have proved useful.

Nevertheless it was Austria who precipitated the tragic drama of 1866. The historian has here to point out a gap in the logical development of events. The mere recital of the facts will not wholly explain the course of history. It is particularly difficult to attribute responsibility when a number of men were acting together. It has often been asked who was responsible for the Austrian measures which inevitably provoked war, but no satisfactory answer has been given. None of the ministers who advised the premature mobilisation which gave Italy and Prussia a pretext for war ever gave an explanation of their policy, chiefly because of their feeling for the Monarchy; they were anxious to avoid separating the Emperor's share in events from their own. This sentiment was peculiar to Austria. In Prussia dynastic feeling was just as deeply rooted; yet there was no hesitation in examining the characters of Frederick William IV, William I, Frederick III, and William II. William I's share in the war of 1866 was fully analysed during his lifetime by some of his closest advisers; the King himself was often able to read that he had not the creative powers of his great minister. In Austria such a thing was impossible; the personality of the head of the House of Habsburg was surrounded, during his lifetime, with a dim religious light, and any discussion of him as an historical character was forbidden by a powerful tradition, which went back to the days of the Holy Roman Empire. It was bound up with the feeling that Austria-Hungary depended more than any other empire on the awe and respect felt for the Dynasty. This silence made the study of contemporary history difficult, but in the eyes of the leading statesmen that did not matter; it strengthened the foundations of the empire.[1]

[1] [The Minutes of the Austrian Council of Ministers, which are now accessible, shed some light on the questions which Friedjung is here discussing. The Council of April 17 discussed what answer was to be made to the Prussian Note of April 15. Mensdorff and Esterhazy both expressed their distrust of Bismarck, but declared that he should be taken at his word and the restoration of the *status quo* accepted. Belcredi, on the other hand, wanted to appeal to the Federal Diet and thus reject the Prussian offer. Finally, Francis Joseph insisted that Austria must avoid even the appearance of being in the wrong and must therefore agree to simultaneous disarmament. On April 21 the Council heard the reasons which made an increase of the army in Italy desirable. Esterhazy was absent, ill; the illness was undoubtedly genuine. Mensdorff was also absent, but Belcredi informed the Council that "Count Mensdorff was in agreement with the calling up of the frontier regiments, and expressed some doubt only over the absolute urgency of the calling up of the fourth battalion" (*i.e.* mobilisation against Italy).

The Council of April 23 was occupied with considering what answer to make to the Prussian Note of April 18, which accepted the idea of simultaneous disarmament. Mensdorff was in favour of a pacific answer, but added: "it is really difficult to say what ought to be done now; the most skilful statesman would be at a loss for a clear, definite answer". Frank, the Minister for War, and Henikstein, the Chief of the General Staff,

Mensdorff was horrified when the Emperor showed him the Austrian General Staff's minute of April 20. In Mens-

both insisted that it was essential to proceed with the mobilisation in Italy, which could not be a threat to Prussia; "it is certain", said Frank, "that when we arm we can speak a language which is bound to have an effect", and Henikstein added that it was unheard of that a state, encompassed by hostile neighbours, should not be allowed to make preparations to defend itself. Belcredi supported this attitude and wanted the questions both of demobilisation and Schleswig-Holstein submitted to the Diet, although he recognised that this would probably cause a conflict with Prussia. Francis Joseph was in favour of answering the Prussian note in a friendly spirit, and of promising to cancel the troop movements in Bohemia; but he added that troops could be brought into the neighbourhood of Vienna without violating this promise and they would be available for an immediate transference later on.

On April 25 Francis Joseph had a "confidential discussion" with his ministers, at which two draft despatches to Prussia were considered. The first agreed to cancel the armaments in Bohemia, though without entering into particulars; the second was to prepare the way for submitting the question of Schleswig-Holstein to the Diet and Mensdorff "did not conceal from the meeting that this document . . . would not be favourably received by the Prussian Government and that the possibility of war could not therefore be ignored". Francis Joseph replied that "it was urgently required to put an end to the present situation, which was becoming more unbearable every day, by an energetic diplomatic action, even if it might result in war".

Esterhazy was absent from all these meetings and in his letters to Mensdorff he praises Mensdorff's efforts to prevent any step which might lead to war, such as his securing the postponement of the departure of the Archduke Albrecht to take up his Italian command. On April 26, when it had been decided by the generals to mobilise on the northern front, Esterhazy writes to Mensdorff: "Our enemies have achieved their object. We are arming—and for a prolonged peace, which will probably compel us to fire the first shot! . . . This war cannot be a defensive war, or still less a conservative war for us. You can console yourself with the thought that you have struggled bravely and with self-control for peace to the very last moment".

On May 1 the Council received from the Minister of War a report of the stage the mobilisation had reached—the army in Italy was completely mobilised and complete mobilisation would take place in the north as soon as Prussia began to mobilise. Extra credits were therefore needed and the Minister of War proposed the immediate issue of 112 dorff's opinion the political disadvantage of mobilisation outweighed everything. He urged a postponement, at any rate until Austria had received the Prussian reply to her disarmament proposals. Mensdorff argued in vain. According to one well-qualified observer[1] Mensdorff advanced his objections at a Council of Ministers at which Esterhazy was not present, having taken to his bed in order to avoid

million of paper money. This was opposed by Mensdorff, because it would have a bad effect abroad: "it will be said that Austria has burnt her boats and wants a war à tout prix". Esterhazy supported Mensdorff; he was sceptical of the reports of the Italian armaments and added: "In order to avoid bankruptcy we must now strive for war. But no one can foresee the extent of this war; it will become a European war and create circumstances which will make the existence of the old Austria impossible and will result in the establishment of a new." Belcredi once more supported a policy of aggression and declared that "the present situation was unbearable and could only lead to the ruin of the monarchy". The Emperor had obviously a certain sympathy with Mensdorff's attitude and declared that he too had at the beginning not believed in the possibility of war; but it was being forced on Austria by others—"war must now be regarded as unavoidable and duty only consists in preparing ourselves well for it in every direction".

There is no sign in these documents that Esterhazy exercised the determining influence for war; indeed he seems rather to have pursued his usual policy of opposing decisive action of any kind and his most definite intervention was on the side of Mensdorff and compromise. The most bellicose of the civilian Ministers was undoubtedly Belcredi, who lost no opportunity of supporting an aggressive policy. But it is abundantly clear that the Council of Ministers played but a subordinate rôle in the affair: the vital decisions were taken in the military cabinet of the Emperor, and the Council was only informed when it became necessary to provide the money for the military actions. Friedjung may have lacked certain details or may even occasionally have been misinformed, but he went to the root of the matter when he pointed to the complete lack of co-ordination between the Ministers and the generals as the source of all Austria's mistakes and misfortunes.

The minutes of the Council and Esterhazy's letters (in the collection called *Rechberg-Nachlass*) are available in the Austrian archives. Extracts from them are published in Redlich, *Das Österreichische Staats- und Reichsproblem*, ii. 771-6, 795-804.—Translator.]

[1] Rechberg, in conversation with the author.

responsibility; but the others were under his influence and
their decision to mobilise against Italy accorded with his
intentions. The order for the mobilisation of the Army of the
South was issued on April 21, and at the same time Benedek
was appointed to the command in the north and Archduke
Albrecht became commander in the south. The previous
plans of mobilisation had postulated a simultaneous
mobilisation of the two armies, and they were now hastily
revised. The strengthening of the Army of the South was
pushed on as energetically as if the enemy had already
crossed the frontier.

Now there was no going back. Immediately after these
decisions the Prussian Note of April 21 arrived in Vienna,
accepting in general the Austrian proposal of disarmament,
and asking for further details. But it came too late. The
mobilisation of the Austrian army in Venetia acted on Italy
like a match to dry tinder. The youth of the whole peninsula
would have volunteered under Garibaldi, if the King had
not himself given the signal for the struggle. On April 27
La Marmora issued a circular to the European Courts, declaring that innocent Italy was in danger from Austrian
aggression. This pathetic appeal was not taken very
seriously in Europe: Lord Clarendon asked the Italian
Ambassador whether he was really expected to believe that
Austria, with all her difficulties at home, was planning
an attack on her neighbours. Nevertheless the Austrian
mobilisation caused a change in European opinion. In vain
Mensdorff assured the Prussian Government on April 26
that Austria would remain faithful to her intention to
disarm in the north, although she was compelled to mobilise
against an Italian attack in the south. Bismarck himself was
surprised at the way Austria had rushed into the trap. For
Prussia could not be expected to distinguish between the
various Austrian corps and regiments which had been
mobilised or their destinations. Benedetti reported on
April 25: "Bismarck is very pleased. The news from Italy

and Vienna may be exaggerated, but he is convinced that Austria will have to abandon the idea of restoring her forces to their peace establishment. This implies, he hopes, that Prussia too will not have to disarm." Bismarck could now prove that it was Austria and not Prussia who desired war, and Roon noted that Bismarck's nerves were normal again —"Otto has slept well for two nights running".

In Austria, Court and people seemed to be in a state of fever. The indignation at being forced into war destroyed the remnants of common sense: Austria was accused of promoting war, and now did her best to merit the reproach. On April 27 the first steps were taken to mobilise the army in the north and soon every trained soldier was being called to the colours. These measures were premature, but understandable: the hunted beast was turning on its pursuers. But far more astonishing was the sudden change of Austrian policy. At the very moment when Austria was assuring Europe that she would make every sacrifice for the integrity of the Empire and when the peoples of the Empire were flocking to the colours for its defence, the Cabinet of Vienna evolved a new plan; in their hatred of Prussia, they proposed to buy off Italy by the surrender of Venice, in order to have their hands free in Germany. Obviously such a plan made it unnecessary to have armed to the teeth against Italy, but it had only occurred to them rather late in the day. On April 30 Metternich was instructed to approach Napoleon and ask him to mediate between Austria and the Italians.

During the disastrous War of 1866 patriotic feeling consoled itself with the thought that the honour of the Empire forbade a peaceful surrender either in the north or in the south. But even before the end of the war it became known that Venice had been offered to the Italians weeks before its outbreak. Even the phantom honour for which so much was being sacrificed was proved non-existent. The war in the south, where the smaller army defeated its superior opponent, was indeed heroic. But it was folly, not heroism, to

propose the surrender of Venice too late—that is, when Italy
was committed to Prussia. If negotiations had been opened
four weeks earlier, Italy could have been separated from
Prussia; but the Austrian Cabinet's pride turned to alarm
too late.

Who should bear the responsibility for this wavering
policy? After the war Mensdorff was at great pains to prove
his innocence and, as he remained in favour, he was able
to get full justice for his pacific efforts in the official account
of the war. But this does not excuse his weakness; it was his
duty to insist on what he thought was right, instead of
giving way to Esterhazy, Belcredi, Biegeleben, and the
General Staff. Mensdorff said later of his relations with
Esterhazy: "I felt my position keenly. I did not understand
politics at all and had often told the Emperor so. But I was
a general and my commander-in-chief ordered me to take
the post; whether I liked it or not I had to tolerate the
assistance of a trained diplomat, who lacked the courage to
accept responsibility himself." When Mensdorff was asked
by the Saxon diplomat, Vitzthum, why he had not resigned
rather than sacrifice his convictions, he replied, "It's no good
your talking, you are not a soldier".[1]

Public opinion then and later made Esterhazy responsible for plunging Austria into the foolhardy gamble
of war. He alone had influence enough to temper the
Emperor's anger with Prussia by bringing home to him the
dangers of war. Formerly Esterhazy had used the worst
hair-splitting methods to avoid any sort of definite decision: but now he was the most urgent and favoured the
rashest steps.[2] When Esterhazy died in a lunatic asylum
in 1890, and the long-pent-up fury of the Austrian press
was released against him, his family consulted Belcredi
as to whether they should publish a defence of his policy.
But it was decided that it was too early for any revelations;

---

[1] Vitzthum, *London, Gastein und Sadowa*, 90 and 230.
[2] Cf. Vilbort, *L'Œuvre de M. de Bismarck*, 202.

until the ruler died whom they had served, the lips of the
statesmen of 1866 were sealed.[1]

The Austrian mobilisation was decisive, because, as
Mensdorff had prophesied, it enabled the Prussian Ministers
to persuade William I to mobilise. The Prussian generals
pointed out that, once Austria had an army ready on the
frontier, there would be the same situation as that which,
in 1850, had led to the humiliation of Prussia at Olmütz.
The King still hesitated; for no amount of argument could
alter the fact that Austria had been provoked and could

[1] [Later research does not altogether confirm Friedjung's harsh
judgement on Esterhazy. There is no evidence that he ever supported
the anti-Prussian policy of Biegeleben and Belcredi, and we know that
at one time he advocated the selling of Schleswig-Holstein; he was
certainly the most steadfast and reliable supporter Mensdorff had in the
Cabinet. Esterhazy was practically the only Austrian Minister who
really believed in the "conservative" system of Metternich, and he
was throughout more concerned with Venice (both as a security for
the Pope and as a jumping-off ground for a new conservative crusade
against Italy and France) than with the affairs of Germany. For him the
war with Prussia was an unmitigated disaster. These considerations do
not, of course, lessen the blame Esterhazy must receive for his constant
hesitations and his hypercritical method, which produced such disastrous
vacillations in Austrian policy.

Friedjung's uncompromising condemnation was largely due to the
information he received from Rechberg. But Rechberg could hardly
be expected to have much understanding for the man who had man-
œuvred him out of office; and in any case, by 1890, Rechberg's imagina-
tion had so transformed many of the incidents of the past that he is
often an unreliable witness even in matters that concern himself. There
was, however, a further reason for Friedjung's attitude. Esterhazy was,
so to speak, the official victim for the diplomatic failure of 1866, just as
Benedek was the official victim of the military failure. Belcredi was
retained in office; Mensdorff was employed later in other important
posts; but Esterhazy was dismissed in disgrace. His had been the greatest
diplomatic reputation in the Empire and his fall was correspondingly
great. But modern research tends to lighten the verdict on both Benedek
and Esterhazy and to place the blame partly on the Austrian system,
but most of all on the man really responsible for Austrian policy—on
Francis Joseph himself.—Translator.]

not possibly desire war. William had accepted his minister's foreign policy, because Bismarck had rescued him from his internal difficulties over the army reform; Bismarck, as he himself said, had served the King, as Jacob had served Laban. If the King now gave way or allowed Prussia to be taken unawares by Austria, monarchical authority would be destroyed in Prussia and in Germany; the Parliament would easily defeat a Government that was weak abroad and Prussia would succumb to the English parliamentary system. Bismarck played off the King's monarchical principles against his unwillingness, and the unwillingness of the Prussian people, to go to war.

Bismarck, in order to make the decision easier, pointed out to the King that Prussia could still negotiate with Austria after mobilising; and that Austria could still, by a reasonable compromise, avoid a war on two fronts. With his knowledge of men and circumstances at Vienna, Bismarck secretly doubted whether the Austrian Cabinet would still want to compromise, but he took the possibility of a peaceful settlement seriously. On May 2 he pointed out to Govone that the treaty between Italy and Prussia bound Italy alone to armed assistance and that Prussia was free to accept any concessions Austria might offer; he added that the Prussian Government would loyally inform Italy in good time and protect her against a sudden attack. But the prospect was not very cheerful for the Italian Government: Italy would have mobilised at great expense merely to assist Prussia's German ambitions, and Venice would remain unconquered.

When the King still hesitated to sign the orders for mobilisation, Moltke and the other generals declared that they could not be responsible for the safety of the state unless the army were put on a war footing. The King replied that he felt his entire entourage would accuse him of treason if he did not give the order to arm.[1] On May 3

---

[1] La Marmora, 182. For the King's anxiety, see Kraft von Hohenlohe, *Aus meinem Leben*, iii. 219-22. "The King's appearance", Hohenlohe

the King issued the first mobilisation orders, which were followed between May 5 and 12 by others, calling out the whole army. All parties at Court and among the Prussian patriots were now silenced, for the honour of the country was at stake. Roggenbach, a minister of Baden, who visited the Crown Prince at this time, found him full of anxiety; he told Roggenbach, as a friend, that it was time for him and the liberals to join up, for "one must always be on the side of one's country".

noted of the parade of May 12, "horrified me. He was ashen-grey and there were deep lines on his forehead. His dreadful seriousness and deep anxiety showed that he was trying to make up his mind to some vital decision".

CHAPTER VII

THE Austrian generals had insisted on mobilisation, not because they were confident of victory, but because they doubted the military strength of the Empire. Just before the battle of Königgrätz, Mensdorff confessed to Motley that during the negotiations between Berlin and Vienna "the military authorities were very dissatisfied, and from the very start of the campaign expected their inadequate preparations to result in grave disaster". The more critical the situation became, the more faults did the Chief of Staff find in the army organisation. It is completely untrue that the Austrian generals were in favour of war in 1866 because they overrated the strength of the army. It was the diplomats who underrated the dangers. This situation recurs throughout Austrian history in the eighteenth and nineteenth centuries, especially in the wars against the French Republic and Napoleon. "The mad, destructive obstinacy" of Thugut, who exhausted the Empire in the series of wars between 1792 and 1800, was strongly opposed in military circles; and before the wars of 1805 and 1809, the Archduke Charles is known to have urgently advised a postponement, because his reorganised army was not yet ready. "The great object of Austria is recovery", he wrote in his report to the Emperor of April 12, 1804; and he resigned his position as President of the Council of

War rather than undertake to create the army demanded by the Emperor in 1805. Metternich alone was skilful enough to spin out the negotiations before the war of 1813, until the army was ready to give the decisive blow at the battle of Leipzig. In 1859, Gyulai's warning against a premature invasion of Piedmont did actually secure the approval of the Foreign Minister, but it was ignored in the Emperor's Cabinet. Those responsible for Austrian policy between 1792 and 1866 were convinced that Austria, as the protector of conservative ideas, must always be ready to fight innovators and disturbers of the peace. But modern ideas were stronger than treaty rights, as the men of 1859 and 1866 had to learn. It is always dangerous for a state to think itself called upon to defend an ideal or divine order of things throughout the world, instead of putting its own interests first. To have compromised in time with Italy, or to have withdrawn from the rigid letter of German federal law, would have been better in 1866 than the war on two fronts. But Esterhazy and Biegeleben thought the war would only result in some slight adjustments of power in favour of Austria or Prussia. They did not realise that a storm was sweeping through Europe—a storm which was to destroy the German Confederation, the temporal power of the Papacy, and with them Austria's predominance in Germany, in Italy, and over Hungary.

Of the Austrian generals, Krismanič alone was full of confidence. He derived his strategy exclusively from a study of the campaigns against Frederick the Great, and these seemed to offer him many analogies to the forthcoming struggle. The enemy was the same, and so was the battle-field; and the quicker Prussian mobilisation was again to throw the Austrians on to the defensive. The warfare of the eighteenth century was dominated by defensive strategy. Twice during the Seven Years' War the Austrian generals— Daun in 1757 and Laudon in 1758—drove Frederick from

Bohemia and prevented any further invasion; and Frederick's Bohemian offensives were successful only in that they achieved a defensive object—the protection of Silesia. Only in the first campaign of 1742 did Frederick dictate peace on Bohemian soil. But Krismanič was ignoring the revolution in the art of war brought about by Napoleon. The armies of the seventeenth and eighteenth centuries were conscript armies, held together only by an iron discipline, and fighting in a rigid, closed line which made desertion impossible. A war of manœuvre resulted, in which each side sought strong defensive positions, and tried to manœuvre the enemy out of his strong positions. Such was the art of Condé, Turenne, Montecuccoli, and later of Prince Henry of Prussia and Daun. Even Frederick the Great only regarded a battle as the last resort, when he had been outmanœuvred, or if the enemy occupied a position which controlled the whole country. Before the battle of Hohenfriedberg he wrote: "There is no way out, as far as I can see, but a battle. In a few hours this emetic will have determined the fate of the patient." The importance attached by the Austrian generals of the time, especially Daun and Lacy, to the choice of a "position" is well known; they would occupy one for weeks or even months, regardless of the loss of time. Laudon, who was a better general, blamed them for never achieving a decisive battle, but he did not dispute their principles. Frederick's theory was the same; and his later campaigns in the Seven Years' War in defence of Saxony and Silesia were based almost entirely on a strategy of positions. In the introduction to his book on the Seven Years' War, he wrote: "The Austrian generals will almost certainly keep to the method of General Daun (which is without doubt the best) and they will be as careful to choose strong positions in the next war as they were in this". His military testament of 1768 is even more explicit: "With the Austrians, a war of positions can be counted on . . . a general engagement is not to be recommended, because a position can only be taken with heavy loss and effective pursuit is impossible in mountainous country. I would fortify my camp and devote all my attention to defeating enemy detachments; for a defeated detachment spreads confusion throughout the army. A number of such small successes is like the accumulation of a treasure—you gradually get rich without knowing how."

A study of the strategy of the time of Frederick the Great is necessary for the understanding of the plan of campaign adopted in 1866 by Krismanič, himself an academic strategist. Napoleon was assisted by the adherence of his enemies to the dogmas of Frederick and in exactly the same way the antiquated principles of Austrian strategy contributed to Moltke's decisive success. With enemies on every side, Frederick had only one method: he stood on the defensive in a strong central position and delivered short, powerful blows against the nearest enemy. Napoleon despised such methods and broke with them completely: only a commonplace ambition, he said, would be content with such small successes.

The "Plan of Operations for the Army of the North", drawn up by Krismanič in April 1866, was a reversion to the ideas of Daun and Lacy. The Austrian generals were chiefly afraid of being surprised by Moltke, as Browne had been surprised before Prague in 1757 by Frederick. Krismanič therefore decided on a concentration of the Austrian army at Olmütz, where, strongly entrenched beneath the walls of the fortress, it could withstand a Prussian attack even before mobilisation was complete. But even when it was ready, it was not to advance to meet the Prussians nearer the frontier; for Krismanič declared that on the seven days' march between Olmütz and Glatz or Neisse, there was no favourable "position" for a battle. Napoleon, or even Laudon, would hardly have admitted that, in a stretch of country covered by seven days' march, there was nowhere suitable to give the enemy battle. The main Prussian attack was expected

from Upper or Middle Silesia; for Krismanič, like the
Austrian statesmen, was preoccupied with Silesia, the
province which was to compensate for the loss of Venetia
and Schleswig-Holstein. It has often been said that in every
important point Krismanič's anticipations were proved
wrong. The Prussians did not come through Neisse, but
through Reichenegg and Trautenau; Bohemia and not
Moravia was the main theatre of war; and the Prussians
wasted no time besieging Olmütz, Josephstadt, and Königgrätz. But this alone is no proof of incapacity; the Prussians
were quite as wrong about the Austrian intentions. They
expected from Benedek a premature attack in Silesia
rather than timid skulking behind fortresses, trenches,
and streams.[1] An enemy's intentions cannot be foreseen,
as Napoleon knew: hence his remark, "I have never had a
plan of operations".

The Austrian generals were not all obsessed with Krismanič's strategical prejudices. The discontent was almost
universal among the officers when Northern Bohemia was
abandoned without a blow; and the conduct of the war
in Italy was not dominated by the defensive idea. The
Archduke Albrecht and Major - General John took the
offensive against an enemy superior in numbers; and
Tegetthoff sought out the enemy fleet and destroyed it.
It would be unfair to condemn Krismanič for not being
Moltke's equal; and many of his guesses were right, as
Moltke's military correspondence shows. He was right to
fear an attempt to surprise the Austrians at their centre
of mobilisation. Had Moltke been solely responsible, as
Frederick II was, he would undoubtedly have tried to do so;
he constantly urged William to declare war on the first day
of mobilisation and attack the Austrians between the
twenty-fifth and fortieth days. And Krismanič was not far

---

[1] It must be clearly understood that this only applies to the Austrian
strategy. Their shock-tactics and their sallies from fortified positions
were in complete contradiction with their strategy.

wrong in expecting the Prussian attack from Silesia. Moltke was for some time in favour of such a plan; Silesia was much nearer Vienna and was a much better base for an aggressive war. Against it, however, there was the fundamental objection that there was only one railway line, so that two weeks would be wasted in the transport of troops. Moltke, therefore, decided in his final plan to concentrate as many troops in Silesia as the railway system allowed, and to assemble the rest of the army on the Saxon frontier by making use of all the other railways. Bohemia was thus to be invaded simultaneously from two sides, and the armies were to unite in the heart of the enemy's country. The Austrian plan was bad, not so much because it was based on wrong assumptions, as because it was rigid and unadaptable. Long after it had become clear that Austria was to be given plenty of time to mobilise, Krismanič kept the army in Moravia, and even when it was nearly as strong as the enemy, hesitated to advance into Bohemia. The geographical difficulties confronting Moltke were quite as great—Bohemia and Saxony almost cut Prussia in two—but he made every effort to overcome them by rapidity of movement.

While Krismanič drew up his Plan of Operations for the Army of the North the two commanders were chosen— the Archduke Albrecht and Ludwig von Benedek. The Archduke's brilliant conduct at the battle of Novara in 1849 had laid the foundation of his great reputation as a general; but the favourite of the army was undoubtedly Benedek. He had acquired a tremendous reputation during the wars of 1848–49 and 1859 for his fearlessness and resolution as a corps commander. Since 1860 he had occupied— and worthily occupied—Radetzky's old position as commander of the army in Italy. Benedek had no theoretical training; his knowledge of war was derived entirely from the battlefield and he regarded the rules of strategy as a sort of secret lore. His strength lay in his freedom from prejudice and fear, and in his frank comradeship with the ordinary soldiers.

Benedek had little confidence in Austria's ability to fight a war on two fronts. As early as 1856 he declared that the day it became necessary would be "the most frightful day of his life";[1] and, incredible as it may seem, in 1866 he sent a message to King Victor Emmanuel before his departure to the north, that he feared the war would be disastrous for Austria. At the Councils of War in March he was shocked to hear that he was destined for the chief command in the north, and he at once rejected the suggestion. He told the Emperor quite frankly that he lacked the ability to direct an army of 200,000 men, especially in a theatre of war which he did not know. He therefore implored the Emperor to leave him in Italy and to give the command in the north to someone more fitted for it. In Upper Italy, he is said to have told Francis Joseph, he knew every tree on the road to Milan, in Bohemia he could not even find the Elbe. If the Emperor left him in Italy he would guarantee the possession of Venice; but he would be no good in the north. He could certainly play the violin, but he did not know how to play the flute. Francis Joseph was in a difficult position, and his insistence on Benedek's appointment is understandable. Public opinion expected the most distinguished general to receive the most important post, although some of the more experienced soldiers doubted whether Benedek was, in fact, fitted to command anything larger than an army corps. Moreover, as I have written elsewhere,[2] "the effect abroad had to be considered; the support of the lesser German states had still to be secured and it was necessary to make them feel that the command of the army was in good hands. Benedek had a tremendous reputation throughout Ger-

[1] According to Prince Hohenlohe-Ingelfingen, in his book, *Aus meinem Leben*.

[2] Friedjung, *Benedeks Nachgelassene Papiere*, 353.

many, while the Archduke Albrecht was practically un-
known; as Pfordten remarked, Benedek in command was
worth 40,000 men. Esterhazy was particularly eager for
Benedek's transfer to the north, mainly because he appeared to be the only man capable of inspiring the discontented Magyars with any enthusiasm. Esterhazy also
argued that dynastic considerations made it essential not
to give the more important command to an archduke,
as his defeat would weaken the Imperial House."

Benedek, however, persisted in his refusal and even
the arguments of his old comrade-in-arms, the Archduke
Albrecht, could not shake him. He was only persuaded to
change his mind by an appeal from the Emperor himself,
as he himself told Wersebe, one of his officers, during the
retreat after Königgrätz. "After the Council of War Benedek was about to set off with a light heart for Verona; but
the same night he was awakened and summoned to the
Emperor's adjutant general. He was told that it had been
decided in the highest quarters to appoint him after all to
the command in the north and he was implored not to
refuse the post: public opinion was demanding him and if
any other commander than Benedek was defeated by the
Prussians, the Emperor would have no choice but to
abdicate. 'After such an appeal', these were Benedek's own
words, 'I should have been a scoundrel not to accept the
command.'" It was Benedek's loyalty to the dynasty
which made him accept the post against his better judgement. "I said openly at a conference", he wrote to his wife
on July 13, ten days after the battle of Königgrätz, "that
Austria was going *va banque*, that I was ready to sacrifice
my honour completely for the Emperor, and that I only
hoped he would not repent having given me the command.
I said in so many words that on the German front I was an
ass, while in Italy I might be of some use."

Benedek had seen the evil effects of orders from Vienna
in the Italian campaigns, and he therefore made it a con-

dition that he should have complete freedom of action;
even the Emperor was to have no control over him. But
this freedom was useless to him, because of his distrust of
his own powers. He needed a Chief of Staff of outstanding
ability to work out the strategical possibilities for him.
Major-General John might have been equal to it; but it was
felt essential to leave John to assist the Archduke Albrecht
in Italy, and Benedek decided to accept Krismanič as his
chief adviser. Overawed by Krismanič's learning, Benedek
let himself be persuaded that it was only possible to fight
on the defensive, against his better judgement and to the
great disappointment of the army, which expected a dashing attack. Once there had been a Benedek, an energetic,
resolute corps commander; now there was only a cautious,
hesitating Commander-in-Chief.

The anxiety of the generals had a deep effect on the
Austrian Government and increased the fluctuations of its
policy. The mobilisation against Italy and then against
Prussia (April 21 and 27) implied a decision to fight; but
within a few days the Cabinet was drawing back and seeking a compromise with Italy. Venice had become for Austria more a burden than a possession; but the empire's
strength was rooted in Germany; and it was from Germany
that Austria had, for centuries, drawn her most valuable
allies. It was therefore decided to offer Venice to Italy and
to concentrate on the struggle for Germany. Austria,
allied with the lesser states, would have a decisive advantage; even Moltke had advised war only on the assumption that part of the Austrian forces would be occupied in
Italy. If Austria settled with Italy she could bring Prussia
to judgement; in the words of Varnbüler, the minister of
Würtemberg, Prussia should be made to experience the
Vae Victis.

The persistent silence of Napoleon caused grave alarm
in Vienna. Prince Metternich, the Austrian Ambassador,

could not persuade Napoleon to declare that he would act against whomsoever broke the peace, and the Austrian Government feared a secret agreement between Prussia and France. The alliance between Prussia and Italy was, as we now know, due to French encouragement; but France and Prussia had reached no agreement. Napoleon, in fact, was indignant with Prussia, because his services with regard to Italy remained unpaid. Things were not going as he had expected. Prussia had still made no offer of territory on the Rhine. Napoleon had strongly advised Italy not to mobilise before Prussia; but Victor Emmanuel, carried away by the enthusiasm of his people, had started to mobilise before his ally. Napoleon said bitterly to Nigra on April 30: "What was the use of asking my opinion and then doing the opposite of what I advised?" La Marmora in alarm sent to Paris the formal declaration that Italy would not take the initiative for war and this was made public in the French Senate.

Napoleon was therefore very pleased at the Austrian request for his mediation on April 30. Austria offered Venice to the Emperor of the French, as, in 1859, she had ceded Lombardy to him; but there was a condition attached— Venice was to be surrendered only when Austria was in possession of Silesia. In return, Napoleon was to secure Italian neutrality in the war between Austria and Prussia. Metternich was delighted with his commission, hoping at last to achieve his ambition of establishing friendly relations between Napoleon and Austria, and he approached Napoleon through the Emperor's old friend, Persigny.[1] Persigny too was delighted with the idea; an alliance with Austria and Italy would destroy Prussia and the fragments of Germany would be there for the taking. But to his surprise Napoleon was cold and unmoved, remarking only that there were other things to consider. Persigny could only think that the Emperor had already got a treaty with

[1] Persigny, *Mémoires*, 385 et seq.

Prussia in his pocket, guaranteeing him an accession of territory. "Then, sire," he said, "I congratulate you; for, if the Austrian offer does not satisfy you, you must indeed hold good cards."

Napoleon regarded the unchecked supremacy of Austria in Germany as the greatest possible danger. Moreover, as he pointed out to Metternich, Italy could not be expected to stand aside, unless Venice was promised to her unconditionally. Napoleon therefore demanded the surrender of Venice to France before the war began; he was anxious to complete his work in Italy and to put her under such an obligation to France that she would leave him undisturbed in Rome. The Austrian Cabinet had gone too far to draw back; it felt that Bismarck had succeeded in putting Austria in the most unfavourable diplomatic position and decided to spring a counter-mine at the last moment. Napoleon was therefore informed that Austria was ready to surrender Venice without compensation and before the outbreak of war—naturally only on the definite condition that Italy remained neutral. The decisive word now rested with the Italian Cabinet.

Napoleon believed he had achieved his desires; he was in a position to choose between the German powers.[1] He could punish Bismarck for refusing to make a definite offer by reconciling Italy with Austria and leaving Prussia exposed to attack. But he would still prefer to come to an agreement with Prussia, because Prussia controlled the territory he wanted on the Rhine. He therefore put the secret Austrian proposals to a most improper use; before he revealed them to Italy, he made threatening hints to Prussia. At a Court ball on May 2 he took Goltz aside and, after pledging him to secrecy, told him that Austria had just made him an important offer but that he would prefer an agreement with Prussia; without beating about the bush he invited Prussia

[1] He is said to have asked a French deputy: "What will you say if I get the left bank of the Rhine for you, without firing a shot?"

to join in the auction. Bismarck had long since instructed
Goltz that in such circumstances he was to say to Napoleon
that everything could be easily arranged if the Emperor
would himself state his claims exactly. Napoleon had always
avoided an answer; he did not want to frighten Prussia off
by asking too much, but equally he did not wish to bind
himself by being too modest. This time he was ready with his
answer: "The eyes of all my country are turned towards the
Rhine".[1]

At all costs Bismarck had to gain time. Without sending
Goltz a direct reply to Napoleon's question he telegraphed
to him on May 3: Prussia must know what the Austrian offer
was, before the Cabinet could decide what promises it could
give Napoleon. Now at last Prussia knew the worst; in a war
with Austria the Rhineland would be at stake. Prussian
honour forbade a voluntary surrender of German territory
and therefore Bismarck had to avoid a direct answer, even
at the risk of driving Napoleon over to the Austrian side.
Impatience with Prussia did, in fact, make Napoleon more
friendly to Austria. On May 4 he revealed the Austrian
proposals to the Italian Minister and added that he would,
of course, transfer Venice to Italy as soon as he received
it from Austria. The greatest obstacle was that for three
months Italy was committed to going to war at Prussia's
bidding. Napoleon enquired whether Italy would be ready
to break her word; if not, he suggested that the negotiations could easily be prolonged until July 8, when the treaty
with Prussia expired. Napoleon was already thinking of a
European Congress in Paris to discuss all the outstanding
difficulties; it might lead to nothing, but it would flatter
his vanity, and would give Italy time to escape from her
commitments to Prussia.

[1] Sybel, iv. 366, and La Marmora are the chief sources for this negotia-
tion. Napoleon also discussed the matter with Loë, the Prussian military attaché, obviously because Goltz refused to be drawn. See Loë,
"Erinnerungen aus meinem Berufsleben", *Deutsche Revue*, i. 295. Cf.
Ollivier, *L'Empire libéral*, viii. 138, and Plener, *Erinnerungen*, i. 73-8.

The Italians were sorely tempted. In return for Venice, Austria was demanding only a sum of money sufficient to fortify the new frontier of the empire. The desire to avoid unnecessary bloodshed, the unsatisfactory state of the army, the economic effects of the war—all favoured an acceptance of the offer. On the other hand, there was the treaty with Prussia. Ironically enough, just at this moment recriminations over the treaty were passing between Berlin and Florence. Bismarck reminded Govone that the treaty did not bind Prussia to support Italy, if Italy started the war, and although William declared that he would feel obliged to come to the assistance of his ally despite the treaty, the Italian statesmen were thoroughly alarmed. Bismarck also let Govone know that he had heard rumours of Italian negotiations with Austria for the cession of Venice. La Marmora consulted the representatives of Italy in Paris and Berlin. Nigra was on the whole in favour of war, but Govone did not attach much importance to the treaty—the accusation of a breach of faith need not be taken very seriously as Prussia was also trying to back out. Moreover, in spite of the alliance Austria's defeat was not a certainty. Govone advised the acceptance of the Austrian offer, unless Italy had an unconditional promise of French protection in case of an Austrian victory.

But the decision was no longer in the hands of the diplomats. The Italian people was eager for another trial of strength with the hereditary enemy, and this time Italy should distinguish herself. Moreover, republicanism was still strong in Italy and La Marmora felt that the revolutionary enthusiasm would become uncontrollable unless it was turned against Austria. He particularly disliked the idea of receiving Venice from the hands of the Emperor of the French; Italy owed Napoleon too much already and had had to pay heavily for his services. Savoy and Nice had been the price of assistance in 1859; what would the price be this time? Then again, if Italy abandoned Prussia, Austria might be victorious in Germany and so become more powerful than ever. The recovery of Silesia might inspire the Catholic Court of Vienna to re-establish the Pope in his old possessions.

In spite of these dangers, the Italian ministers would have reconciled themselves to a compromise with Austria if Napoleon had insisted; but the Emperor recognised that the question was a delicate one and only advised them to gain time. On May 14, therefore, La Marmora resolved to refuse: Nigra was instructed to say that Venice must be ceded direct to King Victor Emmanuel, as the Italian Government did not wish to receive the province from Napoleon, but as the result of a plebiscite. Napoleon, Nigra was to add, would have an honourable share in the achievement by persuading Austria to recognise the principle of popular sovereignty. If Napoleon was annoyed at the rejection of his mediation, he did not show it. He could without much difficulty have exercised sufficient pressure on Italy to have compelled her to accept the Austrian proposals. He did not do so, partly because his illness made him apathetic and incapable of any decisive action, but above all because he wanted a war in Germany, to open the way for French aggrandisement on the Rhine. He had no desire to discourage Prussia or to secure an Austrian victory; he therefore continued to negotiate with Vienna, but made no determined effort to reconcile Austria and Italy.[1] Several of the French ministers saw the dangers of this double game. They wanted Napoleon to declare himself on one side or the other. Rouher, supported by Prince Napoleon,

[1] Most accounts agree that Napoleon wanted a war in Germany and Italy and therefore deliberately avoided ordering Italy to keep the peace. This was the opinion of Bismarck (Persigny, *Mémoires*, 377); of La Marmora, 275; of Gramont, 266; and of Nigra in conversation with the author. Sybel, iv. 399, however, regards the Italian refusal of May 14 as "the undutiful refusal of an ungrateful vassal" and ascribes the consequence that henceforth Napoleon was ready to abandon Italian unity to its opponents; but he provides no evidence for his statement.

favoured an alliance with Prussia, Drouyn de Lhuys with Austria. Rouher's ideas were clear and definite; he argued that France, by promoting the Prussian-Italian alliance, had already committed herself to Prussia. She ought to carry this policy to its logical conclusion and try to secure herself against a future conflict with Prussia, for he knew the defects of the French military organisation. Prince Jérôme, as the son-in-law of Victor Emmanuel and a supporter of the principle of self-determination, was still more eager for a triple alliance of France, Prussia, and Italy. On the other hand, Drouyn de Lhuys, the representative of conservatism, had desired an alliance with Austria, the guardian of treaty-rights, as early as the days of the Crimean War. It was because he disliked the growth of a strong Italian state beyond the Alps that Napoleon had appointed him Foreign Minister in 1862 in place of Thouvenel, who was urging the evacuation of Rome. Napoleon attached great importance to Rome; the Empress Eugenie defended the temporal sovereignty of the Papacy with her tears and he did not wish to disturb his domestic peace.[1] Drouyn de Lhuys distrusted Bismarck, and, while Napoleon was bringing Prussia and Italy together, his Foreign Minister was advising the lesser German states to support Austria. The minister's respect for treaties, of course, ceased abruptly when it was a question of French aggrandisement. When Goltz urged on him that the efforts of France to secure the Rhine frontier would arouse general disapproval and lessen French influence in Europe, Drouyn de Lhuys replied: "We have quite enough influence, it has no longer any attraction for us. We shall not fight again for an idea; but if others gain territory, we must gain in exactly the same proportion; there is no other way."[2]

On May 3 Thiers, the most important member of the

---

[1] See the details in Thouvenel, *Le secret de L'Empereur*.

[2] Sybel, iv. 366. Drouyn's policy is the subject of *Les Quatres Ministères de M. Drouyn de Lhuys* by Harcourt.

Opposition in the Chamber, intervened with a brilliant speech. For four hours he developed the principles on which Richelieu, Louis XIV, and their successors had based French policy: French predominance depended on German and Italian divisions. He warned the Emperor that Italy would soon free herself from French control and then turn against her benefactress, France. He had no knowledge of official policy, but he guessed that Napoleon had been instrumental in promoting the alliance between Prussia and Italy, and he prophesied that Germany under Prussian leadership would one day become the scourge of France. Thiers overestimated the military power of Austria, but he had no desire to see either Prussia or Austria in undisputed control of Germany. In Napoleon's view Thiers was an incorrigible reactionary: it was vain to attempt to resist the nationalist tendencies of the age, and the duty of the statesman was to take all contemporary forces into account and to utilise the desire for national unification as a factor in his policy. Napoleon's reasoning was sound; but such statesmanship needed an energy which he was too ill to provide. He suffered much from fainting fits—once he fainted at his mistress's house and had to be carried back to the Tuileries unconscious—and there is no doubt that the irresolution of his policy was largely due to his physical condition. The worse he became, the more elaborate and fantastic were his visions of the future. Italy was to receive Venice and Austria was to be compensated with Silesia. Prussia would thus be punished for her reserve and the way opened for the advance of France to the Rhine. But Prussia must not be weakened too much; dualism in Germany was necessary for the safety of France. Prussia was needed as a check on Austria and should therefore receive Schleswig-Holstein and other territory in North Germany. The rule of France would extend to the Rhine, not directly—lest she provoke German national feeling—but by means of some small German Duchies under French protection.

Napoleon had thus decided for Austria. Prussia was to lose Silesia and the Rhineland, and for such losses there could be no compensation. All this the Emperor hoped to achieve without shedding a drop of French blood; in other words he wanted the impossible. He replied to Thiers in a speech at Auxerre on May 7, in which he expounded the modern character and revolutionary origin of his policy: he declared that he was "horrified by the treaties of 1815" and announced his intention of tearing them up. He believed that France could achieve this by remaining neutral in the coming struggle, for he assumed that the strength of Austria would be about equal to the combined strengths of Prussia and Italy. Whatever happened, he imagined, he would have plenty of time; when both sides were exhausted by the war he would intervene and dictate his own terms.

CHAPTER VIII

THE DOMESTIC SITUATION IN AUSTRIA AND GERMANY. THE
PRUSSIAN OFFER OF A PARTITION OF GERMANY

THE decision to surrender Venice had come too late to be
of any value. It had, however, this advantage for Austria,
that the war in Italy was no longer of paramount importance, and reinforcements could be diverted to the Army of
the North. During May Austria's position improved. There
was no longer any danger that France would join her
enemies, for Napoleon was increasingly hostile to Prussia.
Within the empire there was a growing enthusiasm for the
war everywhere except in Hungary; and even in Hungary
the Cabinet's conciliatory policy was producing signs of
a change of feeling. Above all, the Austrian army might
expect to be reinforced by 100,000 troops from South
Germany. As late as May 20 Bismarck had been counting
on the neutrality of some of the lesser states, but his plans
for German unity and a German Parliament drove them all
to seek the support of Austria. As the confidence of the
Austrian Cabinet grew, so the King of Prussia became increasingly conscious of his isolation and clung to the hope
of a compromise.

Yet the Belcredi Cabinet, though undeterred by the
pessimism of the generals, might well have been discouraged
by the appalling state of the Austrian finances. Plener, the
Minister of Finance in the Schmerling Cabinet, had made
great efforts to balance the Budget and pay off the deficit,

in order to abolish the discount on paper money. His work had been so successful that the discount, which was no less than 50 per cent at the end of the War of 1859, had fallen by March 1866 to 2 per cent. But the expenditure on war preparations upset the Budget. On May 5, 1866, a decree was issued empowering the Government to issue notes to the amount of 150 million guelders and immediately the discount rose from 4 per cent on April 25 to more than 30 per cent on May 12. This was only a beginning; on July 7, after the battle of Königgrätz, the Minister of Finance was empowered to issue a further 200 millions of paper money. Austria was falling back to the disastrous economic policy which twice already during the century had led her to bankruptcy.

The confidence and enthusiasm of the peoples of the empire was not shaken by the gloomy financial outlook. Prussia's attempt to exclude Austria from Germany excited universal bitterness and silenced the liberal discontent with the suspension of the Constitution and the favour shown to the Slavs. A Styrian lawyer even offered a reward of a hundred guelders for the capture of Bismarck alive or dead. An uneasy feeling ran through Vienna, when on May 23 the digging of trenches was begun on the north side of the capital; but the Government explained that they were not anticipating a siege, but merely preparing a reserve camp for the army. In any case nothing mattered beside the desire for a final reckoning with Prussia.

Feeling was intensified by the Austrian press. Even such a moderate journal as the *Ostdeutsche Post* held it unthinkable that Austria should tamely suffer humiliation by Bismarck: "However much we may desire peace and however dear the blood of our fellow-citizens is to us, yet we say that if the Austrian Government allows itself to be humiliated this time, it must write *finis* so far as Germany is concerned, or make up its mind to face the same situation all over again, and in even worse circumstances, before six months are out".

There was a general overestimation of the Austrian army: the *Neue Freie Presse* put it at a million soldiers, against whom Prussia would have only 450,000. It soon became dangerous to preach moderation. When the *Vaterland*, the organ of the feudal party, published an article during May, warning against an underestimation of the Prussian army and anticipating disaster, the aristocratic patrons of the paper met and compelled the editor, Keip, to resign. The Government newspapers, instead of moderating the enthusiasm, were equally violent, and a special section of the Foreign Office was busy stimulating the press to further excesses against Prussia.

Very different was the feeling in Hungary. After the fall of Schmerling the conservatives—Majlath, Sennyey, and Apponyi—had persuaded the Emperor formally to recognise the Constitution of 1848, but only on condition that it should be revised before it came into force. Deák and the majority in Parliament were ready to undertake the revision, but only if the Constitution was *first* restored. The elections in the autumn of 1865 had given Deák a majority of over a hundred; but he had on his left more extremist groups, such as the followers of Tisza and Ghiczy, who recognised like Deák the need for a connection with Austria, but only in the form of a personal union without any common government, and the Independents who went even further and demanded a complete separation from Austria. Deák hoped that these extreme demands would induce the Emperor to accept his own more moderate proposals. The Government demanded that Parliament should accept the actual position for reasons of convenience, but Deák uncompromisingly replied that legal continuity must come first. "Many employ the word convenience", he said in his speech of February 22, "to avoid keeping the law, whenever it is not in their favour. Convenience is allowed to override the laws and indeed the whole Constitution. We are asked to accept indefinitely this convenient state of affairs, which has already lasted seventeen years. That is not a matter of convenience, it is absolutism." "We demand", he wrote in the Address, "the execution of the laws, for an unexecuted law is a dead letter."

The negotiations made no progress. In a decree of March 3, 1866, the Crown refused to establish a responsible Hungarian Ministry, although it declared its readiness to grant concessions as soon as the royal powers, which had been denied in the Constitution of 1848, were recognised. This however was refused in the next address Deák drafted: "Legislation is the most cherished right of the nation and if this is to mean anything, the laws must be kept until the legislature has constitutionally repealed or altered them. If the executive had the right not to execute laws which had been constitutionally enacted, to suspend them, to substitute others by decree, and to keep the Constitution in mid-air until Parliament alters it, then the executive would in fact be the legislative authority. Your Majesty, we believe, does not wish to maintain absolutism; but such a union of executive and legislative power, if not merely temporary, is really absolutism." The Hungarian Parliament would not even negotiate with the illegal Government. But it went a step further: a commission of sixty-seven members was established to examine, quite independently of the Government, the proposed revision of the Constitution of 1848, and from this commission a smaller committee of fifteen was set up.

These difficult discussions had just begun when the danger of war became acute. In peace-time Deák had been the undisputed leader of the nation. In 1861 the Left had even withdrawn from the Chamber to enable him to carry his famous Address, which they found too moderate. In 1848 Deák, as Minister of Justice, had opposed the extremism of Kossuth, had warned him not to abandon the path of legality, and had left the Cabinet because he disapproved of the rebellion. But although faithful to the dynasty, he had mourned over the defeat of the Hungarian army and the destruction of the Constitution. Now the situation was becoming as difficult as in 1848. The possibility of war revived the influence of Kossuth, and Deák was unable to restrain the conspirators. Deák was not the man to lead or to control a revolutionary party; he was the perfect leader of a constitutional opposition, a man of moderation and self-control, unfitted for troublous times.

In this situation he was asked by Majlath, the Hungarian Chancellor, whether he would advise the Government to keep Parliament assembled during the war or to adjourn it. Deák informed his friends that the Government had no objection to continuing the session, but that it demanded from him, the leader of the nation, a guarantee that the Parliament would not use the opportunity to embarrass the Empire during its struggle. To their astonishment, he then declared that he could not give such a guarantee and that he therefore approved of an adjournment. At the same time he told Majlath that the adjournment was advisable because the Parliament would contest recruiting as illegal, and he did not feel that he could oppose such a view; for if the Emperor waged war as a German Federal Prince, that had nothing to do with Hungary. Eötvös was the only liberal who supported the coming war: he argued that the connection of the Federal lands of Austria with Germany could not be broken, because they rested on the firm bases of history, international law, and nationality. He drew the conclusion that dualism was the only possible constitution for the Austrian Empire, since it would enable the Federal lands to remain German and yet allow Hungary her old independence.

Julius Andrassy, the most outstanding of Deák's supporters and the man whom he nominated as the head of the future Ministry, completely disagreed, however, with Deák's attitude. Andrassy was afraid that once Parliament was adjourned the Government would give no further consideration to Hungary, especially in case of victory; whereas so long as the Parliament sat it could play an important part either by helping or by hindering. Andrassy was unmoved by the danger that the revolutionary party might become master of the situation—it would be fought as ruthlessly as the Government was now being fought. Deák's approval of the adjournment seemed to Andrassy political suicide and for the first time the two men disagreed. Deák was urged to change his mind at a meeting of all his closest supporters, except Andrassy, on June 19. He declared that if that was the opinion of the majority of the party he would write to the Chancellor as they wished. But Gorove, speaking for them all, said: "If you do not yourself agree, we cannot take the responsibility. How could we, when the majority of the nation has placed its fate in Deák's hands?" Deák's original resolve therefore held good, but he persuaded the Chancellor to postpone the adjournment, and used the interval to formulate the basis of a compromise. He wanted to create a "powerful document" which the nation could regard as the programme of reconciliation in case everything went wrong and absolutism was restored. He had to hurry, for on June 24 the battle of Custoza was fought and the Government, full of optimism, decided to adjourn the Hungarian Parliament. The order was issued on June 27, earlier than Deák had expected; but the committee of fifteen had already accepted his draft of a compromise.

The Austrian Cabinet was more successful with the German princes than it had been in Hungary. As always the German Courts put their own interests before the future of the nation; they would have preferred to separate altogether from Austria and Prussia and establish a smaller federation in which their complete sovereignty would be assured. The idea of a trialistic Germany dominated the statesmen of Bavaria, Saxony, and the other smaller states, but the strength of the lesser German princes was in inverse proportion to their ambition. The saying of Ranke applies to them all: "Whoever is unable to protect himself, proclaims himself unfit to exercise full sovereignty, and must surrender part of it to him who provides the necessary protection".[1]

Pfordten, the leading Minister of Bavaria, personally disliked Austria. He regarded himself as the leader of the lesser states in the Diet, and was embittered by the way in which Austria had always left him in the lurch. He was in a curious position. He represented the state which chiefly opposed the Prussian attempt to get control of all the military forces of Germany; and yet he was one of the few politicians of the day who recognised Bismarck's greatness, and he had a very poor opinion of Austria's military strength and of her leading statesmen. His policy was, in consequence, undecided right up to the outbreak of war. At one moment he exchanged confidential letters with Bismarck; at the next, the opinion of Court and people in Bavaria forced him to alter his tone. Before long both sides accused him of unreliability. At the beginning of April he assured the Saxon Cabinet that there would be no war; Austria had no money, the Austrian army was weak and poorly equipped and could do nothing against Prussia; but, he added, if there were a war, Bavaria would have to join with the lesser states against Prussia. At the meeting of the ministers of the lesser states at Augsburg on April 22 his opinion was the same. Some of the ministers still hoped that Austria and Prussia might be left to fight it out alone, and Edelsheim, the minister of Baden, even proposed that the lesser states should establish a federation of their own with a common Parliament. For a long time Bismarck thought that Pfordten would keep Bavaria neutral; but Prince Reuss, the Prussian representative at Munich, had

---

[1] The point of view of the lesser states is put by W. Hopf, *Die deutsche Krisis des Jahres 1866.*

long foreseen that Bavaria would fight on the Austrian side. The ministers of the lesser states met again at Bamberg on May 14, but only formulated some useless proposals for general disarmament. Pfordten's views were clearer, but he created much discouragement by describing Austrian policy as false and unreliable.[1] Bavaria was to prove an obstinate and uncontrollable ally.

The attitude of Hanover was determined by the character and principles of the blind king, George V, who completely dominated Platen, his Foreign Minister. At the beginning of the crisis Hanover had assured Berlin of her neutrality, but on May 5 she called up three year-classes of her reserves. Prussia could not tolerate this, for Hanover's central position directly threatened Prussian security. Prussia therefore demanded a treaty of neutrality, in return for which the integrity of Hanover should be unconditionally guaranteed. Simultaneously there arrived proposals from Austria that the Austrian brigade in Holstein should unite with the Hanoverian army; it was hoped to recruit 10,000 volunteers from Holstein, and so form an army of 40,000 men under Gablenz. On May 13 the Hanoverian Council advised neutrality for fear of Prussian vengeance, and the King ostensibly approved. But in fact George V was unwilling to stand quietly by while the future of his military rights was being decided by war, and he wanted to be ready to participate, if necessary, in the struggle. The Austrian Cabinet sent Prince Charles von Solms, the step-brother of the King and a general in the Austrian service, to Hanover to secure an alliance. He brought with him a letter from Francis Joseph, offering as an inducement territorial acquisitions in Holstein and the

---

[1] After the war Pfordten explained his actions thus: he had foreseen and foretold what was bound to happen, indeed he had proved to Beust at Bamberg that Austria was not in a condition to wage a war. But no one would believe him, indeed he had been called a traitor, so finally he had been compelled to take part in the war.—Friesen, ii. 250.

command over the tenth German Federal Army Corps. King George was tempted, but he was afraid to ally himself openly with Austria; Solms did however persuade him to break off the negotiations with Prussia for a treaty of neutrality, Platen explaining that as a German Prince the King must await the decision of the Diet. This was of little use to Austria, but it compelled Prussia to occupy Hanover in order to secure her own safety. George V was offered the most generous terms, but he preferred any risk to subordination to the House of Hohenzollern.[1]

The situation was very different in Saxony, where the Government was determined to defend its sovereignty to the utmost against Prussia. King John, the most cultured of the German princes, and Crown Prince Albert, a personal friend of Francis Joseph's, possessed in Beust a minister of ability, distinguished from all the other German ministers by his quick comprehension, practical sense, fluency, and resolution. Unfortunately Beust had taken it into his head to enter into a sort of competition with Bismarck. After 1849 he had established a strictly conservative system, but had gradually come round to more liberal views until he became so fond of contrasting Saxon freedom with Prussian oppression that Bismarck hated him more than any other of his enemies. Beust was a real danger; in the lesser German states he had a tremendous reputation as a diplomatic genius and he was in close touch with the Austrian Cabinet. Schwarzenberg called him his best lieutenant in Germany, and there were already occasional rumours of his becoming an Austrian minister. These rumours were still unfounded, for Beust like Pfordten was aiming at creating a federation

[1] These events are treated in detail by Wengen, *Geschichte der Kriegs-ereignisse zwischen Preussen und Hannover* (Gotha, 1866). It is not, however, correct that an agreement for military co-operation was reached between Francis Joseph and King George, although letters were exchanged. In the Hanoverian Cabinet Council of May 14 a letter was drafted to Francis Joseph explaining that the plan was too dangerous, as the Hanoverian army would be soon compelled to capitulate.

of the "third Germany", that is of all the states except
Austria and Prussia. He wanted definite military co-operation with Bavaria and proposed that the Bavarian army
should advance towards the Saxon frontier, to unite with
the Saxons in case of a Prussian invasion. But Pfordten,
hesitating and distrustful as ever, declared that Bavaria
needed her soldiers herself, and in order to avoid complete
isolation Saxony had to ally herself with Austria. Beust was
full of confidence; he assured the Duke of Coburg on April 18
that Austria was superior to her opponent; and on May 5 he
provoked an outburst of indignation in Prussia by appealing to the Diet for protection against Prussian threats.
Saxony was thus ready to bear the brunt of the Prussian
advance.

The Austrian Government had made sure of the
lesser German states. But at headquarters Benedek and
Krismanič watched anxiously over a slow and incomplete
mobilisation. The Austrian army was assembling in Moravia,
because Krismanič had expected the Prussians to invade
Austria from Silesia. By the middle of May it was clear that
he had been mistaken. The Prussians were mustering in a
great semi-circle round Bohemia and Saxony and the
Austrian army was being concentrated too far from the
frontier. Saxony and Bohemia lay open to the invader, unless the whole plan of mobilisation were changed. Krismanič
was not the man to change his mind easily; he argued that a
plan once adopted must be carried through; only when the
army was completely ready should it advance into Bohemia
towards the Upper Elbe. Clam-Gallas, the commander of
the troops in Bohemia, was instructed to fall back on
Josephstadt in case of a Prussian invasion, and the Saxon
Government was informed that the Austrian army would
not be ready in time to come to their help. Benedek expected
the Austrian army to be completely equipped by June 10,
and according to his information the Prussians would be

ready a week earlier, on June 4; in a week they could over-run Bohemia as far as the Elbe.

The Austrian information concerning the Prussian mobilisation was exact to the very day. On May 14 Moltke informed the King that 270,000 men would be ready on the frontier on June 4 and he urged that war should be declared on that day. On May 25 he was still more pressing: he explained that at the beginning of July the Austrians would not have more than 180,000 men and added: "However strong or weak they may be, they will certainly get stronger every day and in a few weeks we may be faced with a new enemy in France. It is essential to defeat our chief enemy first. . . . It is urgently desirable from the military point of view that diplomatic action should have come to an end by June 5." But the King still refused to sanction a sudden invasion of Saxony and a surprise of the Austrian army. He had only given the order for mobilisation because Austria had already started to mobilise, and if the Austrians, as Bismarck and the generals asserted, really intended to attack Prussia, he would fight a defensive battle before the gates of Berlin, where the Prussian generals had made their stand against Napoleon's marshals in 1813. The recollection of the war of 1813 was so strong in him that, when his secretary, Louis Schneider, asked leave to accompany him to headquarters, he replied: "What for? You can easily ride over from Potsdam to Grossbeeren." The Crown Prince was of the same opinion: Austria must be the first to take the offensive. The Prussian army was therefore left in a defensive circle one hundred and forty to two hundred miles long.

Moltke accepted the King's decision uncomplainingly and even defended it to others. He wrote to Bethusy-Huc on May 29: "You are quite right, that a powerful initiative would be the best. The Austrians have six weeks' start of us,[1] but by next week we shall have caught them up. Delay increases their strength and enables them to find allies in

[1] *Sic.*

South Germany, while it exhausts our finances and has a bad effect on our morale. But we are asking our seventy-year-old King to give the signal for a European war, the duration and extent of which cannot be foreseen." And again on June 11 to Blumenthal: "We must not calculate with wishes and hopes, but with realities. Permission to attack cannot be expected for the next week for non-military, but very important reasons."

William's hesitation was justified. The news from Paris and from the German capitals was enough to shake the strongest resolution. Even more alarming was the popular hostility to Bismarck's policy revealed during the Prussian mobilisation. In Silesia Catholic priests condemned the war as an unjust attack on Austria, and in the Rhineland cavalry had to be called out to compel reservists to enter the troop trains. Archbishop Melchers of Cologne voiced the popular fear of French invasion and hatred of a civil war in a letter to the King on May 28, which concluded: "These are the reasons why our soldiers and militia, who only three years ago gladly followed their commander's call, now obey unwillingly and discontentedly". Addresses condemning the policy of the Ministry poured in to the King from all parts of Prussia; only the addresses from Breslau and Halle expressed confidence in his leadership. Bodelschwingh, the Minister of Finance, was the only minister who openly opposed Bismarck and he had to resign; but Schleinitz, who enjoyed the King's confidence, also belonged to the peace party. For a moment, immediately after the mobilisation, Prussia's excellent credit seemed shaken and many merchants refused to accept Prussian notes. It was characteristic of Bismarck that he was quite unmoved by these difficulties. When the Crown Prince warned him of the possibility of a catastrophe, he replied grimly: "What does it matter whether I am hanged, if only the hangman's rope binds your throne fast to the new Germany".

William found his ministers' advice opposed not only by

public opinion, but also by foreign Courts. The Tsar and
Queen Victoria both wrote urging him to keep the peace.
But although the King was slow to make a decision, once
it was made nothing would move him; and he had now made
up his mind to secure the military supremacy over North
Germany. His reply to the Queen of England was completely
in the spirit of Bismarck: he desired peace, and had done his
best to maintain it, but Schleswig-Holstein Prussia must
have. His people, he added, were dissatisfied with the
Government only because so much had been sacrificed to
free the Duchies and Prussia had gained nothing. The English Government was astonished, and Clarendon, the Foreign
Secretary, told Vitzthum that there was not one word of
truth in the letter.[1] The King accepted entirely the ideas of
Bismarck, Roon, and Moltke, regarding them as the real
voice of the misguided people. William recognised the
penalty of failure—the surrender of the Prussian Monarchy
to Parliament and a Constitution on the English model.
Bismarck himself said that the King was resolved to
abdicate in case of defeat and to leave his son to settle with
Parliament.[2] But William was not discouraged. When he
heard that King George of Hanover refused to disarm and
subordinate himself to the military control of Prussia, he
exclaimed, as if this were an act of personal hostility: "I
know, they are all against me, all except Hesse and Mecklenburg. But I will put myself at the head of my army and die
sword in hand rather than that Prussia should again give
way."

Bismarck and the generals saw clearly that the King
would refuse to provoke public opinion in Germany and
Europe by declaring war without further cause. Bismarck
had to find some way of proving finally to the King that
there was no compromise acceptable to Austria. He found it
in the proposal of a partition of Germany between Austria

[1] Vitzthum, 189.
[2] So Bismarck told Unruh, according to the latter's *Erinnerungen*.

and Prussia. The authors of this proposal were the two brothers Gablenz, by birth Saxons, of whom one was an Austrian general, while the other was for some time a member of the Prussian Parliament. Gablenz was one of the Austrian generals who had warned Francis Joseph against a war on two fronts, for he had seen in the Danish War the superiority of the Prussian needle-gun. He proposed to Manteuffel that the Emperor and the King should come to an agreement over the future organisation of Germany.[1] "Then they should assemble all the princes and say to them: this is what we have decided and we call upon you to agree. An army corps would occupy the territory of any prince who refused, a Prussian in the north, an Austrian in the south and all the princes would soon agree. If necessary a Parliament could also be called and, encompassed by a million soldiers, it would also agree. Europe could be told: the affairs of Germany are now settled, and no one would think of intervening against a million soldiers." Anton, the General's brother, also urged this policy on Mensdorff, and with his permission travelled to Berlin to see Bismarck. Between May 13 and 20 Bismarck and Gablenz drafted a Constitution for Germany. To meet Austria's wishes, Schleswig-Holstein was to remain an independent duchy, but a Hohenzollern was to be made duke, and Kiel and Rendsburg were to go to Prussia. The central proposal of the plan concerned the disposition of the armed forces of Germany: "in peace and war the Emperor of Austria is Commander-in-Chief of the South, the King of Prussia of the North". Each of the two empires was to guarantee the other's territory and so Venice would be assured to Austria. Bismarck said later of the proposal: [2] "Nobody could have opposed us. The two German powers were strongly armed and could lay down the law to a Europe which was not

[1] Sybel, iv. 381, was the first to supply a documentary basis for these negotiations.

[2] In a conversation with the author on June 13, 1890.

expecting anything like that. The King of Bavaria would certainly have had to surrender part of his sovereignty to the Emperor of Austria in common with the other South German princes, but the limitation would not have been so great as that which he voluntarily accepted in 1871. This was the reason why we were so shamefaced about these negotiations. Neither we nor Austria, who within a month was Bavaria's ally, could even hint that in May we had been negotiating about a partition of Germany. Naturally I cannot say whether this settlement would have been final or whether a war between Austria and Prussia would not have been necessary later to achieve a permanent arrangement of Germany." According to his own account, Bismarck made a further proposal: "I proposed that, fully equipped as we were, we should turn against France and compel her to surrender Alsace; Austria could then have had Strasburg and Prussia Mainz. . . . Napoleon, with his army weak and demoralised by the Mexican expedition, could not have resisted."

These sweeping proposals are astonishing in their ruthlessness, for they implied a complete desertion of Italy. Certainly Prussia had in the April treaty retained the right to fight or to compromise, as she chose, but the Italians would have had just ground for complaint if, after arming in alliance with Prussia, they had been confronted with Prussian bayonets at Venice. La Marmora and his colleagues have been blamed for entering into the alliance half-heartedly and for not appreciating Bismarck's genius; but they had some justification for anxiety. Napoleon, losing Alsace, would have fared even worse, but he would only have been hoist with his own petard, for he was hoping to make his own profit out of the war between the two German powers. Bismarck made every effort to lull Napoleon into a sense of security; on May 21, the day before Gablenz's arrival in Vienna, he informed Napoleon that German public opinion prevented Prussia from offering him any German territory, but suggested Belgium as suitable compensation.

Prussia's relations with the rest of Germany would have suffered most if Austria had agreed, for the proposed unitary Constitution and the German Parliament would have had to be jettisoned. But Bismarck hoped to compensate the nation by turning its combined forces against France. In any case these are probably idle speculations, for it is impossible to know whether Bismarck ever expected the Austrians to accept these proposals. He certainly thought it unlikely. On May 24 Duke Ernest of Coburg visited Berlin to place his soldiers at the disposal of King William. He found the King, presumably in consequence of Gablenz's negotiations, hopeful of a peaceful solution, the Crown Prince anxious and depressed; but Bismarck told him quite calmly that war was unavoidable and was confident of victory.

The Gablenz mission gave the Austrians an excellent opportunity to gain time to complete their defective mobilisation; for the same reason they welcomed Napoleon's plan of a European Congress, and though the neutral powers knew that his efforts could have no real result, they did not want to reject them. Napoleon drafted a form of invitation, in which the surrender of Venice and the guarantee of the temporal power of the Pope were put forward as the first subjects to be discussed. England and Russia objected that Austria would not come, if the surrender of a province was demanded in advance. The finer-sounding expression, "Austro-Italian dispute", was therefore substituted and the fate of Schleswig-Holstein, and German Federal Reform, were added to the agenda. On May 28 the invitation was presented in this form to the three powers concerned and to the German Diet. Bismarck had no great faith even in the amended proposal; he told the Italian minister that the Congress was a vain phantom and that in his opinion no human power could prevent war. However, neither Prussia nor Italy wanted to appear as the aggressor, and the invitation was therefore accepted, particularly as William held it improper to reject the mediation of the neutral powers.

Prussia was the first to accept, Italy and the German Confederation followed almost immediately.

Gablenz arrived in Vienna on May 23 and the invitation to the Congress was despatched on May 24. Gablenz had an audience with the Emperor on May 25, lasting an hour and a quarter. "He read out his proposals; the Emperor asked questions, and he gave further explanations. Then the Emperor said that it was really regrettable that these proposals had not been made six or eight weeks earlier, when they would certainly have been accepted; presumably Count Bismarck had some deep purpose in making acceptable proposals only when their acceptance was no longer possible. . . . However, Gablenz was dismissed not ungraciously: 'I shall think over this important matter', the Emperor said, 'and let you have my answer; it is at any rate clear that by this agreement Prussia gets the lion's share.' " [1]

The Emperor's words gave Gablenz a presentiment of failure. Mensdorff, the minister whose opinion ought to have been decisive, declared resignedly that towards these fresh projects he was quite open-minded and would do whatever the Emperor recommended.[2] Esterhazy, who had at first wanted a compromise on the lines proposed by Gablenz, was now for a refusal, remarking to Belcredi that the proposals came "somewhat late in the day". The Austrian ministers doubted whether a new alliance with Prussia would be any more durable than the alliance against Denmark, and Bismarck's sudden change from aggressiveness to friendly negotiations aroused their distrust. The Emperor, moreover, had just entered into alliance with many of the German princes; to hand half of them over to Prussia and compel the others to submit to him would be a breach of faith. The Austrian attitude was fundamentally inconsistent: at the beginning of May the outlook had been so black that it had

---

[1] Sybel, iv. 384, according to Gablenz's report.
[2] Friesen, ii. 161.

been decided to buy off Italy with the offer of Venice; since then nothing had changed except the mood of the Austrian Cabinet. The dilettantism with which the Belcredi Cabinet faced its problems, both at home and abroad, lay at the root of the evil. The internal situation should have made the ministers avoid war at all costs; instead they welcomed war as the solution of all their difficulties.[1] Belcredi showed himself completely unfitted for office, and the Duke of Coburg, who knew the Court of Vienna well, described the ministers as gamblers rather than statesmen.[2]

No attempt was made even to spin out the negotiations in order to gain time. Benedek would not be ready to advance into Bohemia until June 10; but the warnings from Headquarters were ignored and on May 28 the Gablenz proposals were rejected. The Prussian General Staff was still afraid that the Congress would prevent the advance of the Prussian troops; the 5th of June, when Prussia would have 270,000 men ready on the frontier and Austria scarcely 200,000, was drawing near.[3] Bismarck told Benedetti on May 29 that the generals would take no responsibility for a further delay of the outbreak of war, which therefore might take place while the Congress was sitting. But the King would take no aggressive action. "He believes religiously", Bismarck said to Govone on June 2, "or rather superstitiously, that he must not make himself responsible for a European war."

[1] Sybel (iv. 390) says that Belcredi and Larisch frankly confessed this to Gablenz, and as this was not denied by Belcredi, Sybel's account was reproduced in the first edition of this book, but with a note that Sybel's report was followed reluctantly. The author had previously asked for enlightenment from Belcredi; but he refused, saying that he did not think it was yet time to give explanations of his actions when in office. However, after the publication of the first edition, Belcredi declared that Sybel's story was an invention, as he had never met or spoken to Gablenz, and never used the expressions which were put into his mouth. He added that, so far as he knew, Larisch too was not acquainted with Gablenz.

[2] Coburg, iii. 484.

[3] Moltke to Govone on June 3 (La Marmora, 259).

Bismarck suggested to the Italians that they might let their impatient volunteers provoke a war or perhaps bribe one of the Croat regiments on the Mincio to attack the Italians—he would see to it that Prussia at once supported Italy. It is not surprising that La Marmora refused to listen and replied that Prussia must start the war.

Austria herself solved her enemies' difficulties. Mensdorff made a last plea for peace and advised the acceptance of the invitation to the Congress; he thought war now inevitable, but he realised that Austria ought to do her best to appear conciliatory. Esterhazy, however, objected that a great power could not allow the sacrifice of one of her provinces to be the subject of a European discussion, and on appeal to the Emperor Esterhazy's view was confirmed.[1] On June 1 Austria declined the invitation to the Congress. She declared that she would attend only if all the powers promised not to discuss territorial acquisitions—an impossible condition as everyone knew—and added that she would not surrender Venice unless she received adequate compensation. "We have been told that Silesia ought to be adequate compensation for Venice. . . . If, in the event of war, our power were increased by striking military successes, we certainly might decide to use our advantage with wise moderation and renounce one province to secure another."

Nobody was more pleased than Bismarck. The French Ambassador was with him on June 4 when the news of

---

[1] [There is little evidence that Mensdorff ever favoured acceptance of the Congress, except in a form which would make acceptance meaningless. There seems to have been hardly any discussion on the subject and certainly no Council was ever held. The proposal of a Congress so clearly assumed that Austria would be called upon to surrender Venice that Austria could not well have accepted the invitation without a complete abandonment of her position as a great power. To have gone to the Congress and then refused all concessions would have merely alienated all the European powers; whereas a refusal of the Congress did not materially weaken Austria's position.—Translator.]

Austria's refusal arrived; without attempting to control himself he burst out: "God save the King!" [1]

[1] On the evening of the same day Bismarck had a long interview with Vilbort, of the staff of the Paris *Siècle* (Vilbort, 211). Bismarck depicted the difficulties he had to encounter with the King's relations and said: "Neither this nor the opposition with which I have had to contend in Prussia can prevent me devoting myself body and soul to the idea of establishing North Germany in her logical and natural form under the aegis of Prussia and I will risk anything, exile and even the scaffold, to attain this end".

CHAPTER IX

THE TREATY BETWEEN AUSTRIA AND FRANCE.
OUTBREAK OF WAR IN GERMANY

As soon as war was certain the Cabinets of Vienna and
Berlin renewed their efforts to make sure of the Emperor
Napoleon. It was Napoleon's growing friendliness towards
Austria which had encouraged the Austrian ministers to
break off the negotiations with Prussia, and Metternich
was now trying to induce France to put pressure on Italy
to remain neutral; there was even a rumour that a fleet
was fitting out in Toulon to force Italy to compromise.
But the Emperor was not willing to go so far; he thought it
wiser to leave Italy on Prussia's side, lest Austria win too
easily. He intended that Prussia should only be humiliated
enough to make her offer him the Rhineland as the price
of his assistance. The Italians, caring much for Napoleon's
support and not at all for the integrity of Germany, urged
Bismarck to make an offer; Victor Emmanuel sent a message saying: "Napoleon wants a meal; give him something,
but not much; then say very firmly that he won't get any
more and he will be content". Napoleon, however, was
confident that he would be able to extort any price he
wanted for his neutrality just before the conclusion of
peace.

Prince Jérôme and Rouher saw with alarm the Emperor's
avoidance of an agreement with Prussia and the Prince
made a determined effort to create an alliance between

France, Prussia, and Italy. He and Nigra drafted for Bismarck proposals for a defensive and offensive alliance between the three states; Prussia was offered the French alliance and France in return was to receive all the land between the Rhine and the Moselle except Mainz and Coblenz. It was naturally assumed in Berlin that the Emperor knew of his cousin's action and it seemed that Bismarck had hinted at Belgium in vain. These overtures, therefore, could not be rejected outright, and Bismarck replied indirectly through Govone. When Govone asked him whether there was no territory on the Rhine which might vote in favour of annexation to France, Bismarck replied: "None—the French agents all report that a plebiscite would not be successful, unless it was manufactured. Nobody likes the native governments or dynasties, but they are all German and want to remain German." Then Bismarck added these ambiguous words: "I am much less German than Prussian and would have no objection to agreeing to the transference to France of all the land between the Rhine and the Moselle. But the King would have very strong scruples and would only agree to it as a last resort: that is, when we stood to win or lose everything."

Did Bismarck mean these words seriously? Nigra thought so, and Benedetti let himself be persuaded that Bismarck was the only man in Berlin who considered the surrender of territory "without prejudice". Bismarck himself later rejected the idea, explaining sarcastically that he had to keep Napoleon in a good humour and therefore told Govone that, if it depended on him, he might be willing to commit a little high treason, but it would be no use, as the King would not allow it. At any rate, the Cabinets of Berlin and Paris never negotiated directly over the matter; Bismarck managed the affair through Italian intermediaries. He held out a mirage of territorial aggrandisement to Napoleon, but he would certainly have resisted any attempt to seize German territory, unless he was in the midst of a war with

Austria. But in order to keep in touch with Napoleon he sent a message asking him to define his minimum demands, while adding that he would settle direct with Austria if the Emperor demanded the whole left bank of the Rhine.

Immediately before the outbreak of war the Prussian Cabinet made a last attempt to get a definite statement: William wrote to the Emperor asking him to promise neutrality. But Napoleon was once more evasive: he replied that it was difficult to foresee all the changing circumstances of war, and that the two sovereigns could rely on each other's loyalty.[1]

The Austrian attempts to secure the favour of Napoleon seemed to be attended with more success. Napoleon's objectives had not changed since the beginning of May. He wanted the emancipation of Italy from foreign, that is, Austrian rule, but not her unification by the inclusion of Rome. Germany was not to be dominated by any one power and, if Prussia or Austria acquired territory, France too must extend her frontier. On May 24 Gramont brought friendly assurances from the Austrian Cabinet to Paris; he returned to Vienna on June 4, and on June 12 a treaty was signed between Austria and France. The most important clause was that Austria agreed to surrender Venice, even if her army were victorious on one or both fronts. It was unnecessary to provide for the possibility of an Austrian defeat, since Venice would then be lost in any case. Austria did not get much in return. Napoleon promised to remain neutral himself and to make every effort to secure the neutrality of Italy. Austria was to lose nothing on her southern frontier except Venice; Italy would take over an appropriate share of the Austrian national debt and pay compensation for the fortresses that were surrendered; and finally, Venice was not to be made a naval harbour.

[1] According to the pamphlet which Napoleon published after his overthrow under the name of the Marquis de Gricourt.

If Austria was victorious she would incur further obligations in Germany. She was not to make any political or
territorial changes without the approval of France, though
Napoleon would not object to any extension of territory—
Silesia was the case in point—which did not upset the
balance of power in Europe and provided that Germany
was not united "under a single authority". Austria did not
promise Napoleon any German territory; but he was gratified
to get a verbal assurance from the Austrian negotiators that
their objectives included not only an increase of territory
and influence for Bavaria, Württemberg, and Saxony, but
the creation of an independent state on the left bank of the
Rhine. Such a buffer state would separate France from her
dangerous Prussian neighbour and would be completely
under French influence.

Austria thus lost Venice whatever happened, and, if she
was victorious, Napoleon was bound to benefit, even if he
did not gain any territory. In return Austria received practically nothing; it was soon clear that she was not even
assured of Italian neutrality. There was only a clause, by
which the Austrian Cabinet set great store, guaranteeing the
present possessions of the Holy See, and even allowing that
under certain circumstances the Pope should regain his
lost territory, the Marches and the Legations. Napoleon
promised not to intervene if ever there was a spontaneous
Italian movement to undo unification. But under no circumstances was the House of Habsburg to profit. The Dukes
of Tuscany and Modena were never to return to their ancient
possessions; at the most they might hope for compensation
in Germany. Napoleon did not expect any reaction in Italy
in favour of the Pope or of the Bourbons; but the strongly
Clerical statesmen of Austria regarded this clause as a real
achievement. The Austrian army in Italy would not be
fighting for Austria, or even for the dynasty, but simply to
secure for the peoples of Central Italy the right to rise in
favour of the Pope.

Beust, who saw the treaty later, described it as the most incredible document he had ever seen, and we can only agree with him.[1] All the clauses were so ambiguous that anything

[1] The text was first published in Ollivier, *L'empire libéral*, viii. 180. [The original French draft of the treaty had this article in relation to Venice: "whatever the results of the war, the Austrian Government promises to cede Venice to France on the conclusion of peace". This clause was rejected by the Austrian Government, which proposed to substitute: "If the fortune of war favours Austria in such a way as to give her an equivalent territorial compensation in Germany the Austrian Government promises to cede Venice to the French Government on the conclusion of peace. If the fortune of war favours Austria in Italy, the Austrian Government promises not to change the *status quo ante bellum* in this Kingdom without an agreement with France." Gramont accepted this change, but it was rejected by Napoleon, for it clearly left Austria with too good an opportunity to escape from her promises after the war. The clause finally agreed upon was: "If the fortune of war favours Austria in Germany, the Austrian Government agrees to cede Venice to the French Government on the conclusion of peace. If the fortune of war favours it in Italy, it promises not to change the *status quo ante bellum* in this Kingdom without an agreement with France." For all practical purposes this is equivalent to the first draft; the only circumstances in which Austria could retain Venice would be if the war in Germany went neither against her nor in her favour, which was wellnigh impossible. But the Austrian Government consoled itself, as Friedjung has described, with the additional clauses, which guaranteed the temporal sovereignty of the Pope and committed France to non-intervention in Italy.

The ministers, of course, realised that the treaty was very unfavourable to Austria, but they could see no alternative. The decisive consideration was the information of Napoleon that he could reach an agreement with Prussia if Austria refused. Francis Joseph informed the Council of June 11 that Napoleon had said: "Prussia had offered him the surrender of the Rhine provinces and the agreement with Prussia only needed his simple acceptance—the result would be an active intervention on his side with all his force". Napoleon was, of course, saying exactly the reverse to Bismarck, but unlike the Austrian ministers Bismarck did not give way to panic. It was in fact a repetition of the diplomatic manœuvre by which Napoleon had induced Francis Joseph to agree to the armistice of Villafrancha in 1859—the same transformation of possibilities and probabilities, some of them with very little foundation, into certainties, and on the Austrian side the same unquestioning acceptance of Napoleon's unconfirmed statements. Esterhazy seems to have been the could be read into them—only the arrangements for the surrender of Venice were clear and precise. The whole document is indeed the last testament of the old Austrian system of government. The possession of Silesia was worth a war; but why should Austria make this achievement more difficult by fighting Italy at the same time, not for the sake of Venice, but for the sake of the Pope? The old Austria had regarded herself as the protector of the Papacy, but neither Kaunitz nor Thugut nor Metternich would have allowed the integrity of the Papal States to outweigh Austrian interests. The war in Italy could only be justified as a serious effort to defend the frontiers of the empire. Such an effort was no longer contemplated, but prejudice forbade direct negotiations with Italy. Italy was an illegitimate creation and therefore the mediation of that most legitimate monarch, the Emperor Napoleon, had to be employed. The Monarchy was committed to a war on two fronts over a question of etiquette.

Napoleon had every reason to be satisfied with the treaty of June 12. He had never intended to abandon his neutrality and Austria was paying him heavily to do what he would

only minister who did not accept Napoleon's information unreservedly and he merely remarked: "It is questionable whether Napoleon's threat to intervene with his whole force is seriously meant, whether the pistol is really loaded".

The Council agreed that the treaty must be accepted and the Emperor stated in conclusion: "Napoleon had said that the interests of Austria and France were identical apart from Venice and that there was nothing to prevent these two powers forming a close alliance once this bone of contention was removed. Whatever value might be attached to these statements it was undeniable, that Napoleon was at the moment master of the situation and that it would be more than rash to drive him into the camp of two powerful and bitter enemies by a brusque rejection of his proposals. The thought was particularly painful to him that the army in Italy would now have to fight for something which the greatest heroism could no longer save."

Council minutes of June 11, in the Austrian archives K.Z. 2119, and published in Redlich, ii. 804-8.—Translator.]

have done in any case. Italy would get Venice and he had the prospect of extending his influence to the Rhine. It must be borne in mind that he rated the military power of Austria higher than that of Prussia. He wanted to insure himself against Habsburg supremacy in Germany and he did so by securing a promise that France should be consulted on the reorganisation of Germany.

After the treaty had been signed, Napoleon began to feel guilty about Italy. He had secured Venice for her, but he had exposed Central Italy to certain dangers, however remote, and he anxiously concealed the contents of the treaty from Nigra. This silence frightened Victor Emmanuel into sending his son-in-law, Prince Jérôme, to ask Napoleon for more precise information. This Napoleon did not vouchsafe, but there was some comfort in Napoleon's assurance that Austria was committed to the surrender of Venice. Nigra wrote optimistically: "The war begins under favourable auspices and the situation could not be better".[1] There remained a cloud on the horizon: though ignorant of the terms of the treaty, Nigra shrewdly suspected that Napoleon would not object if the Austrian army established the Pope in his old possessions. "In that case," he added, "it would be difficult for France to send troops to Italy to take away from the Pope the provinces restored to him by Austria." From now on Napoleon gave the Italians the impression that he was favouring Austria. He warned La Marmora not to begin the war and even advised Victor Emmanuel not to put all his strength into the struggle. So Napoleon did his duty by the Austrian alliance, though without much benefit to Austria; for her honour and her unity Italy was bound to fight with all her might.

After the conclusion of the Austrian treaty, Drouyn de

---

[1] In a memorandum written in June 1866 for the Prince of Carignano, a cousin of Victor Emmanuel's, in which Nigra summarises the negotiations he had conducted. See Rothan, 422. It is an important historical document.

Lhuys advised his master to insure himself by a similar treaty against a Prussian victory. But Napoleon's ambitions were too great to be revealed to King William: he could not ask Prussia to cede her territory on the left bank of the Rhine to a buffer state, still less to France herself. Napoleon's apologists, such as Émile Ollivier, his partner in misfortune in 1870, have argued that Napoleon's respect for national rights prevented him from aiming at the German Rhineland. This is only true in that he concealed his ambitions, for fear of frightening William into the arms of Austria. The treaty of June 12 shows his intentions clearly enough: he wanted to weaken Prussia and open his way to the Rhine.[1] That is the reason why he avoided a formal agreement with the Prussian Cabinet and remained content with the verbal promises of Bismarck and Goltz to consult France before a final reorganisation of Germany. Such promises, unconfirmed by the King, were of little value; but Napoleon was confident that he could control Prussia whatever happened.

On June 11 Napoleon published a sort of manifesto to

[1] This is the answer to Ollivier (viii. 645) who criticises me for saying that Napoleon was annoyed at the Prussian rejection of his demands. Napoleon, Ollivier declares, never made any demand. Nor did I say he did, but I showed that Napoleon *expected* definite offers from Prussia and turned against Prussia when they did not come. I cannot, however, agree that Napoleon never aimed at German territory and honestly desired the Congress in order to assure the peace of Europe.

[Friedjung's contention is now amply confirmed by the evidence of the Austrian archives. As shown in the previous note, Napoleon told the Austrian Government that he could get a promise of the Rhine from Prussia if he wanted it, and undoubtedly Napoleon really believed this. Whether he could, in fact, have got such a promise from Prussia is, of course, a very different matter. Napoleon's German policy is the subject of Oncken's *Rheinpolitik Kaiser Napoleons III von 1863 bis 1870*, a selection of documents from the Austrian and Prussian archives and from those of the South German states. The introduction has been published in English under the title of *Napoleon III and the Rhine*. The selection of documents is unfortunately tendencious.—Translator.]

Europe, which was read out in the Chamber. He indicated
his aims in the oracular style which he loved: "For our part,
we should have liked a closer union, a stronger organisation,
and a more important rôle for the lesser states of Germany;
more cohesion and power in the North for Prussia; and for
Austria the preservation of her great position in Germany.
We should also have aimed at the cession of Venice by
Austria in return for equivalent compensation." The objects of the Emperor's policy, the manifesto continued,
were the balance of power in Europe and the maintenance
of the work of France in Italy, and the Emperor did not
desire any territorial acquisition unless—and here was an
important qualification—the balance of power was upset.
"But is not the moral force of France enough to secure
these two interests? Will she be compelled to draw the
sword? I think not." Here lay Napoleon's fundamental
mistake, and he repeated it when he asserted that, however
the war ended, French interests "were secured by the
declarations of the powers involved, so that none of the
questions which affect us can be settled without the agreement of France".

This reference to all the powers involved made Europe
believe that Napoleon had an agreement with Prussia,
when in fact he had only a few friendly and empty words
from Bismarck. Only the invasion of Prussia by the armies
of Austria and France could have compelled her to give
up Silesia and the Rhineland in return for compensation
in North Germany; only armed mediation could have compelled Germany to surrender the Rhine; only a great military ruler could have humiliated Prussia and checked
Austria. But the French arsenals were empty and, for fear
of opposition in the Chamber, Napoleon did not even dare
to propose a loan for their replenishment, still less to raise
the inadequate annual conscription. Napoleon had come
to the throne by force; and only force could intimidate
Europe and secure his rule. He let himself be surprised by

the War of 1866, unprepared, with an army that was
rotten to the core.

The Austrian Cabinet considered the diplomatic campaign at an end. Napoleon had been won over, the lesser
German states were all arming against Prussia, and Hungary was apparently satisfied with the prospect of the
recognition of her Constitution. It was only regrettable
that the lesser states were all arming independently of
Austria and that Saxony alone recognised the need for
close military co-operation. The Kings were all determined
to pursue a war policy of their own and the hesitations of
Bavaria, or rather of Pfordten, did Prussia the invaluable
service of dividing the considerable forces of the "third
Germany". Pfordten had been nominated to represent the
German Confederation at the proposed Congress, and his
ambition was galled at losing this honour when Austria
refused to attend. He bitterly denounced "the unreliability
and duplicity of the Austrian Government", and wrote to
Bismarck proposing the dissolution of the German Confederation, thereby encouraging Bismarck to hope after all
for Bavarian neutrality. As late as June 1 Pfordten proposed
a resolution in the Bavarian Chamber, demanding a Parliament from the lesser states as "the first step towards
a general German Parliament". But meanwhile, public
opinion was forcing Bavaria to mobilise in order to resist
the danger of Prussian hegemony.

It was essential to persuade the lesser states to commit
themselves to Austria. There was only one way of doing so.
The German princes had been deeply offended when Austria and Prussia had withdrawn Schleswig-Holstein from
the jurisdiction of the Diet; they could, however, be ap-
peased if Austria now submitted the question of the
Duchies to the Diet. Austria was ready to do this, and to
make sure of public opinion she went still further: she
decided to consult the representative assembly of Holstein

on the fate of the Duchies, knowing that it would declare in favour of the Duke of Augustenburg and against Prussia.

These were definite acts of hostility against Prussia, for the treaty of January 16, 1864, was still in force, by which Austria and Prussia were to dispose of the Duchies jointly and Denmark had surrendered the Duchies jointly to the two states. William, though averse from war, had always declared that the submission of the question of the Duchies to the Diet would be a breach of the treaty and he was still more offended by the appeal to the popular assembly in Holstein. Nevertheless, on June 1 Austria appealed to the Confederation, on the grounds that all attempts to reach an agreement with Prussia had failed, and summoned the Estates of Holstein. Nothing could be more welcome to Bismarck and to the generals who were trying to persuade William to declare war. They pointed out that the rights of Prussia were being trodden underfoot and added the argument, which carried great weight with the King, that Austria was allying herself with the Revolution against the Prussian Monarchy. Bismarck made the most of his opportunity. A few days later he issued a circular violently provocative to Austria. "There is no longer any doubt that the Imperial ministers desire war at any price, partly in the hope of successes on the battlefield, partly to overcome their internal difficulties, and actually with the expressed intention of restoring the Austrian finances either by an indemnity from Prussia or by an honourable bankruptcy." At the same time Prussia appealed to public opinion by publishing in the *Staatsanzeiger* of June 5 the clause of the treaty of January 16, 1864, by which the fate of the Duchies was to be determined by the two powers jointly. The breach was now complete and it only remained for Bismarck to induce Austria to show herself as the aggressor.

The Austrian Cabinet did not fail him. Benedek's delay was causing impatience at Vienna, particularly in view of appeals for help from Saxony, and the Emperor, therefore,

sent his adjutant, Lieutenant-Colonel Beck, to Olmütz,
to prompt Benedek to advance at once. In view of Francis
Joseph's promise to leave Benedek an entirely free hand,
Beck was to say that he brought no orders but only advice;
he was, however, to point out to Benedek the nearness of
war and the desirability of meeting the Prussians in Bohemia, if not in Saxony. But Benedek and Krismanič were
not to be moved: the army was not completely mobilised
and was short of provisions; an advance from Moravia
before everything was ready would only cause confusion.
Headquarters were still anxious for delay, but it was too
late for the Foreign Office to draw back; on June 6, the
day that Beck arrived in Olmütz, the Governor of Holstein
carried out his instructions and summoned the Estates of
Holstein to meet on June 11 at Itzehoë.

This attack on his sovereign rights made King William
at last resolved on war with Austria. He told Beust five
years later that he only gave the order to attack after
a long struggle with his ministers and after eight sleep-
less nights, because the Austrian armaments forced him
to it. Embittered by the "faithlessness" of Austria, he
forgot the hostilities with which his Government had
pursued Austria ever since the conclusion of the Italian
alliance. In answer to Archbishop Melchers of Cologne he
wrote: "Austria has torn up the Treaty of Gastein and
handed over to the Diet the question of the Duchies, which
ought to be settled by us and not by the Diet at all; she
has laid herself open to the charges of perfidy, lying, and
breach of treaty. . . . I have wrestled with my God in
prayer in order to know His will and at every step I have
acted as my conscience dictated and for the honour of
Prussia." And on June 8 he said to the Italian minister:
"Fortunately I have a clear conscience. I havè been often
accused of wanting war for the sake of ambition; but
Austria's refusal to attend the Congress, her breach of the
Treaty of Gastein, and the violence of her press have shown

everyone who is the aggressor." This was the King's mood when he gave the order to use armed force against the Austrians in Holstein.

As soon as Gablenz summoned the Estates, Manteuffel informed him that he would not hesitate to occupy Holstein to secure the rights of Prussia. On June 7 Prussian troops occupied those parts of the country which were not held by the Austrians; and on June 11, when the Estates were to meet, they entered Itzehoë and arrested the Austrian commissioner. Manteuffel announced that he would occupy Altona the next day, and Gablenz, who had concentrated his troops there, was compelled to retire over the frontier into Hanover. Bismarck was very annoyed at Manteuffel's moderation. "If only there had been an exchange of shots", he said impatiently to the Italian minister. But as La Marmora observed with justice: "I do not see how Manteuffel could have fired on the Austrians, when they had retreated without fighting". On June 10 Bismarck said to the Hungarian General Türr: "I have not yet succeeded in convincing the King that war is immediately necessary. But what does it matter. I have put the horse at the ditch and . . . he must jump."[1]

Since force had been employed against Austrian officials and troops, Austria recalled her Ambassador, Karolyi, from Berlin. At the same time she appealed to the Diet, declaring that Prussia had broken the Treaty of Gastein and invoking Article 19 of the German Federal Act which afforded the injured party protection against attack: the Diet was to mobilise the seven army corps, which apart from the three Prussian corps was the total force at Germany's disposal, and to nominate commanders to them. The whole federal power was to be employed to punish Prussia and even states which were still unarmed were to be called on to mobilise.

Bismarck, too, was acting and with greater effect. On June 11 he sent to the German princes his draft of the

[1] General Türr in the *Deutsche Revue*, Feb. 1900.

future German Constitution: Austria was to be excluded, a Parliament was to be elected by universal suffrage, and, in the hope of winning over Bavaria and appeasing France, military supremacy was to be divided between Prussia and Bavaria. "It is unreasonable", Bismarck wrote in an accompanying letter to the Duke of Coburg, "to demand that one generation or one man, even my most gracious Sovereign, should make good in a single day what our ancestors have been ruining for centuries". Bismarck frankly admitted that the new Prussian Germany had some similarity with Rome, who "right at the beginning of her history earned considerable odium by the Rape of the Sabines. I do not think the German Rome will avoid some violence towards the Sabines, although I would like as little as possible." Bismarck had no illusions about the responsibility for giving the signal for violence and he did not shrink from the consequences. He was planning with General Klapka, one of the Hungarian leaders in 1849, the creation of a Hungarian corps, and Türr, another Hungarian, was sent to Serbia and Rumania to prepare a rising against Austria.

In North Germany Bismarck's appeal to public opinion began to have some effect. The contrast between Bismarck's plan for German unity and Napoleon's programme of keeping Germany divided for ever into three, made many liberals feel that Bismarck might after all achieve something for them. Bennigsen, the President of the National Association, even had an interview with Bismarck and shortly afterwards carried in the Hanoverian Chamber a resolution urging the King to remain neutral. The representative assemblies in Darmstadt and Nassau refused the money for a mobilisation against Prussia. Even more important was the fact that Bismarck entered into negotiations with the more moderate leaders of the opposition in the Prussian Chamber. Twesten and Unruh were willing to support Bismarck if the right of the assembly to control the budget was recognised, and they drafted for Bismarck a speech from the throne, in which the King was to admit this right. Soon afterwards Bismarck told Unruh that the Government agreed with the proposal, but that the King was afraid that after the war Parliament would again cut down the number of his regiments. Bismarck implored the Opposition to abandon its hostility, if only for a time: he agreed, he said, with the justice of their complaints, but a seventy-year-old King could not be expected to change his opinions easily, and the interests of the state and the great German Fatherland must come before everything.[1]

Where the appeal to national feeling did not suffice, Bismarck was prepared to use even more ruthless methods. The Grand Duke of Baden personally favoured Prussia, but the opinion of his subjects was driving him into war. To his astonishment, Bismarck advised him to declare himself on the other side and put himself under the protection of France, a service which Napoleon would only too gratefully perform. The Grand Duke was rightly horrified at the idea of inviting Napoleon to interfere in the internal affairs of Germany and by his refusal did his country a very valuable service.[2] On June 14 Duncker, the Mayor of Berlin, was sent to Bennigsen with the message that Hanover was to be occupied by Prussian troops and that Bismarck intended to place Bennigsen at the head of the new Government of Hanover. Bennigsen, of course, rejected the proposal. "If I had accepted", he wrote later, "everyone in Hanover would have denounced me as an ambitious traitor, and rightly."

Meanwhile the Austrian action at the Diet was taking its course. The Austrian proposal was technically illegal, as Biegeleben with his knowledge of federal law must have known. The Austrian complaints of the breach of the Treaty of Gastein could not in any way concern the Diet, which was

---

[1] Unruh, *Erinnerungen*, 342. Cf. the account in Poschinger, *Fürst Bismarck und die Parlamentarier* (Berlin 1895), 26-36.

[2] Lorenz, *Kaiser Wilhelm und die Begründung des Reichs*, 52, 566.

not a party to it. Furthermore, the Federal Act did not prescribe the immediate execution demanded by Austria, but a long-drawn-out and tedious process, with military measures only as a last resort. In vain did Beust deplore the attempt to involve Austria's allies in a breach of the Federal Constitution; all that he could do was to get a more or less acceptable amendment drafted by Pfordten. The Prussian delegate at Frankfort made no attempt to resist the Austrian proposal; but the Prussian Government warned all the lesser states by telegraph that a vote for mobilisation would be regarded as a *casus belli*.

The decisive vote was taken on June 14, not on the Austrian proposal, but on the Bavarian amendment, which conformed to federal law and which did not mention Prussia. Bavaria merely proposed the mobilisation of the four army corps of the lesser states; the Austrian and Prussian contingents would not be affected and such a step could not be construed as a breach of the peace. This proposal, which was supported by Austria, was carried by nine votes to six.[1] Then Savigny rose and formally declared that the discussion of the Austrian proposal had constituted a breach of the Federal Act and therefore announced the withdrawal of Prussia from the Confederation. Prussia had scarcely better legal grounds for her action than Austria; for, as the Bavarian delegate pointed out, it was not the doubtful Austrian proposal but the Bavarian amendment which had been accepted, and there had therefore been no breach of federal law. Savigny made a mistake in not withdrawing at once from the hall and so was compelled to listen to the declaration of the President that the with-

[1] There voted for the Bavarian proposal: Austria, Bavaria, Hanover, Württemberg, Saxony, Electoral Hesse, Hesse-Darmstadt, Nassau, Meiningen, Frankfort. Against: Prussia, Luxemburg, the two Mecklenburgs, Weimar, Coburg, Altenburg, Brunswick, Oldenburg, Schwarzburg, Anhalt, Hamburg, Lübeck, Bremen. The vote of the sixteenth Circle (Lichtenstein, the two Reuss, the two Lippes, and Waldeck) was doubtful. Baden abstained.

drawal of Prussia was null and void, since the Confederation was indissoluble.

But constitutional forms do not determine the fate of a nation. When they have lost their meaning a new organisation must be created, sometimes by peaceful agreement, more often by the sword; and it was to the sword that William now appealed. In the night of June 15-16 Bismarck had a conversation with Lord Augustus Loftus, the English Ambassador. At midnight, as they were strolling in the garden, Bismarck exclaimed: "Our troops are even now marching into Saxony, Hanover, and Hesse. It will be a bloody struggle and perhaps Prussia will succumb, but whatever happens she will fight bravely and honourably. If we are defeated I shall not return here; I shall die in the last charge. You can only die once and death is better than defeat."

The hostile resolution of the German Diet acted on public opinion in Prussia like a blow. When a city councillor of Berlin said in the anteroom of the chamber that he hoped that Prussia would be defeated, there was a storm of disapproval and cries of "throw him out!" And on June 14 troops marching through the streets were greeted for the first time with wild cheering.

CHAPTER X

THE War of 1866 decisively settled the German question, because Austria accepted it as a final verdict on the history of three hundred years. This was the price of the long suppression of all freedom of thought and conscience which had followed the expulsion of the Protestants; exiles like Kepler and Amos Comenius could not be replaced by the pupils of the Jesuits. The provinces south of the Danube had been the only part of Germany to escape the ravages of the Thirty Years' War, but they had declined spiritually and economically ever since, while the rest of Germany had been slowly recovering. In consequence, when Maria Theresa and Joseph II set themselves to restore a shattered Austria, they had been hampered everywhere by the lack of competent assistants; in spite of this they had given the Monarchy such a renewal of strength that it had been able to withstand the storm of the French Revolution, while the Prussia of Frederick the Great had collapsed after Jena. But then under Francis I the empire had relapsed disastrously into the policy of repression.

Throughout all these changes the army remained the backbone of the empire. It is remarkable, for instance, how little its spirit was shaken by the defeats of 1809, in striking contrast to the Prussian army after Jena or the French army after Leipzig. The Austrian army, thanks to the spirit

195

of Wallenstein, who created it, and thanks to the Protestant-ism or anti-clericalism of many of his successors, never entirely succumbed to the obscurantist clerical influences which dominated the civil administration. But during the reigns of Maria Theresa and Joseph II even the army began to suffer, as the higher commands fell more and more ex-clusively into the hands of the Austrian aristocracy; there was an increasing lack of determination and initiative, and an increasing unwillingness to punish incompetence in any member of a great family. As in every state governed by an aristocracy, a man's family secured his promotion and bore the responsibility for his mistakes. Francis II accepted this as inevitable: when he appointed Radetzky Chief of Staff after the battle of Wagram, he said to him: "Your char-acter is a guarantee that you will not deliberately make mistakes; as for the usual blunders, if you make them I am quite used to it".[1] And before the battle of Wagram the Emperor remarked with gloomy fatalism: "I know things will go badly on the left wing, for there Rosenberg is in command".[2]

The Archduke Charles had fought against this system persistently, but in vain. The victor of Aspern, like his two gifted brothers the Archdukes John and Joseph, was fated to be distrusted by the Emperor because of his ability. Archduke John had organised the rebellion in the Tyrol in 1809, and prepared another in 1813 without the Emperor's knowledge; Francis, fearing that he was planning to make himself King of Rhaetia, exiled him for years from the Tyrol. Archduke Joseph, the Palatine of Hungary and

---

[1] Radetzky, *Mitteilungen des k.k. Kriegsarchivs*, 1887, i. 69.
[2] Gentz, *Tagebücher*, i. 92. Gentz reports Radetzky's pessimism after the War of 1809 (*Tagebücher*, i. 183): "He spoke to me also—and in a manner which astonished me in a man so calm and self-controlled—of the ideas which are beginning to circulate in the army concerning the incapacity of the Emperor and of the advantage which would result from a complete change of dynasty".

the most popular man in the country, was accused of friendship with the Hungarian opposition and was therefore never consulted on Hungarian affairs. The reorganisation of the army by Archduke Charles after 1801 was hampered and cut short by the wars of 1805 and 1809; and after 1809 he was never employed in the army again, although he would have been a far better commander than Schwarzenberg, who was more a diplomat than a soldier. Radetzky, Schwarzenberg's Chief of Staff in 1813 and 1814, was forgotten after the war and employed in subordinate positions until 1831, when Frimont, his old comrade in arms, appointed him as his second in command in Italy; and it was only the accident of Frimont's early death which placed Radetzky at the head of the army in Italy.

Even these mistakes did not shake the spirit of the army. The highest commands were reserved almost exclusively for the sons of the 600 ruling families, but most of the officers were drawn from old army families or from the middle classes, and they all looked upon the army as their only home. This single-hearted devotion made it possible for the corps of officers to assimilate the various races of the Monarchy into a single unified whole. In Austria, as in all the other states of Europe, except Prussia, there was no universal obligation of military service. Each year 310,000 to 320,000 young men reached their twentieth year, but only 85,000 of them were conscripted; they were then supposed to serve for eight years as soldiers and for two years in the reserve. Actually, as a result of financial difficulties, they were dismissed much earlier; the infantry served from one and a half to three years, the engineers and artillery from four to six, and the cavalry somewhat longer. In theory there were thus ten annual classes of 85,000 men, and diplomats loved to talk of the army of 900,000 men at their disposal. In fact there was hardly half that number—the faulty organisation, the losses in the wars of 1859 and 1864, and other causes resulted in an army of 460,000 men all told. Of these a considerable number was needed for garrison duty: Vienna, and even more Hungary, could not be completely denuded of troops. There remained a field-army of 310,000 to 320,000 men, 74,000 concentrated in Italy and the remainder under the command of Benedek. Owing to the lack of any militia, there was no reserve; and attempts to create one were undertaken only when the war had already started.

The army reforms of 1862 had produced a very different state of affairs in Prussia. Every year 63,000 men were conscripted to serve seven years in the line, that is, three in the standing army, and four in the reserve. Prussia had thus in theory 441,000 and in practice 355,000 men available for active service. Garrison duty could be left to the *Landwehr*, and when 50,000 men had been diverted against the federal states and 9000 for the protection of Upper Silesia, the Prussian army in Bohemia was still practically the same size as the Austrian, although Austria had 35 million inhabitants and Prussia only 18 million. Moreover, since every Prussian conscript served with the militia until his thirty-sixth year, and sometimes until his thirty-ninth, Prussia had an enormous reserve of trained soldiers. All these could, if necessary, be incorporated into the field-army; and Moltke declared after the war that, if France had joined Austria, Prussia could have put 600,000 men into the field.

The Prussians had other and even greater advantages. They had a General Staff and a cadre of officers whose knowledge of military theory and practice was constantly kept up to date, and every soldier in their army had had the benefit of elementary education. The fire of their needle gun was three times as rapid as that of the Austrian muzzle-loader. Above all, their tactics were immeasurably superior. Until the French Revolution every European army had fought in line. The soldiers were driven forward by blows from their officers and even cavalry had sometimes to urge them on from behind; there could be no room for individual initiative. The French Revolution created a new sort of army, lacking in parade ground discipline, but full of enthusiasm and patriotism. The French generals, adapting their tactics accordingly, employed skirmishers to surround the enemy and followed them up with the tremendous weight of the column, which broke once and for all the line of the old monarchies. These were the tactics exploited by Napoleon and later imitated by the Prussians; and the Archduke Charles had based his reform of the Austrian army on similar ideas, though the Austrians characteristically concentrated on defence and developed a system of fighting in scattered groups. Later experience has shown that this more open formation was, in fact, the right way to meet modern improvements in artillery and rifle fire; but it demands from even the most subordinate officer an initiative and intelligence which the Austrian officers lacked. In the War of 1859 the French shock tactics had left the Austrians completely helpless, despite the superiority of the Austrian fire, and after the war the Austrian generals drew the mistaken conclusion that the French victory had been entirely due to the bayonet charge of massed columns. Austrian military training was revolutionised; musketry drill practically ceased and the men were exercised only with the bayonet. They were told that the bayonet was not only an aggressive weapon, but even the most suitable for defending a position, and during the War of 1866 the Austrians often charged out of woods or down hills which they were defending without firing a shot at the advancing enemy.

The Prussian General Staff drew the opposite conclusion from the War of 1859: they argued that a well-directed rifle fire would have stopped the French charge and therefore concentrated on fire control in their army training after 1859. The Austrians were well aware of the superiority of the Prussian fire, but they believed that it could be overcome by a shock attack even heavier and more massive than the French charges of 1859. When the Germans were faced with the same problem in 1870, they overcame the superiority of fire of the French *chassepot* by fighting in even more open formation and offering no clear front to the enemy. It was, of course, too late for Benedek to change the tactics of the whole army once the war had begun, and it must be said in his defence that, after the experience of the first engagements, he did all he could to reverse the previous instructions and especially to minimise the effect of the Prussian fire by the skilful use of his superior artillery.

In spite of all these preliminary disadvantages the Austrian army was successful in its first battle at Custoza, and the victory seemed a good omen for the outcome of the struggle. The Commander-in-Chief in Italy, the Archduke Albrecht, was the son of Archduke Charles and the most intelligent and the best trained of the Austrian generals; and as Chief of Staff he had John, the best organiser in the army. It is true that the Austrians only numbered 74,000 against their opponents' 165,000, but they were absolutely confident of continuing the series of victories over the Italians begun in 1848. After the French Revolution it was generally thought that a people striving for national unity was irresistible; but in the history of the nineteenth century no nation achieved independence without foreign aid, and Italy was only unified in the teeth of an unbroken succession of military defeats. Victor Emmanuel, who was in supreme command, distrusted La Marmora and Cialdini, his two leading generals, and they distrusted one another. Worse still, they could not agree on a plan of campaign. Cialdini argued that there was no hope of defeating the Austrians in the famous quadrilateral and therefore wished to avoid a direct advance from the west across the Mincio. He preferred to cross the Po behind the Austrian lines, so drawing the enemy away from his fortresses and compelling him to fight in the Venetian plain. La Marmora disagreed on the grounds that after crossing the Po the Italians would still have the Adige in front of them and would be exposed to a

flank attack from the Austrians. He clung so persistently to
the policy of a direct advance across the Mincio that Italian
Headquarters finally took the almost invariably fatal step
of trying to combine both plans. The army was to be divided;
La Marmora was to operate on the Mincio and Cialdini to
advance across the Po.

Moltke, it is true, loved to take his enemy between two
fires. But this strategy, which was so successful in Bohemia,
needed the energy and ability of a Moltke. La Marmora was
no Moltke; moreover, since he knew that the treaty between
France and Austria guaranteed Venice to Italy whatever
happened, he was unwilling to risk the Italian army. As one
of his colleagues remarked, the conflict was more an affair
of honour than a real war. The Prussian Government had
more than one grievance against its Italian ally. Bismarck,
leaving no stone unturned, had entered into negotiations
with the Hungarian *émigrés* and also with the Serbs, in the
hope of raising an insurrection in the heart of Hungary
and provoking an invasion of Austria from the south. This
was only possible if the revolutionaries were encouraged
by the presence of a regular force and Bismarck urged La
Marmora to land Garibaldi and his volunteers on the coast
of Dalmatia. La Marmora was conservative by nature; he
believed, quite rightly, that Kossuth and his followers had
no longer enough influence to raise an insurrection in
Hungary, and, above all, Napoleon was against the plan,
having no wish to see his new ally, Austria, further hampered
by a rebellion within the empire. La Marmora therefore
decided to send Garibaldi's volunteers not to Dalmatia but
to the Tyrol, where they were useless to the Prussians, since
they did not compel Austria to withdraw a single man from
Bohemia, whatever embarrassment they might cause to the
Archduke Albrecht. There is no doubt that the Italians
were completely justified in their refusal; there was no hope
of provoking a rebellion among the Southern Slavs, and in
any case it was doubtful if the incompetent Italian fleet

could have effected a landing. Nevertheless, Usedom, the Prussian minister, continued to urge a more ruthless conduct of the war; his Note to La Marmora of June 17 declared that "if Venice was to be permanently secured to Italy, Austrian power must be struck to the heart".[1]

Before La Marmora joined the King on the Mincio he visited Bologna to co-ordinate his plans with Cialdini; but in fact the two generals parted with widely differing intentions. Cialdini thought that the army on the Mincio was going to confine itself to a demonstration, while he crossed the Po and took the Austrians in the rear; La Marmora for his part intended to cross the Mincio and fight the Austrians before Cialdini could secure the distinction of defeating them. The Archduke and John met the threat of a double advance with a strategy that was clear and precise. The essential object was to prevent the two enemy armies from uniting. It was therefore decided to attack the more exposed army on the Mincio during the five days it would take Cialdini to reach the Adige. Immediately after the declaration of war, on June 20, the Austrian army advanced into the Quadrilateral, in readiness to cross the Mincio and engage La Marmora.

But La Marmora saved them the trouble. He believed that the Austrian army was still behind the Adige, for he credited the enemy with his own timidity and incompetence. On June 23 the Italian army crossed the Mincio and advanced on a wide front into what they believed was a

[1] [Friedjung is at great pains in this and other passages to emphasise Bismarck's ruthless use of any and every weapon against Austria, as exemplified in his attempts to organise a revolt in Hungary. But Friedjung did not know or omitted to add that the Austrian Government was ready to employ similar methods and that it entered into negotiations with the King of Naples in order to provoke an insurrection in Southern Italy. It is true that it refrained from organising a Neapolitan corps on Austrian soil, but only because it feared complications with France. The King of Naples was granted a million francs. Council minutes of May 14 (K.Z. 1496) and Redlich, ii. 804.—Translator.]

defenceless land. The Archduke's plan was bold and simple. The whole weight of the cavalry was to be thrown against the Italian right wing, so as to give the impression that the main army was here, while at the same time an infantry attack was to be launched southwards on the Italian left: in the centre the bulk of his force was to stand on the defensive until the Italians had been drawn into the trap and completely surrounded.

The battle of Custoza on June 24 did not work out entirely as the Archduke hoped. For one thing La Marmora did not intend to advance beyond Custoza; to this extent he adhered to his original arrangement with Cialdini only to make a demonstration. The Austrian attack therefore did not burst on an army in full march. Still more decisive were the characters of the subordinate Austrian generals: Rodich, on the right wing, who ought to have attacked at all costs, proceeded cautiously and methodically, so that the Italian left was not pushed back until the afternoon, while Hartung in the centre, who ought to have done all he could to tempt the Italians further into the trap, delivered one assault after another on the hill of Custoza. The plan of surrounding the Italians on all sides and inflicting a crushing defeat at small cost broke down and the Archduke had to alter his dispositions in the middle of the battle: the decision was not gained on the wing, but in the centre, at Custoza, where a frontal attack drove the Italians back in the evening in full retreat towards the Mincio. La Marmora made the Austrian victory all the easier by losing his head at the very beginning of the battle; as early as midday he was heard to exclaim: "What a defeat, what a catastrophe! Worse even than 1849!"

Credit for the victory must be divided between Archduke Albrecht and John. It was John who had supervised the organisation and drawn up the plans, but it was the Archduke who carried them out undismayed by the vastly superior numbers of the enemy. The calm decision to take the offensive and ignore the army of Cialdini, and the swift attack on La Marmora were measures worthy of the great Napoleon. Once and for all the Archduke showed that his reputation was not due merely to his Habsburg birth. It is true that military laurels were more easily won in Italy than in Bohemia, where the greatest talent could hardly have prevented a Prussian victory, although it might have made it less decisive. But after 1866 the Archduke deservedly ranked as one of the great generals of Austrian history and as the equal even of his Prussian contemporaries.

The Austrians did not at first appreciate the completeness of their victory and prepared to renew the battle next day. Even when they learnt that La Marmora had retired over the Mincio, they did not pursue him, but turned to meet Cialdini's advance over the Po. Cialdini, however, on receiving the news of the battle of Custoza, immediately retired to join La Marmora and the Austrians were able to advance into Lombardy, though with the intention of avoiding a pitched battle. Telegrams from Vienna were warning the Archduke to save his men, and once the Italian armies had united he dared not risk an attack on a force numerically so superior.

Then the battle of Königgrätz forced the Austrians to withdraw their victorious army to defend Vienna, and Austrian supremacy in Italy was at an end. To the very last the Italians had been unable to shake that supremacy single-handed. The Archduke, by bringing 50,000 fresh, confident troops to the Danube and organising an army of 200,000 men for the defence of the capital, prevented Austria from being crushed as France was crushed five years later. Therein lies the historical importance of the battle of Custoza. It was not just an episode in military history; it was the proof that Austria could still assert herself as a great power, despite the loss of her hegemony in Germany and Italy.

CHAPTER XI

THE opening of the war found Prussia very badly placed strategically. The attitude of France was uncertain, the Southern states had declared for Austria, and the straggling southern frontier of Prussia was cut in two by Saxony and North Bohemia; the main army was covering Berlin, while the second lay far away in Silesia, and there were few troops to spare for the conquest of the German states. Moltke was insisting on an immediate offensive to shorten the three hundred-mile front and bring the two armies into closer contact, but to the very last moment the King thought in terms of a defensive war. It was the decision of the German Diet on June 14 which destroyed William's irresolution, and it was the King himself who ordered the occupation of Hanover, Electoral Hesse, and Nassau.

Prussia was confronted with three groups of enemies of varying strength. The Austrians, united with the Saxons, had 261,000 men in Moravia and Bohemia; 18,000 Hanoverians reinforced by 7000 Hessians divided the western from the eastern provinces of the Monarchy; and there were 94,000 scattered South German troops who would hardly become dangerous before the end of June and could therefore be disregarded for the time being. To deal with the most immediate danger 48,000 troops were detailed to surround Hanover, and either drive the Hanoverian army south or compel it to surrender.

On the morning of June 15 the courts of Saxony, Hanover, and Hesse-Cassel were presented with an identical Prussian Note, containing three demands: their armies were to be restored to the peace establishment of March 1; as soon as elections for a German Parliament took place in Prussia, their Governments must organise similar elections; and finally, their rulers were to renounce part of their full sovereignty by accepting the Prussian proposals for the reform of the German Constitution. If the princes complied with these conditions, Prussia would guarantee their possessions. The German princes had been unwilling to give up any of their sovereignty to the people in 1848 and equally unwilling to surrender it to Austria at the meeting of the princes in 1863. Nor were they prepared to surrender any of it to Prussia now. The smaller states, however, were helpless; and realising this, the three Grand Dukes of Mecklenburg and Oldenburg, the Duke of Brunswick, and the free cities of Hamburg, Lübeck, and Bremen accepted the Prussian proposals. Duke Ernest of Coburg-Gotha, who had already recognised the military supremacy of Prussia by the Convention of June 1, 1861, joined in with enthusiasm, but most of them were playing for safety: if Prussia won, their territory was safe, and if Austria won, the treaty with Prussia became null and void.

The princes who did not take this prudent course—Hanover, Hesse-Cassel, and Nassau—paid for their mistake with their thrones. King George of Hanover thought that he could negotiate as an independent power between Austria and Prussia, allying himself with the one who offered most. King John of Saxony alone acted honourably and straightforwardly. He realised what was at stake, allied himself openly with Austria, and threw all his strength into the struggle on her side; and by this sincerity and honesty he did more to preserve his throne than the other North German princes by their vacillation. The Hanoverian Cabinet retained its delusions to the end. Platen, when asked

if the Prussians would not invade Hanover on the day after
the anti-Prussian vote in the Diet, replied that Bismarck
would never break the federal law and that there must be
a six weeks' interval before hostilities opened—as though
Prussia had any intention of observing the tedious formalities of the antiquated Confederation. Even the arrival
of the Prussian ultimatum the next day did not shake
King George; he told the Prussian minister that such demands were equivalent to mediatisation and that he would
rather lose his throne. He was still confident that he could
withstand the Prussian attack and he was too proud even
to make a treaty with Austria. Public opinion in Hanover,
however patriotic, disapproved of such obstinacy. A deputation from the city council petitioned the King on June 15 to
come to an agreement with Prussia; and the Estates carried
Bennigsen's resolution in favour of neutrality. The King's
reply was unchanged—as a Christian, as a monarch, as a
Guelf he could not do otherwise; it was his duty to defend his
royal authority and to hand it on undiminished to his son.

The Prussians soon put their threats into execution. They
occupied Hesse without difficulty, since the Elector sent his
army to join Prussia's enemies in the south and trusted
in his divine right to protect his Grand Duchy. This
proved inadequate to the occasion: he was taken prisoner
on June 19 and his country was taken over by Prussia. The
Prussians entered Hanover on June 17 and could have
immediately surrounded the Hanoverian army. But the
Prussian commander, Vogel von Falckenstein, let himself be
diverted from his main objective, first by his desire to occupy
Frankfort and drive out the Diet, and then by a rumour
that the Bavarians were advancing from the south. The
Hanoverian army was even able to defeat part of the
Prussian army at Langensalza. It was not until June 29
that Falckenstein obeyed Moltke's ceaseless telegrams from
Berlin, and concentrated against the Hanoverian army,
which was immediately forced to capitulate; the men were

disarmed and sent home, the officers were sent on leave, and the King and his sons were allowed to choose any residence outside Hanover. They never saw their home again.

Nothing injured the cause of the Confederation more than the perpetual vacillations of Bavaria. Prince Charles, who was to command the army, wanted the closest co-operation with Austria and sent General von der Tann, his Chief of Staff, to Vienna to draw up a convention. Tann agreed that the Bavarian army should advance into Bohemia and place itself under the supreme command of Austrian Head-quarters. But Pfordten strongly opposed this policy; he was still hoping for his "third Germany" under Bavarian leader-ship, and he despised the military power of Austria. He declared it unthinkable to leave Bavaria to be overrun by the Prussians, while the Bavarian army fought Austria's battles in Bohemia, and won over even Prince Charles by his arguments. Blome argued in vain that a purely defensive attitude would be worthless at the decisive moment. When Beck, the Emperor's adjutant, arrived in Munich to work for the junction of the two armies, Pfordten told him obstinately that Bavaria was not the vassal of Austria. "Then you", prophesied Beck, "will certainly be defeated on the Main, and we, perhaps, in Bohemia." On June 18 the Austrian Government was officially informed that the Bavarian army would concentrate on its own northern frontier.

While Prussia overran Hanover, Benedek, to everyone's astonishment, dallied in Moravia. He was determined not to repeat the mistake of 1859 of invading the enemy's country with insufficient forces, and he was completely dominated by Krismanič's faith in defensive strategy. Bohemia, running up between Saxony and Prussian Silesia, was a natural base for an offensive, but the Austrians had never made use of it because the Prussians had always been ready first. It was even better adapted to a defensive campaign, as had been proved in the War of 1778. After that war Joseph II had built the fortress of Josephstadt just where the mountain roads reach the Elbe and there, twelve days' march from Olmütz, Krismanič now proposed to concentrate the Austrian army. Clam-Gallas, the commander in Bohemia, was instructed to unite with the Saxons to form an army 60,000 strong in a defensive position behind the Iser, but to fall back on the main army if he was seriously attacked. Benedek did not intend to fight a decisive battle until the whole army was concentrated at Josephstadt: then he could await the Prussians or advance to meet them in case they hung back.

This plan, had it been promptly executed, might well have led to victory. The Austrian army would have been able in its central position to turn its full strength against each of the scattered Prussian army corps and defeat them in detail. But on June 10 the army was not nearly ready to advance; it was still 40,000 to 50,000 men short of the expected total, it was short of provisions, it was short of ammunition for the artillery, and it was impossible to move until the reserve magazines had been prepared. Benedek and Krismanič ought undoubtedly to have advanced whether the army was completely ready or not; they had 200,000 men at their disposal and they were not going to advance into a desert, nor even into hostile country, but into the rich province of Bohemia, where ample supplies could have been obtained. Time was the all-important consideration; a day gained was worth all the reserves and supplies that they lacked. The Austrian generals could, of course, answer that they had warned the Government over and over again against precipitating the struggle. The diplomats who had provoked the outbreak of war instead of trying to postpone it, were responsible for Austria's present inability to help her Saxon ally.

Albert, the Crown Prince of Saxony, had first intended to satisfy honour by making a stand against the Prussians before retiring into Bohemia. He decided, however, that the Austrians were too far away and that he had therefore better husband his strength for the decisive battle. The Prussian troops met with no resistance when they crossed the Saxon frontier on June 15, and on June 17 the King slept in his capital for the last time. Early the next morning he summoned Beust from his slumbers to tell him: "I have slept little and thought over everything. I hope we shall win and there might be then some idea of recovering the territory we lost in 1815. But that is not my wish. We should only perpetuate old enmities and secure bad, because unwilling, subjects." Beust said that the question could be left open and decided according to the event; privately he thought that it had hardly been necessary to wake him up so early.

The Prussians thus reached their first objective without striking a blow. The possession of Saxony would make the concentration of their scattered forces very much easier, and they had certainly expected the Austrians to support the Saxon army. When, on June 11, the Prussian General Staff at last realised that the Austrian army was still in Moravia, Moltke could only conclude that Benedek intended to invade Silesia to hold it as a pledge against Venice; and Moltke did not think that the advance of the main Prussian army from Dresden would turn him back. "A dashing general like Benedek", he wrote, "will not be induced by that to abandon his operations in Silesia." The army of the Crown Prince, which had been brought into closer touch with the main army, was hastily moved back into Silesia and reinforced with a fourth army corps. The Prussian armies were more widely separated than ever, and a rapid concentration at Josephstadt would have placed the Austrians right in between them. It was a heaven-sent opportunity for a far-sighted and determined general; but Krismanič only deduced from the Crown Prince's movements that the Prussians were about to invade Moravia, and still further postponed his advance from Olmütz.

At the Imperial Court, Krismanič's deliberate preparations were watched with the greatest impatience. Francis Joseph had promised Benedek not to interfere in military matters, but he had expected an energetic leadership of quite a different order. On June 16 he could restrain himself no longer and telegraphed to Olmütz: "Events in Germany make it urgently desirable to begin operations. But since military considerations are decisive, I leave it to you to choose the moment to advance and await telegraphic information of your decision." Benedek wired back that the advance had already begun, and wrote a long report on the same day to explain and justify the concentration in Moravia. The army, he concluded, was at last completely equipped, but it was still inferior in number to the enemy: only when reinforced both by the Saxons and Bavarians would he feel justified in seeking out the Prussians and offering battle; in that case he believed that he could count on victory. The tone of the despatch was gloomy and pessimistic.

Benedek left for the front on June 22; by June 28 it was hoped to have five army corps concentrated at Josephstadt. Even Krismanič was in a hurry now, for it was essential to take up the central position before the Prussian armies effected a junction. Now that it was at last on the move the Austrian army was full of confidence, and spirits were rising at the prospect of a battle. They underestimated their opponent and trusted blindly in the effectiveness of their shock tactics. Everywhere the advancing army was greeted with enthusiasm. In the eyes of Germany the ambition of Prussia and, above all, of her chief minister had provoked a civil war; the peoples of Austria felt that the empire had been compelled to draw the sword in defence of its position as a great power, and, except for the Magyars, every race in the Monarchy enthusiastically supported the war.

The victory of Austria was generally expected throughout Europe, and more especially in France. Having defeated Austria in 1859, the French flattered themselves that Austria was inferior only to themselves. Napoleon, though he did not altogether share the self-confidence of his people, certainly expected a prolonged struggle, and this miscalculation was the primary cause of his fall four years later. The rulers in Prussia and Austria shared the popular view: William went into the war with deep misgiving—almost with despair—while Francis Joseph was confident of his right and power. Their advisers were more clear-sighted; Bismarck, Moltke, and Roon were certain that Prussia could win; and the Austrian statesmen and generals had feared and doubted, though none of them had the ability to avoid war. Mensdorff had done his best, however ineffectively, to secure a peaceful solution, and none of the Austrian generals expected to win; even Krismanič only hoped for a successful defensive war.

In the last resort the course of history is determined by deep-lying forces; but these are often lessened and even neutralised by the incompetence or the ability of individuals. Italian unification, seemingly inevitable, was postponed for a generation by the genius of Radetzky. And although all German history since the seventeenth century had been preparing the way for the triumph of Prussia, the great opportunity of 1849 had been lost by the hesitations and indecision of Frederick William IV. Now the position was reversed; genius and energy were on the side of Prussia and were accelerating the final stages of a long historical process. A struggle between Austria and Prussia for the supremacy over Germany was inevitable, and the eventual victory of Prussia was almost equally inevitable. But that struggle might well have been postponed and it might have been fought in circumstances much more favourable to Austria. It was Bismarck who provoked the conflict and who made Prussia's victory sure.

CHAPTER XII

THE first steps of the Prussians were dilatory and indecisive. For a long time Moltke hesitated, expecting an Austrian attack on Silesia and it was not until June 19 that he finally dismissed this danger from his mind. The Crown Prince's army, which had been moving aimlessly up and down the Silesian frontier awaiting an Austrian offensive, was ordered to advance straight into Bohemia. Moltke was taking the risk of invading the country at two widely separated points and his two armies were only to be united in the face of the enemy. Napoleon I had sharply criticised the very similar strategy of Frederick the Great in 1757, and military theorists, especially in France, were equally disapproving of Moltke's strategy in 1866. Moltke was well aware of the theoretical defects of his plan, but it was his only hope for a complete victory. The King's hesitation had postponed the Prussian offensive so long that the lost ground could not be made up without taking risks; to unite the two armies before crossing the frontier would be safer, but it would give the Austrians time to advance in force to the defence of North Bohemia. He himself described his plan of campaign as "the carefully arranged and energetically executed remedy for an unfavourable but inevitable situation".

On June 23 the Prussian armies began their advance. The objective for both sides was the plateau between the Elbe and the Iser, to the north of Josephstadt. The Prussian

213

First Army under Prince Frederick Charles, united with the smaller army of the Elbe, was to reach Jičin [1] by June 29 and there join the Second Army under the Crown Prince, which was to invade Bohemia from the east. The dangerous moment for the Prussians—the "crisis" continually referred to in Moltke's letters—must come when the Crown Prince emerged from the mountains on the east of Bohemia. The Austrian army concentrated at Josephstadt at the foot of the passes might well be able to throw its entire strength against him, and defeat him heavily before Prince Frederick Charles could relieve the pressure on him by a flank attack. Moltke hoped to meet this danger by a rapid advance, so as to take the Austrians between two fires before their concentration at Josephstadt was complete; but here he underestimated both the difficulties to be encountered by the Crown Prince in the Bohemian mountains and the speed of the Austrian advance. Krismanič had indeed delayed too long to secure all the advantages of the central position, but once begun, the advance was energetically carried out and the Austrians reached Josephstadt earlier than Moltke expected. The Prussian delay in declaring war had made Benedek take a less gloomy view of the Austrian prospects and on June 24 he said to some of his officers: "I believe I shall beat them after all". With this new confidence Benedek rejected his earlier intention of tamely abandoning North Bohemia to the Prussians. Clam-Gallas and the Saxons were ordered to make a stand on the Iser, and there the first engagement was fought on June 26; but Clam-Gallas, one of those aristocratic commanders who had done so much harm in the past, made no attempt to carry out his orders, and allowed two of the bridges over the Iser to fall into the hands of the Prussians without striking a blow.

It was vital that Benedek should make up his mind to attack one of the enemy armies and carry through the attack swiftly and unflinchingly. He had originally intended

[1] [Pronounced Yitchin.—Translator.]

to fall upon the Crown Prince's army as it emerged from the mountains, rightly expecting it to be the first to appear on the scene. But on June 26 Krismanič drew up a new plan, the famous "secret plan" of Benedek. He now argued that, although the Crown Prince was nearer, his army, still protected by the mountains, offered no single front against which to throw the whole weight of the Austrian army. He therefore proposed to contain the Crown Prince with 60,000 men on the right flank, and to advance with the main army to meet Prince Frederick Charles on the Iser. There he would be able to concentrate in overwhelming numerical superiority for the decisive battle; and if once the road to Berlin was opened by an Austrian victory the Crown Prince would be compelled to retreat, whatever temporary successes he might have achieved.

Energetically carried out, this plan might well have been successful; it was in fact the method which enabled the Archduke Albrecht in Italy to beat an army twice as large as his own. But in Bohemia the energy was on the other side; Krismanič was so obsessed with the idea of keeping the whole army united that he would never allow an advance until every division was ready, while the co-ordination of the Prussian movements was so perfect that the Austrians immediately found themselves threatened in the flank whenever they made up their minds to advance against either army. The "secret plan" had to be postponed almost at once. On the morning of June 26 Benedek, determined to fight a decisive battle against Frederick Charles, telegraphed to Clam-Gallas, instructing him to hold the line of the Iser at all costs; and in obedience to this command the Austrians and Saxons attempted in the afternoon to recapture the lost bridges, though without success. At midnight came another telegram from Benedek, saying that the defence of the Iser need not be prolonged to the utmost. The change was due to the rapid advance of the Crown Prince, which upset all Krismanič's calculations. Krismanič had indeed no intention of changing his plan; he had refused to alter his dispositions even at the request of the Emperor, and he was certainly not going to let the enemy's movements interfere with his strategy. He had merely decided to postpone the advance against Prince Frederick Charles until he was more certain of the exact position of the Crown Prince. "This step", Benedek telegraphed to the Emperor's Adjutant-General, "is only a temporary postponement of the offensive and I shall take the offensive as soon as the army is fully concentrated and I have ascertained the position of my opponent, which I hope will be the case in a few days."

In spite of the slow and methodical advance, Krismanič had managed to concentrate the Austrian army between the two Prussian armies which were still separated by a seven days' march. There was a splendid opportunity to defeat one of them before the other could come up, but not if he wasted "a few days" investigating the position of the Crown Prince. The Prussians were advancing with bewildering rapidity. By June 27 the heads of the three columns in which the army was marching from Silesia had reached the point where the passes emerged on the plain; and here took place the first serious engagements of the war. At Nachod the most southern column under Steinmetz won a complete victory over the Austrians, and demonstrated for the first time the superiority of the Prussian tactics. The needle-gun wrought havoc among the massed ranks of the advancing Austrians, who lost almost 5700 men, while the Prussian casualties only numbered 1122. At Nachod too the Prussian officers showed their superiority; the Austrian officers were brave enough, but since 1859 they had been taught that all their duty lay in leading their men to a direct attack on the enemy and they were left little scope for initiative. The Prussian companies were much more flexibly handled, and it has been well said that the chief credit for Prussia's victory belonged to the company commanders.

It was, however, on June 27 that the Austrians achieved their one success. While Steinmetz was defeating the Austrians at Nachod the most northern column of the Crown Prince's army under Bonin was heavily repulsed at Trautenau, after fierce fighting, by a strong Austrian force under Gablenz. For once fortune favoured the Austrians: Gablenz, formerly commander in Holstein, was abler and more experienced than Bonin, who had never been under fire, and he was not so pedantic a slave to shock tactics as were the other Austrian generals. Trautenau was the only battle of the war where the Austrians carried out a flank attack, and it was successful. As always throughout the war the Austrian artillery and cavalry showed themselves superior to the Prussian; the Prussians were so afraid of losing their guns that they kept them too far from the scene of action to be effective, whereas the Austrians did not hesitate to bring their massed artillery right into the heart of the battle. Trautenau and Custoza were the last victories of the Austrian shock tactics, and they were bought at a great price; in both battles the Austrian losses were nearly double those of their opponents—in other engagements they lost three times as many as the Prussians. No army could go on winning battles at that rate: capable leadership and Prussian mistakes might have made possible a few partial victories, but in the long run the muzzle-loader and the bayonet charge were bound to go down before the needle-gun and open formation of the Prussians. Even at Trautenau there was no hand-to-hand fighting; the Austrians owed their success to the moral effect of repeated charges, which not even the murderous fire of the Prussians could check; but the long death-roll made the victory almost as discouraging to the Austrian troops as a less costly defeat.

The following day, June 28, was the real crisis of the war. The Crown Prince's army was very unfavourably placed. Steinmetz had fought his way out of the mountains only

to expose himself to an overwhelming attack from the main
Austrian army; Bonin's column had been driven back up
the pass and had even spent the night on the Prussian
side of the mountains. In consequence more than half the
Guard, who composed the middle column, had to be sent
to help Bonin renew the attack on Trautenau, and only
scanty reinforcements were available for Steinmetz. Here
was a magnificent opportunity for the Austrians to exploit
the interior lines which Krismanič's concentration at
Josephstadt had secured for them. The whole weight of their
army could be directed against the Crown Prince while
Prince Frederick Charles was still at least two days' march
away at the Iser. But Benedek and Krismanič had determined to fight Prince Frederick Charles first and nothing
would induce them to change their minds. Benedek had
been much impressed with the accuracy and precision with
which Krismanič had conducted the advance and concentration of the army; and Krismanič's faith in his own
strategy never wavered. Benedek revealed his subservience
to Krismanič's theoretical knowledge in a remark to the
Archduke Joseph during the retreat of the army through
Upper Hungary a month later: "You know, Your Imperial
Highness, you should never think yourself less clever than
other people. At Josephstadt I said to myself: the best
thing for me is to attack the Crown Prince with all my
forces, and then in came Krismanič to talk about primary
and secondary forces—a victory over the primary force
necessarily produces a victory over the secondary, but not
vice versa, and the primary force was beyond Jičin." This
cannot, of course, absolve Benedek from responsibility:
however right his instinct may have been, he did not
follow it.

The events of June 27 did, however, compel Austrian
Headquarters to modify the "secret plan" to a certain
extent: two corps under the Archduke Leopold and Festetics were sent to reinforce Ramming against Steinmetz,

and it was decided to postpone the advance of the main
army to the Iser until the following day. Krismanič had
learnt nothing from the defeat of Nachod; he still thought it
possible to contain the Crown Prince with 70,000 men while
the Austrian army crossed his front on its way to the Iser;
he refused to attempt to defeat him decisively. The wrong-
headedness of this strategy stands out clearly. Even if the
Crown Prince could have been held back in the mountains,
and Prince Frederick Charles had been decisively defeated
on the Iser, the Austrians would then have had to retrace
their steps in order to fight the Crown Prince. Then why
not, as many of the Austrian officers themselves asked, deal
with the Crown Prince before advancing to the Iser and so
avoid marching to and fro? Krismanič undoubtedly missed
an almost certain chance of defeating Steinmetz, but it is
only fair to add that neither he nor Benedek can really be
held to blame for the decisive defeat of June 28, since
so many of their most important orders went astray or
were disobeyed. The lack of punctuality, efficiency, and
obedience among the subordinate commanders and officers
was the worst fault of the Austrian army; it is not too much
to say that throughout the war it was rare for any of Benedek's orders to reach his subordinates promptly, and it was
to this that the final disaster was largely due.

On the morning of June 28 Benedek drove out with his
staff to Skalitz to examine the position of the Prussian
divisions which had been victorious at Nachod the day
before. He was received with wild enthusiasm. Already
excited by the hurried concentration of three army corps
and the thunder of a long-range artillery duel forward by
Skalitz, every officer and man believed that the Commander-
in-Chief had come up to direct a decisive battle. Never again
were the Austrians to be given such a chance. They had
70,000 men on the spot; Steinmetz had only 30,000 and
could expect no reinforcements from the Guard in the

centre. But Benedek was determined to fight Prince Frederick Charles and no one else; after a brief reconnaissance he decided that the Prussians were not preparing to attack, but were trying to get into touch with the Guard in the centre. He refused to be carried away by the enthusiasm of his troops for battle and, raising his voice so that all the officers standing by could hear, he declared that there must be no serious fighting here, as he was determined to abide by the decisions he had already made. Ramming and the Archduke Leopold were ordered to retire and march towards the Iser; the corps of Festetics alone was to remain to cover his flank and check any casual Prussian attack by artillery fire. Having made these disastrous dispositions Benedek returned to Headquarters to prepare for the march to the Iser; at six o'clock that evening the instructions which had been drawn up the previous day were despatched to the various commanders, and Francis Joseph was informed that the army would soon be in motion for the decisive battle.

But the orders for the advance were never executed, for before the messages were even sent off two of the covering army corps had been heavily defeated. Steinmetz did not behave as Benedek had expected; he knew even better than the Austrians how precarious his situation was, and he determined to escape from it not by retreat or by delay, but by a bold attack upon the Austrian position. In accordance with Benedek's orders, the Archduke Leopold was carrying out a dilatory retirement in preparation for the march to the Iser, when he saw the Prussians advancing; against all orders he ordered his men to halt. He felt it dishonourable to retire before an advancing enemy and altogether underestimated the Prussian forces; he did not even trouble to inform Ramming or Festetics of his intentions and in consequence only 14,000 Austrians were engaged. Although they were fighting a defensive battle, the Austrians again relied on bayonet charges and sent wave after wave of massed men into the Prussian fire. The result was a complete rout: the whole corps was sent flying back to seek protection under the walls of Josephstadt and to spread consternation throughout the army. For by now the inferiority of the shock tactics had been overwhelmingly demonstrated. The men felt that their leaders were incapable; and many of the bravest officers, who had fought in 1848, 1849, and 1859, declared that such a superiority of weapons, tactics, and leadership was irresistible.

Worse was to follow. The defeat of Skalitz was largely due to the failure of the Archduke Leopold to obey orders or even to make proper preparations for battle once he had decided to fight. But almost at the same time came the news that Gablenz, the victor of Trautenau, had been defeated and his communications with the army at Josephstadt severed. In the morning of June 28 Gablenz had occupied a very favourable position; Bonin had been driven back on to Prussian soil and the Austrian corps was free to occupy the mouths of the pass by which the Guard would emerge on to the plain. But Gablenz had been deeply shaken by so costly a victory, and the confidence of both officers and men had been undermined. Gablenz had asked Benedek to cover his communications with Josephstadt by throwing a few battalions into Prausnitz which was threatened by the advance of the Prussian Guard. Through a misunderstanding his staff assumed that his request had been granted when in fact Benedek was keeping every available man for the march to the Iser. Gablenz had to oppose the central column of the Crown Prince's army with the exhausted troops who had suffered so heavily at Trautenau the day before; he had seen the folly of the bayonet charge as a means of defence and he now attempted to fight a real defensive battle—to meet the Prussian advance with rifle fire from small scattered groups. But the Austrians had never been taught to fire, they knew nothing but the bayonet charge, and did not know how to receive an attack.

After heavy fighting they were driven back in disorder, and as nothing had been done to secure Prausnitz, Gablenz had to draw off westwards and lose all touch with the main army.

The orders for the "secret plan" had therefore to be cancelled almost as soon as they had been despatched, and at eleven o'clock that evening the march to the Iser was abandoned. The Austrian army had almost lost the advantage of its central position. The distance between the two Prussian armies was rapidly decreasing; the Crown Prince had fought his way out of the mountains, and was now in a position to deliver an overwhelming flank attack if Benedek tried to move against Frederick Charles. The great opportunity of June 28 had been lost. King William said later to Govone: "If the Austrians had been in position six hours earlier my son would have been held by the throat and would never have been able to emerge on to the plain, while Bonin was already in retreat. . . . We had laid our plans well, but it was the great strategist, God, who helped us that time." The Prussians had fully realised their danger and had overcome it by their energy and daring. But although the Crown Prince had accomplished the most difficult part of his task and united his three columns on enemy soil, the Prussians did not entertain extravagant hopes; they had been victorious, but only against isolated divisions and their two armies were still widely separated. Benedek might yet fling the whole Austrian army against the Crown Prince before the army of the Elbe could get within striking distance, and the Prussians were preparing for a much more severe struggle on the following day.

This was indeed the only hope of victory for the Austrians —to attack the Crown Prince trusting in a numerical superiority of practically two to one to overcome the inferiority of tactics and weapons. They might, of course, be defeated, but the alternative was even worse—to stand helplessly by while the Prussians united to form a single army of overwhelming strength. Austrian Headquarters, however, had already abandoned all thought of an offensive. Krismanič had always hankered after a defensive war of positions, and the defeats of June 28 enabled him to convince Benedek that a successful offensive against the superiority of the Prussian weapons was impossible. The defensive position which Krismanič now occupied was the one used by Joseph II and Lacy in 1778—the plateau of Dubenetz, overlooking the valley of the Elbe and the road from Jičin, along which Prince Frederick Charles would have to advance to effect a junction with the Crown Prince. Dubenetz is protected to the east by the fortress of Josephstadt, but it is open towards the west and here the Prussians would have had to undertake a flank attack, while the Crown Prince was attacking in front—the exact reverse of what took place at Königgrätz some days later, but in all probability with the same result.

Moltke was perfectly aware of the Crown Prince's danger; he met it unhesitatingly by ordering the advance to be continued regardless of the risks, even urging the Crown Prince to accept battle, if necessary, with the entire Austrian army. But on June 29 only two minor engagements were fought, for the Austrians were busy taking up their new position at Dubenetz. Ordered at one moment to advance to the Iser, brought back to engage the Crown Prince, despatched once again to the Iser, and now recalled to Dubenetz, the Austrian army was already in confusion. Krismanič attached such importance to keeping the army united and under a single control that he insisted on directing all the operations himself; and by June 29 his control had largely broken down. Great masses of Austrian soldiers had spent the last four days in marching round and round Josephstadt and each other until they were in a state of complete exhaustion. Nevertheless, by the morning of June 30 the Austrian army had consolidated itself on the heights of Dubenetz and the Austrian generals anticipated with confidence a frontal attack from the Crown Prince, of the kind they themselves would have undertaken in similar circumstances. But Moltke had no intention of presenting the Austrians with a victory. The Crown Prince had done all that was required; he had advanced successfully into Bohemia without being defeated by the united Austrian army, and now he was to await Prince Frederick Charles.

Prince Frederick Charles had not advanced with the impetuosity of the Crown Prince, although he was faced with a much weaker enemy. On June 26 the Prussians had secured the passage of the Iser and the Prince had then given his forward divisions a day's rest. Even on June 28 he did not push on to join the Crown Prince at Jičin, but allowed himself to be diverted into an attempt to surround the Austrian and Saxon troops at Münchengrätz—an attempt which failed because Clam-Gallas and the Crown Prince of Saxony were already falling back on Jičin, to establish contact with the main army. Moltke, increasingly impatient at these delays in the advance of the First Army, ended them with a telegram in the early morning of June 29: "His Majesty expects the First Army by an *accelerated* advance to relieve the Second Army, which is at present in a difficult position despite a number of successful engagements". Prince Frederick Charles at once recalled his scattered divisions and prepared for an immediate advance towards Jičin.

Here Clam-Gallas and the Crown Prince of Saxony had passed the night. Having received no orders from Benedek since June 27 they still believed that he intended to take the offensive against Prince Frederick Charles; his last message to them had been, "Army headquarters to Miletin on June 29, to Jičin on June 30". A request for further orders was unanswered, as the telegram reached Josephstadt the day after Benedek had left, and before the field-telegraph to Dubenetz was working. Clam-Gallas and the

Saxon Prince had no idea that Benedek had abandoned all thought of an advance and was anxiously awaiting their arrival in order to close up his left wing. At 2 P.M. on June 29 they received by courier the General Order for the advance on the Iser, dated June 27, issued at 6 P.M. on June 28, and cancelled a few hours later. Though puzzled by the incompetence which caused a message dated June 27 to take two days to reach them, they were confirmed in their decision to hold Jičin at all costs until the main army arrived the next day. The allies therefore met the Prussian advance with a fierce resistance all along the line.

The sound of heavy gun-fire brought a belated messenger hurrying to the Saxon Crown Prince. Count Sternberg had left Headquarters early that morning with Benedek's vital instructions to Clam-Gallas and the Saxons to withdraw at once without fighting, since the advance of the main army had been abandoned. On the way, hearing that Crown Prince Albert was expected at the castle of Milicowes that evening, he decided to wait for him there to give him the message. There he remained all day, and it was not till 7.30 in the evening that he reached the Headquarters of the Saxon army, at the most critical moment of the battle. The two commanders could see no alternative but to perform that most difficult of all manœuvres, the disengagement of their troops from the midst of battle. The Crown Prince showed himself equal even to this, and withdrew the Saxons in good order. But Clam-Gallas lost control both of himself and his army. The Prussians were not yet present in overwhelming force, but Clam-Gallas insisted on retreating the whole night through until he reached the protection of the walls of Königgrätz, behind the main army itself. The Crown Prince, deserted by his ally, was unable to retreat through Jičin and had to withdraw towards the south, quite out of contact with Benedek at Dubenetz. The defensive position of the Austrians was now untenable, for their flank was completely exposed on the western side. They no longer had the advantage of interior lines; instead they were in danger of being attacked on two sides simultaneously. The Prussians had to be left to unite their two armies undisturbed. Benedek decided to take up a new defensive position further south and the Austrian army began to retreat, defeated already in spirit.

CHAPTER XIII

THE BATTLE OF KÖNIGGRÄTZ

THE news of the first Prussian victories, which reached Berlin on June 29, revolutionised public opinion in Prussia. Hitherto the war had been unpopular and even the King had not felt sure of victory; now cheering crowds surrounded the royal palace and for the first time Bismarck himself was received with cheers. Moltke decided that it was time to transfer Headquarters to the seat of war, in preparation for a decisive battle, though he had still no knowledge of the Austrian intentions and did not yet realise how near the Prussians were to victory. Roon wrote to his wife on July 1: "Our rapid advance, which has enabled us to win various battles every day from the 27th to the 30th, must now proceed more gently, or our men will die of exhaustion. The junction of the two armies seems to have been secured; now we can await events with every chance in our favour." Moltke even hoped to surround the Austrians in their position at Dubenetz, and instructed Prince Frederick Charles to strike at Königgrätz, in the Austrian rear, without waiting to join the Crown Prince. But the retreat of the Austrian army foiled this attempt.

Francis Joseph had been left in almost complete ignorance of the movements of his army. On June 27 he had been told that everything was in readiness for a decisive advance to the Iser, on June 29 that the offensive had been abandoned and that the army was taking up a defensive

position at Dubenetz, and finally on the afternoon of
June 30 came a telegram: "Débâcle of the First and of the
Saxon Army Corps compels me to retreat towards Königgrätz. Headquarters near there to-morrow." The Emperor
at once took counsel with Mensdorff, Franck, and Esterhazy, and resolved to appeal for French mediation. The
treaty of June 12 had promised the cession of Venice only
after the victory of Austria in Germany; Metternich was
now to offer to surrender Venice immediately, though he
was to add that Austria had not abandoned hope, and was
preparing for a decisive battle. At the same time Francis
Joseph decided to send his adjutant, Beck, to Headquarters
to examine the position, with a view to the Emperor's
taking over the command of the army himself.

Beck found Benedek gloomy and pessimistic. The Commander-in-Chief was convinced that the Austrian army,
already shaken by the Prussian victories, was not fit to
fight a battle after the disorder and confusion of the night
retreat to Königgrätz. He could see nothing for it but a
further retreat beyond the Elbe, to Olmütz or perhaps to
Vienna itself. He even telegraphed to the Emperor on the
morning of July 1: "I implore your Majesty to make peace
at any price. Catastrophe of the army unavoidable." It
seemed impossible to the Emperor to surrender completely
without a battle; he replied the same day: "Impossible to
make peace. Retreat if necessary," and his adjutant added
the question: "Has a battle taken place?" an addition which
the Emperor approved. Technically this telegram left
Benedek entirely free to decide what was best; he could
not say that he had been ordered to stand and fight. But
the question at the end of the telegram indicated clearly
the Emperor's wish: better a lost battle than no battle at
all. The Emperor still showed entire confidence in Benedek;
and, when he learnt that Benedek had lost all faith in
Krismanič, a new Chief of Staff was at once appointed.

There can be no doubt that a retreat to Olmütz or

beyond, however disgraceful, was the right policy. Since it
had already been decided to surrender Venice, the victorious
army of Italy could have been brought north, and the
Archduke Albrecht and John could have taken over the
command with confidence unimpaired by defeat. Such a
policy would also have given Napoleon, who had no wish
to see Prussia completely victorious, time to intervene as
mediator; but it would not have accorded with the traditions of the house of Habsburg. Ferdinand II encompassed by rebels, Maria Theresa in conflict with all the
armies of the Continent, Francis in his ceaseless wars
against Napoleon, all had put their fortunes to the test on
the battlefield, however unfavourable the circumstances.
Austria's position in Europe did not rest so much on great
victories as on her defensive strength. She had lost provinces, but only after long and fierce resistance. Never did
she abandon a position without a struggle as Prussia did
at Olmütz, or as Russia was to do at the Congress of
Berlin. There was in Austria no articulate public opinion,
and the determining factor was therefore the honour of the
empire and the dynasty; a ruling house, especially when it is
sure of the allegiance of its subjects, will always prefer
a battle to a voluntary humiliation. Benedek received no
further communication from the Emperor after the telegram of July 1; but the feelings of the Court had been made
unmistakeably clear to him and, more than anything else,
determined him to fight. The army had recovered from its
disorganisation of the previous day, the Saxon contingent
had renewed contact with the main army, and Benedek
was a little more hopeful. On July 2 he telegraphed to
the Emperor that he was preparing to fight a defensive
battle to the north of Königgrätz. Having learnt from the
previous battles that shock tactics were useless against
the Prussian fire, he now instructed his men to fight a
real defensive battle. There were to be no more massed
bayonet charges; the enemy fire was to be answered by

groups of Austrians firing consecutively; and it was hoped that the superiority of the Austrian artillery would neutralise the Prussian rifle fire. But Benedek's real opinion is revealed by the detailed instructions for the possibility of a retreat, which accompanied the General Orders for the battle.

Moltke too was making preparations for a decisive battle. He was still uncertain as to the Austrian position, for it seemed impossible that so impetuous a general as Benedek would remain on the defensive if he had his whole army available. Moltke was therefore inclined to believe that the bulk of the Austrian army still lay east of the Elbe and behind Königgrätz. After long debate it was decided that the Crown Prince should remain on the east bank, while Prince Frederick Charles forced a passage over the Elbe in face of the enemy. The two armies were not united, in the hope that the double attack might surround the Austrians and compel them to surrender. When Frederick Charles began his advance to the Elbe on July 2 he encountered unexpectedly strong enemy forces, as the Austrians moved up to occupy the heights of Chlum and Lipa. He decided on his own responsibility to attack them in force next day, and sent to the Crown Prince to ask for the co-operation of the Prussian Guard against the enemy's right flank. At the same time his Chief-of-Staff went to inform Moltke of his intentions. Moltke, dragged from his bed at ten o'clock that night, at once realised that the whole Austrian army was on the west bank of the Elbe and that this was his opportunity to fight a decisive battle. Orders were sent at midnight to the Crown Prince to cross the Elbe with his entire force and hasten to the assistance of the First Army. It was a daring plan, for the troops of the Crown Prince had to accomplish a march of at least five hours before they could go into action; a few accidental delays might enable the Austrians to defeat Prince Frederick Charles before the Crown Prince could attack

their right wing. But Moltke could not afford to waste a
day closing his two armies, lest the Austrians escape.
There was no time to lose. On July 1 it had been announced
that the French Ambassador, Benedetti, was on his way
to the Prussian Headquarters; and the decisive victory
must be won before France could intervene to rob Prussia
of the fruits of success.

The two Prussian generals lost no time in advancing.
Prince Frederick Charles did not yet realise that he was
confronted by the whole Austrian army, but he knew that
it would be some hours before the Crown Prince could
arrive on the battlefield and that meanwhile his army
would have to bear the brunt of the fighting. The Prussian
advance, at first successful, was soon halted by Benedek's
skilful dispositions and above all by his brilliant handling
of his artillery. Against the Austrian superiority of numbers
the Prussians could make no progress, and in some places
they were engaged for five hours without gaining a foot of
ground. Benedek's spirits began to rise as he saw a possibility of defeating Prince Frederick Charles before the
Crown Prince appeared and he called up his reserves for a
decisive counter-attack upon the Prussian centre. But unwelcome news from the right wing robbed him of his chance.
The two corps of Counts Festetics and Thun had been
posted on the right to defend the northern flank against the
first attacks of the Crown Prince, while Benedek won a
victory in the centre. But a defensive position against an
enemy not yet in sight did not interest these two aristocrats; they ignored Benedek's orders and tried to win the
battle themselves by attacking the Prussian left. They also
disregarded Benedek's amended tactical instructions and
sent their men forward in the old massed columns which
had already proved so disastrous. Benedek dared not leave
his right flank uncovered while he attacked in the centre.
He ordered a reserve corps to fill the gap created by the
unauthorised attack of Festetics and Thun and sent orders

to these two generals to break off their attack immediately and retire to their original position. But to sacrifice this reserve corps meant abandoning all hope of delivering a decisive blow in the centre, and the order to the reserve was almost immediately cancelled in the hope that the two original corps would still suffice to cover the flank. Once again Benedek was committing the fatal sin of hesitation and delay, just as he had wavered until too late between attacking the Crown Prince and advancing to meet Prince Frederick Charles. As a result of his contradictory orders the reserve spent the whole morning marching and countermarching in the rear of the army without taking any part in the battle. There was no decisive blow on the Prussian centre, but the Austrian flank remained unprotected, for the two aristocratic generals persisted for another hour in their useless offensive against the Prussian left before obeying Benedek's peremptory orders to retire.

Even now, when the guns of the Crown Prince could already be heard in the distance, Benedek might have secured the victory by a swift, determined attack on the Prussian centre. There was a moment when he seemed to have made up his mind; turning to his staff he exclaimed: "Well, shall we let fly?" No one dared to answer and the order was never given. Benedek had begun the battle convinced that Austria was already defeated; he seemed incapable of taking any decision and anxiously husbanded his reserve in the belief that it would be needed to cover a retreat. He displayed none of the energy and initiative which had distinguished him in the Italian wars; and his hesitation deprived the Austrians of what little chance they had of victory. Prussian Headquarters were far from confident; it was clear that the centre was making no headway, and troops who had been on the march since early morning with nothing but a cup of coffee to sustain them could hardly be expected to withstand a powerful counterattack. The King began to despair as no message came

from the Crown Prince; and Prince Frederick Charles
prepared to bring up his last reserves for a final attempt on
the Austrian position. But Moltke restrained him, never
wavering for a moment in his strategy of occupying the
mass of the Austrians in the centre, while the decision was
reached on the two wings. In the early morning he had told
the King, "Your Majesty will win to-day not merely the
battle, but the campaign", and he meant to make his
words good. Bismarck related later that, noticing that
Moltke had run out of cigars, he offered him his own
case, with the two last cigars in it; he was relieved to
see that Moltke carefully examined them and chose the
better one.

Moltke had intended to surround the Austrian army by
driving in both its wings and thus compel it to surrender.
The flank attacks succeeded as he had planned, and his
strategy was completely successful. But it had not the
crushing effect of the later campaigns against the French,
because the Austrians managed to escape from the trap
before it closed. At one o'clock the army of the Crown
Prince launched its attack on the Austrian flank. The two
Austrian corps on the right, exhausted by their earlier
offensive and with their front still facing the west, were
driven back in disorder and the Prussian Guard stormed
victoriously on to the heights of Chlum, right behind the
Austrian centre. Benedek's position was now untenable
and he ought to have begun his retreat at once; but on the
capture of Chlum he threw all caution to the winds and
made the most desperate efforts to recover it. The retreating soldiers were rallied for a fresh attack and, when that
failed, the whole reserve was flung against the advancing
Prussians. This tardy resolution was in vain; as the Austrians fell back, repulsed from Chlum, the Prussians began
to break through against the Saxons on the left. The
Austrian army was in danger of being completely surrounded. The road from Sadowa to Königgrätz was the

234 STRUGGLE FOR SUPREMACY IN GERMANY CHAP.

only line of retreat; and it was already crowded with men
and horses and threatened on both sides by the Prussians.
The reserve, which ought to have covered the retreat, had
already been used up in the futile attack on Chlum; and but
for the brilliant conduct of the reserve cavalry which was
still intact, and the failure of the Prussians to make the
best use of their cavalry, the Austrian retreat would have
become a rout.

The Prussian centre had begun to advance as soon as the
Austrians were seen to be diverting their fire against the
pressing danger from Chlum, and the Austrian centre was
already in full retreat when Benedek was urging his reserve
to the final counter-attack. This desperate effort succeeded
in holding the Crown Prince in check until the main
body of the Austrian army had escaped from the closing
trap; and the Austrian artillery by remaining in action
until the last possible moment led the Prussians to believe
that there was a strong reserve of infantry supporting it.
There is no doubt that the Prussians, through inexperience,
failed to exploit their victory completely. Prussian Headquarters had been so impressed by the prolonged struggle
in the centre that they did not think their men capable of
pursuing the enemy; and after the strain of waiting for the
Crown Prince, everything was forgotten in joy and relief
when he at last arrived. As Stosch, one of the Crown
Prince's generals, wrote: "We were none of us experienced
enough in great victories, and instead of continuing the
pursuit at all costs, we rode round and round the battlefield drunk with victory". Moreover, Moltke's nerves gave
way under the strain and he collapsed with fever; even on
the next day he did not realise the greatness of his victory,
and declared that the armistice, which the Austrians were
demanding, would be very welcome to the exhausted
Prussian troops.

The Austrian army was, however, as much shaken by
its own loss of morale as it could have been by any Prussian

pursuit. The cavalry could rightly feel they had done as
well as the enemy, and the artillery had shown itself definitely superior; but the infantry had lost faith in everything—in their weapons, in their leaders, in their tactics,
and in themselves. None could be braver than the Austrian
infantry in attack, but there their energy was exhausted
and during the retreat they lost all discipline. Austria's
political and military mistakes, the insistence on shock
tactics, the suppression of all initiative, the disastrous
choice of commanders, had their inevitable consequence;
the imperial system, by crushing all spiritual and moral
independence, had deprived the army of confidence and
self-reliance. All through the night the defeated troops
streamed back through Königgrätz, a disordered mass
that had long lost all respect for its officers; the whole
structure of the Austrian army seemed to have vanished
in an hour, and the moral effect of the wild flight across the
Elbe was almost greater than that of the appalling losses in
battle. The Austrians lost about 13,000 killed and 17,000
wounded, while about 13,000 were taken prisoner. Together
with the Saxons they lost in all 44,393 men. The Prussians
lost 9172, of whom 1935 were killed.

Bismarck said later that the battle of Königgrätz put the
German clock right for a century. Austria could not fight
another battle. It is hard not to sympathise with the tradition in the Austrian army that the battle was only lost
by chance: if only, it is said, the Crown Prince had arrived
two hours later, the main Prussian army would have been
already in flight. But this view will not stand closer exam-
ination. Though the army of Prince Frederick Charles
could not make headway against the Austrian centre,
it was strong enough to withstand any counter-attack,
unless the Austrians had already been victorious on both
wings. Moltke even hoped that the Austrian centre would
advance, so as to enable the Crown Prince to cut off its

retreat.[1] The night after the battle he said to some of his officers: "I am not entirely satisfied with our victory. I should have liked the Austrians to have advanced here in the centre, and then we should have had them absolutely in a mouse-trap."

Single battles are often decided by what is called chance. But the superiority of the Prussian army, and especially of its leaders, was so great that the Austrians would not have won a decisive victory even if they had forced Prince Frederick Charles to retreat, and July 3 would not have been the last day of the war. The Austrian army had fought bravely and honourably to the last: there was no Austrian collapse after Königgrätz like the French collapse after Rossbach or the Prussian collapse after Jena, and the victor was left almost as exhausted as the vanquished. Nevertheless the war was at an end, for more than an army had been defeated at Königgrätz. The disorganisation of the Austrians as they retreated was an inevitable consequence of the system of government followed in Austria since the Counter-Reformation. There was no attempt to renew the struggle, because Austria realised that she herself was the essential author of her own defeat.

[1] See Moltke's views in Appendix IV.

CHAPTER XIV

THE INTERVENTION OF NAPOLEON AND THE
CONTINUATION OF THE WAR

THE first news Francis Joseph received of the defeat was a telegram from the commander of Königgrätz, announcing that swarms of fugitives were trying to enter the fortress. It was not until half-past four in the morning that news came from Benedek himself. Benedek's telegram read like an accusation, with its opening references to his own prophecies of disaster three days before. The Commander-in-Chief doubted if he would be able to rally the army at all; it was retreating in complete disorganisation towards Olmütz, and it might not be possible to resist the enemy even there.

There was only one hope—to recall the Archduke Albrecht's victorious army from Italy to resist the Prussians; and this could only be done if Venice was surrendered at once. Austria had been willing to surrender Venice before the war started; and 130,000 men had been sent south merely to defend her honour. Now that the Prussians had defeated the northern army, the Austrian Government realised its mistake. The immediate surrender of Venice had already been decided on June 30, and on July 1 Archduke Albrecht was warned not to waste his strength in ambitious offensives. The next day Napoleon was asked to mediate to secure an armistice in Italy. Napoleon, alarmed at Prussia's rapid advance, welcomed the oppor-

tunity to act as arbitrator and formulated his conditions
on July 3: if Venice was surrendered to him immediately
and unconditionally, he would act as mediator and secure
an armistice with both Italy and Prussia. Napoleon hoped
by this action to make a deep impression on Prussia; he
believed that he was on the verge of achieving all the
ambitions which he had nursed before the war.

The news of the battle of Königgrätz on July 4 completely altered the situation. There were no longer two
well-matched armies in Bohemia, between whom Napoleon
could mediate without resorting to arms himself ; only a
French army could bar the road to Vienna. The same day
the Austrian Cabinet formally decided to surrender Venice
to Napoleon immediately and unconditionally, and Archduke Albrecht was ordered to prepare to evacuate Italy
and transport his whole army to the Danube. Austria had
in fact no alternative and it was probably wise to flatter
Napoleon's self-esteem ; but the empire would have been
spared much suffering if a reconciliation with Italy had been
directly negotiated before the war.

Napoleon had counted originally on an Austrian victory
and had provided Prussia with Italian help in order that
Austria should not become too powerful.[1] He had never
imagined that Austria could be defeated so rapidly and so
completely. All his plans had gone astray, for he could
no longer appear as Prussia's saviour and exact his reward
of territory on the Rhine. Napoleon had always avoided
opposing the movement among the neighbouring peoples
towards unification; he now found himself compelled to
deny his favourite principles of nationality and stand in the
way of the unification which Germany desired.

When Napoleon first gave Metternich to understand that
he seriously intended to intervene, he was quite sincere;

[1] Rouher said in the legislative chamber on March 16, 1867: "It was
assumed that Austria would win and that Prussia would have to pay
for her folly and pay heavily".

and he was confirmed in this policy by Drouyn de Lhuys, the Foreign Minister,. who had desired a less adventurous and more conservative policy before the war, and who now insisted that the treaty settlements must be asserted and Austria preserved. In pursuance of this policy telegrams were despatched during the night of July 4/5 to the Kings of Prussia and Italy, announcing that Austria had surrendered Venice to Napoleon and had accepted his mediation, and urging them to conclude an armistice in order to prevent further bloodshed. This alone was enough to make the Prussians fear that Napoleon was prepared to support his mediation with armed force. But Drouyn went further: he proposed that the Chambers should be summoned and asked for a credit of 500 million francs, to establish an army of 100,000 men on the frontier, and that Benedetti should be sent to Prussian Headquarters to prevent an advance on Vienna. Thus armed, France could put forward her conditions, and in the event of Prussian aggrandisement she could secure territory on the Rhine.

Napoleon had helped to promote the war in order to weaken the two German powers: this objective could now only be secured by intervention. Napoleon himself realised this, and wrote to Metternich, agreeing to send a fleet to the Adriatic, in order to check any further Italian offensive.[1] Austria's hopes began to revive; her united armies were still a considerable force, and if France supported them with an army on the Rhine, Prussia would have to renounce the full fruits of her victory. But an influential party in Paris violently opposed the conservative policy of Drouyn de Lhuys. Prince Napoleon, Rouher, and La Valette regarded the unification of Germany and Italy as inevitable and

[1] Gramont, *L'Allemagne nouvelle*, 297. On July 11 Tegetthoff was ordered to prepare for the reception of the French fleet. [Metternich telegraphed to Esterhazy on July 9 that the French fleet had sailed for Venice. He added that Napoleon had sent a telegram to Victor Emmanuel: " If, after you have Venice, you think of trying to advance any further, you will find me barring the way".—Translator.]

strongly condemned useless opposition to the sacred principle of nationality; and Prince Napoleon, as son-in-law of Victor Emmanuel, had in addition a genuine affection for Italy. This group had failed before the war to persuade the Emperor to ally himself with Prussia and Italy, but they were determined that at least France should not fight on the other side.

These differences of opinion were clearly shown in the discussion on the evening of July 5, at which Drouyn de Lhuys and Rouher were present, together with the Emperor and his wife. Since Rouher remained silent, Drouyn's report and suggestions were accepted; the decree summoning the Chamber for an extraordinary session had already been drafted for insertion in the *Moniteur* when suddenly La Valette, who had not been invited to the discussion, came into the room; [1] and his arguments made Napoleon hesitate. La Valette warned him not to humiliate the young Italian state by closing the gates of Venice and Verona to the Italian army: Victor Emmanuel, he urged, had allied himself with Prussia on Napoleon's advice, and the Emperor could not now forbid him to fulfil his promises to Prussia. Suppose Italy published the documents showing that Napoleon had supported the treaty of April 8? La Valette's arguments were unsound, for France had to consider her own interests and not those of Italy; and to secure Venice for Italy without further bloodshed was in accordance with the principles on which Napoleon had based his Italian policy. After a short discussion with the Empress and Drouyn in his private room, Napoleon announced that his decision was unaltered, and Drouyn withdrew, expecting to see the decree published in the *Moniteur* the next morning.

But during the night Drouyn's opponents made another attempt to shake the Emperor, and Prince Napoleon added his efforts to those of Rouher and La Valette. They warned

[1] Rothan, *Affaire de Luxembourg*, 43, according to information from La Valette.

him that his Foreign Minister was leading France towards an incalculable European war. They spoke of Austria with the utmost contempt, Prince Napoleon in particular being convinced that she was on the brink of collapse and was valueless as an ally. They succeeded in converting Napoleon, who ordered the decree not to be published. Prince Napoleon went still further, for he instructed the Hungarian *émigré*, Seherr-Toss, who was just setting out for the Prussian camp, to warn Bismarck against a premature peace or armistice. Austria, the Prince said, was cringing in defeat, but revengeful in victory, and would exact a heavy retribution at the first opportunity unless she was crushed completely.[1]

Drouyn's astonishment, when he opened the *Moniteur* the next morning, was indescribable. He sent for Dalloz, the director of the paper, and asked him why he had not inserted the decree, only to be told that Napoleon had countermanded it during the night. Drouyn had no intention of provoking a war. He believed that a mere threat from France would compel the Prussians to compromise; and if it failed, the Emperor would still be able to stop at threats or take up arms, as he wished. Drouyn recognised that it would be rash to ask now for Rhenish Prussia. But France might secure compensation in Belgium, the Bavarian Palatinate, or Rhenish Hesse, especially as Bavaria and the two Hesses were at war with Prussia; even if this failed, she could at least prevent the establishment of a united Germany on her borders. There were countless openings, if only the Emperor would act with energy.

Marshal Randon, the Minister of War, when he heard that Napoleon had rejected Drouyn's proposal, is said to have exclaimed: "It is we who were beaten at Sadowa!" Randon was already preparing for a powerful military demonstration: one army of 140,000 men was to be established on the Rhine, while another of 110,000 was to be organised at Lyons for use against either Prussia or Italy.

[1] Cf. Kienast, *Die Legion Klapka*, 109.

This scheme was laid before the Emperor, but he had abandoned the idea of armed intervention and put it aside.[1] The Minister of War was deluded if he really thought that within four weeks he could create a field-army of 250,000 men, which represented a total army of 450,000; such figures were as imaginary as those with which Lebœuf led the Emperor and the country astray in 1870. In 1866 France could certainly not have mobilised a larger army than that of 1859, which numbered 150,000, and that only after many weeks. Drouyn, however, was not thinking of war, but only of a military demonstration of a very elementary nature. When the Minister of War mentioned the large number of troops of which he could dispose, Drouyn exclaimed: "400,000! That is too much; 40,000 men are enough. The *gardes champêtres* would suffice."

The real problem was whether Prussia would dare to fight a war on three fronts, against Austria, France, and South Germany. Certainly the Prussians had the best weapon; as *The Times* wrote, "Needle gun is king", and this had a great moral effect throughout Europe, especially on Napoleon and the French army. The difficulty of the problem is best shown by the different opinions later expressed by the two men chiefly responsible for Prussian policy. Bismarck, when he was attacked in the Reichstag (January 16, 1874) for organising the Klapka legion against Austria, defended himself by saying that he had to use every possible means to compel Austria to make peace,

[1] *Mémoires du Maréchal Randon*, ii. 148. Randon defended himself against the accusation that France could not put an army into the field after Königgrätz, in a memorandum, written in April 1867, in which he attempted to show that France had 450,000 men available at that moment. He circulated it among his friends and published it in October 1870 after the fall of the Empire; it is reproduced in his *Mémoires*, ii. 219-41. Drouyn defended his policy by the publication of *Documents pour l'histoire contemporaine*. The answer to this, written by Lachapelle under the inspiration of Napoleon, is referred to and used by Rothan, *La politique française*, 226.

because Napoleon was threatening to intervene. He continued: "Although France had then very few troops, a small
French reinforcement would have been enough to transform
the considerable, but unorganised, forces of South Germany
into a really effective army, so that we should have been
compelled to cover Berlin and give up all our gains over
Austria". Moltke took the opposite view in the Reichstag
on April 3, 1867: "We were stronger after Königgrätz than
before it and we had 664,000 men under arms"; and in
August 1866 he was of the opinion that the Prussian army
could deal with both France and Austria simultaneously.

Napoleon had thus some excuse for hesitation. He could,
of course, have refrained from intervention altogether and
left Germany free to determine her future Constitution;
and by doing so he might well have established a lasting
friendship between the two countries. A monarch ruling by
hereditary right would have suffered no loss of prestige by
remaining neutral, just as the Tsar remained neutral in
the wars of 1866 and 1870, and Napoleon himself recognised
that this was the most effective and most dignified policy.
But his domestic position drove him on towards intervention; French ambition had been provoked by the success
of Prussia and Napoleon had in the last resort no alternative but to accept the Prussian challenge. For four years,
until 1870, he hesitated to draw this conclusion, and this
hesitation destroyed his dynasty.

Napoleon was deeply discouraged by the failure of his
first attempts to alleviate the Austrian position. The French
indeed regarded the surrender of Venice to their Emperor
as a token of their prestige in Europe, and celebrated it by
illuminating Paris on July 5. But the news was very unwelcome to Italy. Napoleon's demand to Victor Emmanuel
to halt his army on the Po and the Mincio was an interference with the conduct of the war, and the Italian army
and people were incensed at this claim to treat Italy as
the ward of France. Even the vacillating La Marmora

realised that it was out of the question to desert Prussia
and accept Venice as a present from Napoleon. Ricasoli,
the Prime Minister, was not called " the proud baron " for
nothing. When Malaret, the French minister, excitedly
demanded an armistice, he quietly asked if Malaret meant
to threaten him. Malaret, unable to discover from his instructions whether or not Napoleon was prepared for extreme measures, felt that he had gone too far.[1] Ricasoli
pointed out that Italy was bound not to lay down her arms
before her ally, and refused to be deceived by Malaret's
impudent assertion that Napoleon had already secured
Prussia's agreement to an armistice. Visconti Venosta, the
Foreign Minister, refused with equal firmness to desert
Prussia, declaring that he would never be "such a swine".
In vain Napoleon declared that Venice was now French
property and must not be invaded by Italian troops. Italian
opinion was not pacified until Cialdini crossed the Po, and
even the appearance of a French commissioner could not
check the advance of the Italian army. The Italians easily
occupied Venetia, since the Austrian army had already
withdrawn, and the Parisians, recently so proud of their
Emperor, now remarked contemptuously that Napoleon
was not strong enough to prevent the bridegroom entering
the bridal chamber.

Prussian Headquarters at first knew nothing of the
"patriotic preoccupations" of the Cabinet of Napoleon III.
Bismarck had managed to hold off French diplomacy until
the battle of Königgrätz; but on the night of July 4 came
a menacing telegram from Napoleon, announcing that he
had agreed to mediate and recommending the conclusion
of an armistice. Prussia seemed to be in danger, as Bismarck's enemies had prophesied, of having to fight for her

---

[1] See the despatch of Malaret in Harcourt, 276. Cf. Sybel, v. 223. It
appears, however, from the eighth volume of *Lettere e documenti del
Barone Ricasoli* that Ricasoli attached so much importance to the French
alliance that he would have given way if Napoleon had not been so weak.

existence on the Rhine and the Danube simultaneously. The Prussian leaders were very depressed and began to anticipate a reversal of the fortunes of war. Bismarck therefore grasped all the more eagerly at a new weapon to force Austria to a speedy peace. He sent for the Hungarian exile, General Klapka, and told him that the organisation of a Hungarian legion was to be seriously undertaken; the Hungarian prisoners were to be transferred to Silesia and there Klapka was to try to recruit them for an invasion of Hungary. Bismarck declared that he did not aim at the destruction of Austria, but only at a rapid conclusion of peace; but since he anticipated further fighting, he was ready to give the Hungarians a chance to show that their boasts were not empty words.[1]

The Prussians were slow to exploit their victory, and it was not until July 5 that they realised how complete was the disorganisation of the Austrian army. Then at last Moltke recovered his energy. He proposed that Prince Frederick Charles should press on towards Vienna, while the Crown Prince moved eastwards towards Olmütz to hold Benedek in check. There was, of course, the danger that Benedek might summon up the courage to attack the numerically inferior army of the Crown Prince. In that case the Crown Prince was to retreat into Silesia, while Prince Frederick Charles hastened to his assistance, until the Austrian army was completely trapped, as happened twice to the French during the War of 1870.

There were some misgivings at Prussian Headquarters

[1] A few days later Bismarck received Seherr-Toss and said to him: "You regarded me as a Junker, as a reactionary. Appearances are deceptive. I was depicted to the King as a democrat in disguise and I could only win his confidence by showing him that I was not afraid of a conflict with the Chamber in order to carry through the essential army reforms. This struggle has cost me my nerves and my strength. But I have defeated them all! all!" and Bismarck mentioned three royal ladies who had caused him particular difficulty.

over the plan of disregarding Napoleon's threats to the
Rhineland and advancing into the heart of the Austrian
Empire; but Bismarck and Moltke realised that the nearer
they got to Vienna the higher would be the final reward of
victory. Bismarck's part was to convince Napoleon that
military intervention was both superfluous and dangerous.
The Emperor's telegram of July 5 therefore received a
conciliatory answer; the King declared at once that he accepted French mediation, and promised to define more
exactly the conditions on which he was prepared to conclude an armistice. The contrast between this soft answer
and Italy's defiant refusal did much to appease Napoleon.
This was followed up by the despatch of Prince Reuss to
Paris on July 7: he was to say that Prussia could not conclude an armistice until she knew what concessions Austria
would eventually be ready to make; otherwise her victory
would be fruitless. The Prussian aims were broadly defined
as the exclusion of Austria from the German Confederation
and Prussian territorial expansion in North Germany
sufficient to link up her detached provinces. Goltz meanwhile was left without instructions and with a free hand to
use his influence on Napoleon. Seldom has a diplomat succeeded better. On July 8 he was still anxiously reporting
that Drouyn de Lhuys was doing his utmost, in conjunction
with Metternich, to bring about an open alliance with
Austria. But from then on the reports from Paris became
increasingly favourable. Although there was a danger of
French intervention until the very end, after the middle
of July the King and Bismarck were gradually convinced
of Napoleon's fumbling uncertainty and of his fatalistic
acquiescence in the course of events.

The feebleness of Napoleon's policy can only be explained
by the illness which crippled his body and impaired his
resolution. Napoleon was overwhelmed with advice from
all sides. Public opinion demanded that he should arrest
Prussia's victorious course. Metternich and his gifted wife

did all they could to persuade him to mobilise in Austria's favour. Goltz on the other side laboured ceaselessly to convince him that Prussia would never do anything to offend the honour of the Emperor or of France. The Empress, as an avowed supporter of Austria, overwhelmed Goltz with reproaches about Prussia's arrogant exploitation of her victory. Nevertheless Goltz's efforts were not without effect. With remarkable skill he hinted his disapproval of Bismarck's policy, and even suggested occasionally that he might be summoned to succeed Bismarck and put right his mistakes. He told Napoleon that he personally regarded the French claims for an increase of territory as justified, and so left the Emperor in a state of agreeable uncertainty as to Prussia's intentions.

Goltz was strongly supported by Drouyn's enemies, Rouher, La Valette, and Prince Napoleon; indeed their cooperation with him and the Italian minister almost amounted to conspiracy. They supported the allied cause at Court; they kept Goltz informed of the Emperor's mood before he had an audience; and they gave him full details of their conflict with Drouyn in the Cabinet. Prince Napoleon was led completely astray by his sentimental devotion to Italy and to the principles of nationalism: be believed that Italian policy would be guided by gratitude to France and not by self-interest, and even denounced Austria as a "corpse" with whom France must avoid an alliance. Rouher was more balanced and sensible; but he too believed that it would be possible to acquire a little German, or at any rate Belgian, territory, through a friendly agreement with Prussia. The Emperor had a great respect for the Germans, whom he called "the race of the future", and would undoubtedly have avoided a decisive struggle with them, had he been strong enough to keep French policy entirely in his own hands. But he realised that French vanity demanded an increase of territory and so tried to compromise with the principles of nationality by seeking compensation for France in Belgium. It remains inexplicable that he presented his demands to Prussia only after the conclusion of the armistice with Austria. It is possible that he had only just realised that the survival of his dynasty depended on fresh conquests. More probably he hoped first to make Prussia grateful for services rendered, and failed to realise that Bismarck's ruthlessness would never be bound by an obsolete debt of doubtful gratitude. He was at this moment particularly ill and lost both judgement and dignity. In the discussions of July 10 and 11 he again decisively rejected Drouyn's advice: "The whole policy of July 4", he exclaimed, "rested on a mistake; we must make haste to abandon it". In the ensuing negotiations with the Prussian and Italian ministers he confessed weakly that he was powerless to interfere in the destinies of Europe.

The Austrian army had spent the night after Königgrätz in a state of disorganisation and confusion, anxiously awaiting another Prussian attack. But during the next two days order was restored; the Prussians were resting and re-organising, and the natural discipline of the Austrian army reasserted itself. Benedek had sent Gablenz to Prussian Headquarters on July 4 to negotiate an armistice, but without empowering him to conclude an agreement, so that he was merely told that the King was ready to grant a three days' armistice in return for the surrender of the fortresses of Königgrätz, Josephstadt, and Theresienstadt. The next day Mensdorff arrived at Austrian Headquarters and instructed Gablenz to agree to the surrender of the three fortresses in return for an eight weeks' armistice and the free withdrawal of the garrisons. Encouraged by this confession of weakness, and already informed of the proposed transference of the Army of the South to the Danube, Prussian Headquarters were unwilling to give the Archduke Albrecht time to unite his two armies. Gablenz therefore

was not received by the King, but was informed by Moltke
that the terms were unacceptable.

Mensdorff realised that not even reorganisation at Olmütz
would enable the army to resist the enemy's advance, and
he advised Benedek to fall back directly on Vienna for the
defence of the capital. But Benedek, fearing that the army
would go to pieces on the one hundred and forty mile
march to Vienna, insisted on re-equipping his troops at
Olmütz which was only half that distance. This diversion to
Olmütz was useless unless a stand was to be made there; it
would merely delay the retreat across the Danube which was
the last resort. Finally, as a compromise, six infantry corps
and the Saxons, protected by a cavalry division, retreated to
Olmütz; one corps was sent by train to Vienna to occupy
the trenches in front of the city; and four cavalry divisions
were to fall back slowly towards Vienna and hold the
advancing Prussians in check. These operations were
carried out during the next few days and, thanks to the
splendid performance of the cavalry, the infantry reached
Olmütz on July 11, practically unmolested.

Meanwhile, on July 10 the Archduke Albrecht had been
appointed Commander-in-Chief of all the forces of the
Monarchy, and at last a spirit of energy and determination
showed itself in the supreme command. The Archduke
decided to concentrate all his forces beyond the Danube to
fight a defensive campaign for the river and the capital.
He had already telegraphed to the Emperor on July 9 that
it would be better for Benedek's army to fall back on
Vienna at once, in order to effect a junction with the
southern army. Benedek would have preferred to stay in
Olmütz with his seven corps, while the Archduke's four
corps covered Vienna; but this did not suit the Archduke's
plans and Benedek was ordered to begin his march to the
Danube without delay. His position in Olmütz was becoming more precarious every day; the Prussian cavalry was
already threatening the single railway line, and succeeded

in cutting it on July 15; and the Crown Prince, realising that the Austrians were incapable of further aggression, had moved his army south of Olmütz, almost across the direct line of retreat to Vienna. The Archduke Albrecht, observing this, telegraphed to Benedek on July 13 instructing him to retreat into Hungary and join the troops on the Danube by way of Pressburg rather than run the risk of an engagement. But Benedek feared that the week he would lose by going through Hungary would make him too late for the decisive battle on the Danube. He therefore determined to trust his luck once more and to retreat along the river March right across the front of the enemy. The first two corps began their march on July 14, and got past the Prussian army with little loss; but on the following day the Prussians launched a fierce attack on the marching columns. The Austrians suffered heavy losses—1600 against 135 of the Prussians; they lost much of their artillery; the Prussians were able to throw their army right across the March; and, worst of all, it was made clear that many of the Austrian infantry had lost all stomach for fighting. The same evening Benedek learnt that the army of Prince Frederick Charles had reached Göding lower down the March. Before long he would be attacked by the Prussians in front and rear, and there was nothing for it but to retreat over the Little Carpathians into Hungary. In this way Benedek's army made its escape, but its junction with the troops of the Archduke was considerably delayed, and the strategical position of the Prussians was now infinitely more favourable.

CHAPTER XV

THE Austrians were convinced that deep-lying causes rather than a series of unlucky accidents were responsible for their defeat. It was as Austrian patriots had prophesied for years; Austria, by abandoning the policy of Joseph II and crushing all independence of thought and action, could no longer compete with the rising nations on her borders. Her weapons had become rusty; her tactics and her strategy were antiquated; the learned professions were exempt from military service and the well-to-do could buy themselves out; and the consequent lack of educated elements in the army was intensified by the backwardness of popular education. The Court was swayed by favourites and the governing aristocracy was unequal to its task; it had not even been able to provide properly equipped soldiers. The Austrian press was full of contemptuous criticism of the Government responsible for the disaster, and cynical verses were in every mouth. In the *Wiener Abendpost* of July 9 the Government attempted to defend itself: it was declared that public opinion had forced the appointment of Benedek on the Emperor, and the press was accused of first exciting the most exaggerated ideas of victory and then preaching pessimism. The papers answered that their patriotic outbursts had been provoked by the instructions of the Government, and that they had obeyed in spite of the fact, as the *Presse* wrote, that "the public recognised that a German war was being waged by a Czech Ministry, that the inventor of compulsory Czechish in Bohemia accorded ill with the black, red, and gold flag over the federal palace in Frankfort, and that Count Maurice Esterhazy and the German Parliament, which Austria intended to call after the war, were irreconcilable opposites".

Yet there was little apparent change in the capital. The theatres and places of amusement continued to flourish, and Strauss's concerts in the Public Garden were as popular as ever. L. A. Frankl, in a letter to the poet, Anastasius Grün, tells of the day on which the news of Königgrätz reached Vienna: "It is dreadful to have to say it, but the same evening two thousand Viennese were present at a summer carnival. Does not such scum deserve its fate? I, myself, after wandering for hours in the Prater, went into a garden-restaurant to get something to eat. It was crowded with prosperous men and women, eating and drinking. Suddenly there came in some painted whores, who began to play the harp and sing the most miserable ditties; the company applauded and encored many of the songs. I said to myself, have I dreamt it all, have we really been defeated?" [1] Nevertheless there was a strong undercurrent of discontent. After the surrender of Venice to Napoleon a hostile crowd held up the carriage of the Duke of Gramont; and even the Emperor did not escape. As he drove out one day to Schönbrunn, the crowd in the Mariahilferstrasse, instead of saluting him, greeted him with shouts of "Long live the Emperor Maximilian". The Emperor never forgot that the same crowd, which used to bow humbly before him in the days of his glory, had reproached him in his misfortune with the name of his brother, then Emperor of Mexico, who was credited with liberal sympathies.

The Emperor's principal anxiety was Hungary, for the German and Slav lands, despite their complaints, never refused further sacrifices of blood and money. It was only

[1] *Briefwechsel zwischen Anastasius Grün und L. A. Frankl* (Berlin, 1897), 195.

seventeen years since Hungary had risen in arms against
the Habsburgs, and although Deák and the majority of the
people now disapproved of the revolution of 1849 and
desired a compromise, the radical parties might well make
an attempt to exploit the situation. The supporters of a
personal union, and the followers of Kossuth who desired
complete separation, were in fact preparing a rebellion.
Klapka's officers were given a banquet in Berlin, at which,
it was alleged, Prince Frederick Charles was toasted as the
future King of Hungary; and their passes to Silesia were
inscribed "to Neiss for the purpose of army organisation".
Komaromy, a former member of the Hungarian Parliament, had directed the conspiracy in Hungary and dis-
tributed the money received from the Prussian Government. In Florence Count Csaky was making extravagant
promises to the Italian Government, assuring them that
the whole of Hungary would rise at the first signal. It has
been seriously argued that Hungary was ripe for rebellion,[1]
and it must be admitted that the Prussians could have
organised a revolt against Austria once they had pene-
trated into the heart of Hungary. But only a Hungarian
insurrection in the rear of the Austrian army before the
appearance of the Prussians in Hungary could seriously
influence the course of the war by compelling the Emperor
to detach one or two army corps for its suppression.
Nothing of the kind took place, and the 20,000 men left
in Hungary at the beginning of the war were perfectly
capable of preserving order. Prussia and Italy spent money
enough in trying to provoke a rebellion—Prussia provided

[1] Kienast, *Die Legion Klapka*, 161-5. Kienast is very hostile to both
Hungary and Prussia, and, against all the evidence, he ascribes to Bismarck the intention of breaking up the Austrian Monarchy, although he
does not explain why Bismarck declined Kossuth's assistance. It is
incomprehensible that the Austrian Government allowed the writer of
such a book to see the most secret documents, especially those from
which the conclusion might be drawn that many of the Hungarian regiments were unreliable.

1½ million francs and Italy 60,000—but they got very little for their pains, and the Hungarian exiles accused each other of converting the money to their own uses. It would, however, be a mistake to overlook the symptoms of dis-affection, which might have developed into something more serious: the Italian prisoners were greeted enthusiastically in Kecskemet as brothers and comrades; the red feather, the old badge of insurrection, was seen once more in the hats of the young men of Pest; and in most districts it was found impossible to carry out the special conscription ordered during the war.

Deák knew what was afoot, and warned the hotheads that Austria could, in the event of an insurrection, make peace with Prussia and Italy, and bring 300,000 men to suppress it. The more moderate of the conspirators were not aiming at the overthrow of the House of Habsburg, but merely hoping to compel the Emperor to grant their con-stitutional demands; and in the same way Bismarck did not wish to destroy the Austrian Empire, but merely to distract it by a Hungarian revolt. Both Bismarck and the leaders of the conspiracy were thus anxious to keep the movement out of the hands of Kossuth, who was proposing to offer the crown of Hungary to Prince Napoleon; and that was the reason for the small part played by Kossuth in 1866. Deák, though informed of these plans, was powerless to oppose them, and advised the adjournment of Parliament in the hope of keeping his own party out of the storm. There was very little chance of an insurrection in Hungary, but the activities of the conspirators among the soldiers in Bohemia were more dangerous. Their efforts, at first un-successful, were helped by the moral effect of the needle-gun; and many of the Hungarian regiments fought half-heartedly even as early as the battle of Königgrätz. There was a still stronger temptation for the Hungarian prisoners of war and many of them succumbed to it; but the emissaries of Klapka were often met with a storm of disapproval, and there were fierce conflicts with knives between the loyal and the disloyal in the Hungarians' prison camps. Klapka's efforts were on the whole completely insignificant.

In these circumstances it was decided to make a direct appeal to Hungarian loyalty; the Empress Elizabeth was to take up her residence at Pest, as though she felt safer there than anywhere else. Her reception at the railway station on July 10 surpassed all her expectations; not only the officials, but all the leading men of the country, were there to greet her. Deák, Andrassy, and their friends were all present, for Deák held it cowardly to turn in her misfortune from the Empress to whom he had formerly paid homage. She was received with still greater enthusiasm when she returned to Pest with her children on July 13: a great crowd surrounded the station and greeted her with a storm of cheers. But despite these manifestations of sympathy, Hungary gave no help towards the war. Deák held to his principle that recruiting was illegal unless sanctioned by Parliament; the most he would do was to keep silent about it. The Emperor sent Sennyey to ask Andrassy what his demands were. Andrassy replied without circumlocution: "The first demand is that you should make room for those who possess the confidence of the nation: you must call Deák to power and responsibility". Sennyey jumped up and exclaimed: "Do you really expect the Emperor to send for you and your friends? Things are not so bad as to make us run away and leave you to enter in triumph." In spite of the enthusiasm for the Empress, matters remained at a deadlock, though the Government was now assured that there would be no Hungarian insurrection, even though the Magyars might be hoping for a Prussian victory to produce the restoration of their Constitution. And Bismarck actually wrote to Goltz on July 9 that a guarantee for the Hungarian Constitution might well be included in the terms of peace.[1]

[1] Sybel, v. 251.

Austria's enemies realised that she depended chiefly on the support of the German Austrians, and they hoped to win over the Slavs, as well as the Magyars, by promising them greater freedom from Vienna. A proclamation was issued to the "inhabitants of the glorious Kingdom of Bohemia", written on the assumption that they were all Slavs, and concluding: "If our righteous cause is victorious, the moment will perhaps have come for the Bohemians and the Moravians, *as well as the Hungarians, to accomplish their national ambitions.* May their fortunes then prosper for ever!" The Germans of Bohemia read this promise with dismay; their German brothers from Prussia were offering to make the Slavs masters in a land in which they too had equal rights. The Germans might be proud that no offer was made to tempt them from their allegiance but they realised for the first time that Germany was prepared to make them strangers in their own land. Many of the best and most patriotic Germans in Austria despaired of the future of their country. Anastasius Grün wrote to Frankl on July 26: "*Finis Austriae!* Whoever has carried in his heart, as I have, the picture of an Austria free, cultured, and prosperous, and whoever has cherished the conviction that these aims could be achieved by simple, but straightforward methods, will read this sentence with bitterness and dismay. But I can see no other conclusion. It is not the greatness of the disaster and disgrace which has befallen us, but the conviction that our rulers are unteachable, that has forced this belief on me. . . . May Germany in the future compensate our children and grandchildren for this loss which they will not feel as we do.   But *finis Austriae!*"

Such pessimistic views, though widely held, ignored the firm foundations of the Austrian Empire. Frankl replied to his friend that the spirit of Germany was so unlike that of Austria that the absorption of Austria into Germany was impossible: "The temperaments of the North German and of the German Austrian are so opposed, Protestantism and

Catholicism are so foreign to each other, the very products
of the soils are so unlike, that I do not think even a plebiscite
would unite German Austria with Germany, provided that
we had a wise and progressive Government—though there
is little hope of that". The Germans were cast down by the
loss of their dominant position in the empire, and the star
of the Magyars was clearly in the ascendant; as was said
later by a parliamentary speaker, the larks of Hungarian
freedom rose into the heavens from the bloody field of
Königgrätz. The Slavs too might look forward to a brighter
future; the hated Unitary Constitution of 1861 had been
suspended in 1865, and the Germans had lost their majority
in the provincial assembly of Bohemia. Just before the war
the Emperor received a loyal deputation and held out to
them the prospect that he would have himself crowned
King of Bohemia. At the same time the Diet in Prague took
steps to make the University Slav and to introduce Czechish
as a compulsory language in all the schools, even in the
German districts. Immediately after Königgrätz there were
signs of a reaction in favour of the Germans; the Emperor
had a long audience on July 19 with Prince Charles Auersperg and Prince Colloredo-Mansfeld, the leaders of the
constitutional party among the German nobility, and there
were rumours of a change of Ministry. But these rumours
were at once denied, and the Imperial Proclamation of
July 10 did not mention the Constitution; it announced the
Emperor's firm intention not to alter anything in the
domestic situation, but to devote all his energies to fighting
the enemy.

As a result of this a powerful movement was set on
foot for giving expression to the wishes of the German
Austrians. Kolatschek, a member of the Austrian Parliament of 1848 and now of the City Council of Vienna, had
already drafted an Address to the Emperor on July 6, full
of the ideas of the year of revolution: it demanded that
a Liberal Ministry should be formed, that the Austrian

and Hungarian Parliaments should be summoned, that the Government should prepare elections for a German Imperial Parliament and proclaim the fundamental rights of 1848. This was too much for Zelinka, the Mayor, and he persuaded Kolatschek to withdraw his untimely proposal. But feeling that something must be done to express the disturbed public opinion, he led a deputation to the Emperor on July 10. Unfortunately he raised two quite different issues: he first voiced the popular fear that Vienna might be besieged and taken, and begged the Emperor to treat Vienna as an open town; it was only after this that he represented to the Emperor the popular desire for the replacement of the prevailing absolutism by free institutions. Consequently the Emperor assured him that the trenches were so far away from Vienna that the city would not be affected even in the event of a battle, and in reply to the principal issues gave only a general promise to consider the wishes of the people.

The Mayor's action was received with mixed feelings in the capital. His expression of the political discontent was welcomed; but his timid anxiety lest Vienna might be involved in the war was strongly criticised. The *Presse* declared that he ought rather to have asked for 160,000 rifles, with which to arm the citizens. Meanwhile the city was in a state of continual alarm. Steamships were being loaded day and night to carry the gold reserve, the archives, and the imperial treasure to Komorn. Food prices were rising, and housewives were laying in stores in preparation for a siege. Among the workers, unemployed through the complete stoppage of trade, there was a rumour that the Bohemian factories were working full time in order to satisfy the needs of the Prussian army. The City Council decided to organise a Civic Guard of 20,000 men, to keep order in the interval between the withdrawal of the Austrian army and the arrival of the Prussians; but there was everywhere a lack of energy, and recruiting for the regular army left few volunteers over for the Civic Guard.

The Imperial Proclamation of July 10 disappointed those who awaited the promise of a Constitution, but its manly tone and unshaken courage made a deep impression, especially abroad. Napoleon, the Emperor announced, had offered his mediation in order to prevent further bloodshed and this mediation Austria had accepted. "I am ready", the Emperor continued, "for a peace under honourable conditions, to put an end to the bloodshed and horrors of war; but I will never agree to a peace which shakes the foundations of My Empire as a great power. In that case I am determined to fight to the last and I am confident of the support of My Peoples. . . . Austria has suffered misfortune, but she is not humiliated or broken. My Peoples! Trust your Emperor! The peoples of Austria have never shown themselves greater than in misfortune." The proclamation to Hungary was equally confident, though more moderate: "I firmly believe that the warlike sons of Hungary, inspired by their hereditary loyalty, will hasten to enrol themselves voluntarily under my banners to help their fellow-countrymen and protect their threatened Fatherland".

The brave words of this proclamation were soon seconded by the Archduke Albrecht's energetic preparations for the defence of the empire. On his arrival on July 13 he greeted a deputation from the City Council of Vienna with the words: "Courage, gentlemen, only courage, and do not lose hope. He who abandons hope abandons himself." If Napoleon had kept his word and prevented the Italians from invading Venetia, the whole southern army of 120,000 men could have been transferred to the Danube. As it was, 38,000 men had to garrison the fortresses of the Quadrilateral and Venice; 17,000 were needed for the defence of the Tyrol; and one corps, 27,000 strong, was left to prevent the Italians penetrating into the heart of the Monarchy. 57,000 men were thus available for the defence of Vienna; one corps of the northern army and most of the cavalry were already covering the capital; the Saxons and another corps were already entraining for Vienna; and the main body of the northern army, 92,000 strong, was with Benedek at Olmütz. Austria could thus count on roughly 200,000 men for the defence of the Danube. The Archduke made every effort to concentrate his forces as quickly as possible in front of Vienna, and his stern discipline did much to restore the morale of the defeated army of Bohemia. The weakest point was the lack of reserves, and attempts were made to organise a popular militia; but except in the Tyrol, the traditional centre of loyalty to the Habsburgs, and Dalmatia, where the local volunteers were eager to try conclusions with Garibaldi's red shirts, these efforts were attended with little success.

Austria's isolation might well have daunted the stoutest spirit. Napoleon, in his first burst of irritation at Italy's ungrateful disobedience, had indeed promised Metternich to send a fleet to Venice, and for some days Mensdorff kept the Emperor's letter prominently displayed on his desk. But the hope of French help soon died. The change in French policy was first revealed to the Austrian Government by a despatch from Drouyn de Lhuys to Gramont which, after stating that Prussia demanded the exclusion of Austria from the German Confederation as the first condition of an armistice, added: "The Emperor thinks that in the present circumstances the continuation of the war would be the ruin of Austria". Napoleon, product of a revolution, could not appreciate the strength of the historic tradition which still made Austria formidable, as Bismarck and Deák well knew. On July 11 Drouyn further informed Metternich of the French intentions. He wrote: "We possess no clear statement of the preliminary basis on which Prussia would sign an armistice; we only know that the exclusion of Austria from the German Confederation is the *sine qua non*. . . . The Emperor thinks that only an armistice and negotiations offer you any chance of a favourable outcome. His Majesty is determined not to involve the French nation

in a war as a result of the present crisis." The promised
assistance of Napoleon had thus dwindled to a few empty
words.

The Austrian answer was worthy of her traditions and of
her European position: "The Emperor Francis Joseph must
know the other conditions of the preliminary terms before
he agrees to the exclusion of Austria from the Confederation.
If some of these conditions are unacceptable—if for instance
they include any cession of territory, Austria would rather
appeal to the fortunes of war and, if necessary, perish
honourably, than buy her safety at such a price."

France soon renewed her ineffectual attempts at mediation. Benedetti had now appeared at Prussian Headquarters,
and to meet his wishes the Prussian generals formulated,
on July 12, their conditions for a three days' armistice:
the Austrians must withdraw over the Thaya, that is into
Lower Austria, and both sides must pledge themselves not
to move their troops during the armistice. These terms
would have left Benedek immobilised at Olmütz, and the
army of Italy scattered between the Po and the Danube.
Austria immediately rejected them and prepared for the
worst. It was possible that the Archduke might be defeated
in front of Vienna and so forced to fall back on Komorn
in Hungary. This raised the question whether it would
be possible to carry on a war against Prussia in a still un-
reconciled Hungary. Deák and his friends had made no
secret of their desire for a compromise, and Francis Joseph
now resolved to accept the hand which they held out to
him.

Deák, the man of compromise and constitutional methods,
had watched with alarm the growing symptoms of dis-
affection; once again, as in 1848, he felt powerless to control
the extremists. He had therefore withdrawn to his estate
in the country, and it was here, on July 17, that he received
the Emperor's letter summoning him to Vienna. The mo-
mentous interview between Deák and the Emperor took

place on July 19. Francis Joseph asked what Hungary wanted and Deák gave his famous answer—Hungary asks no more after the battle of Königgrätz than before it. He explained to the Emperor that it was impossible to alter the system of government before the conclusion of peace, but that then it should be undertaken without delay. The Emperor replied that he was willing to establish a parliamentary Ministry in Hungary and asked Deák to lead it. Deák humbly declined; but he promised his full support to any Government which would put his principles into execution. He also recommended Count Andrassy, whom he had once described as the man appointed by Providence to be Prime Minister of Hungary, as the best leader for the new Government. Deák's declaration that Hungary asked no more now than before the defeat was quite sincere. But it must be pointed out that Hungary would have had to be content with much less if Austria had been victorious. The draft conditions for a compromise drawn up by Deák before the war represented the maximum which he believed the Hungarians could ever achieve; and now he was to make this maximum a reality.

The Emperor received Andrassy the same day. Andrassy agreed with all Deák had said, except that he urged the Emperor not to wait for the conclusion of peace, but to put the Constitution into force immediately. Reconciliation with Hungary, he declared, was the only way to get better terms of peace, and it was essential not to give the impression that the ruler preferred to accept an unfavourable peace rather than restore the Hungarian Constitution: the empire possessed two dominant nationalities, the German and the Hungarian; it had been founded on their union, and on their union it could be rebuilt. The Emperor was deeply impressed by these interviews; and it is understandable that he preferred Deák's advice and postponed the fulfilment of the Hungarian wishes until after the conclusion of peace. He saw Andrassy again on July 28, but the decisive negotiations which were to create the Dual Monarchy only began later.

The Germans of the Austrian empire met with a very different reception, when they tried to express their wishes. The Town Council of Salzburg had addressed the Emperor, petitioning for the restoration of the Constitution; the Council of Graz expressed the conviction that the strength of the empire was not destroyed, but would reassert itself as soon as the government was entrusted to men of progressive ideas. And finally the City Council of Vienna prepared an Address accusing the system of goverment, but assuring the Emperor that the citizens of Vienna would support him in this hour of danger; let him call to the guidance of the state men in whose actions and ideas the people had confidence. This Address was presented on July 23; the armistice with Prussia had already been signed and Deák had been received by the Emperor, so the Germans, too, hoped that better days were in store for them. But the Emperor's answer was extremely ungracious. The Emperor, the Mayor reported to the Council, was grateful for the expressions of loyalty, but would like to see deeds corresponding to the words; under the present circumstances he would ignore the fact that the Council was not competent to present Addresses, and regard the Address as the opinion of its individual members; His Majesty, the report concluded, had the greatest desire to see the restoration of a constitutional system, but in this he must consult not merely the wishes of the inhabitants of Vienna but the needs of the whole Monarchy.

The report of this audience produced great indignation and many of the councillors threatened to resign. It was clear that there would be violent speeches, and the Mayor resolved to avoid them by expostulating humbly with the Emperor himself. He therefore begged for a second audience and there recounted the effect of the Emperor's words on the people of Vienna. He reminded the Emperor of the city's efforts during the war. "I emphasised especially", he reported to the Council, "that my position was not that of an official, that I was not only bound to maintain the bonds of sympathy and loyalty between the citizens and the dynasty, but that I had also a duty towards the citizens and that this duty was to bring the feelings of the people to the knowledge of His Majesty". The Emperor answered soothingly that he had never doubted the patriotism and self-sacrifice of the population of Vienna, especially in this difficult time.

The discontent was abruptly silenced on July 26 by the proclamation of a state of siege, by which all political activities and all serious criminal offences became subject to martial law. The Government was at some pains to justify the taking of such a step on the very day that the preliminaries of peace were signed at Nikolsburg; the official newspaper explained that martial law had been proclaimed solely in order to control the foreign elements that were crowding to Vienna. The truth is that the defeats of 1859 and 1860 had revived the discontent with the absolutist state, and that the Government was determined to put an end to agitation. It did its utmost to make the people of Vienna feel that they were in disgrace, and characteristically did not even trouble to publish the news of the conclusion of the armistice on July 21, but left the Austrians to discover it from a paragraph in the *Moniteur*.

Fortunately the conduct of military operations was in more competent hands, and the Archduke Albrecht had done everything possible to ensure the defence of the Danube. Vienna was ringed round to the north with earthworks and fortifications, and equipped with heavy artillery, so that a direct Prussian attack on Vienna was hardly possible. To prevent surprise, strong detachments of cavalry patrolled the whole course of the river from Linz to Pressburg, and the Archduke intended to concentrate his main force half-way between Vienna and Pressburg, in readiness for an attack on either bridgehead. Pressburg, as yet but feebly garrisoned, was obviously the most vital point; for Benedek's connection with Vienna would be severed if it fell into the hands of the Prussians. The Archduke and John had at first thought of throwing Benedek against the Prussian flank to give the southern army time to arrive on the Danube and enable the fortifications to be completed. Benedek, however, replied that his men were exhausted by constant marching ever since the battle of Königgrätz and were no longer strong enough for any sort of offensive; he hastened, therefore, to place them where they might be invaluable in defence, and on July 20 his advance columns began to arrive in Pressburg.

The Prussians too were hastening towards the Danube and on July 19 the advance guard of the army of Prince Frederick Charles halted at the village of Wagram, only two days' march from Vienna, on the ground occupied by the Austrians on July 5, 1809. Moltke was uncertain of the Austrian strength, and therefore delayed the advance of the Prussian First Army until the Crown Prince came up to its support. Practically the whole of the Austrian southern army was now on the Danube, and within a day or two Benedek's main army would reach Pressburg. It was the concentration of forces which precedes a great battle; and the Archduke Albrecht did not despair. Everything possible had been done to make the defence of the capital more successful than the campaign in Bohemia.

CHAPTER XVI

THE TRUCE

DURING the week which followed the battle of Königgrätz the threat of French intervention hung over Prussian Headquarters like a thundercloud. In spite of Goltz's encouraging report on the conflict of views at the French Court, there remained the possibility that Drouyn de Lhuys would get his way. The interruption of telegraphic communications between Prussian Headquarters and the outside world was another, and most important, factor in the succeeding negotiations; for Bismarck did not learn until the middle of July that Goltz had overcome the pro-Austrian party in Paris. Prince Reuss had been sent to Paris to give a general explanation of Prussia's intentions and Napoleon was waiting impatiently for more detailed information. On July 9 Bismarck sent Goltz more definite instructions: our political needs—the essential sentence ran—are limited to the control over the forces of Northern Germany; and it was expressly stated that the inclusion of the South was for the moment impossible. It was a very moderate presentation of Prussian ambitions: Hanover was to surrender East Friesland, Saxony the district of Leipzig, Darmstadt, the district of Upper Hesse. But Goltz was to hint at an alternative—the direct annexation by Prussia of Hanover, Saxony, the two Hesses, and Nassau—and to ask Napoleon what compensation outside Germany France would then demand. This plainly pointed to Belgium; for Prussia, Bismarck wrote,

was determined to defend German soil at all costs. If France
were to threaten Germany, Prussia would appeal to German
national feeling, disinter the Constitution drafted by the
Frankfort Parliament of 1848, and then accept the French
challenge. France could choose between peace and friendship and a national war. As Bismarck remarked on another
occasion, if a revolution was unavoidable, it was better that
it should be in Prussia's favour.

The evolution of the Prussian programme of annexation
in 1866 has been often discussed. Soon after the arrival of
Napoleon's threatening despatch William defined his aims
as "supremacy over all Germany", and a few minor conditions. On these grounds William has been praised for his
German national spirit, and the later programme—the
annexations and the establishment of the North German
Confederation—has been condemned as a departure by
Bismarck from this great ideal. This is a misunderstanding
of the phrase, "supremacy over all Germany". William was
thinking of annexations and the command of the military
forces, and not of constitutional changes. Two circumstances determined the decisions of Prussian Headquarters
in the following days. One was the recognition that Napoleon
would not tolerate the subordination of South Germany to
Prussia and the consequent limitation of Prussian ambitions
to North Germany. The other was the gradual realisation of
the decisiveness of Königgrätz, which resulted in an increasing determination to make the most of the victory by large
annexations in the north.

Bismarck still did not know what the Prussian representatives in Paris could achieve, when Benedetti arrived at
Headquarters on July 12 to urge the immediate conclusion
of an armistice. To meet his wishes the Prussian generals
formulated conditions, which were, however, rejected by
Austria, because they forbade the movement of troops
during the armistice. During these negotiations Bismarck
and Benedetti reviewed the whole situation. Benedetti was

in an awkward position, not knowing his master's real intentions. He therefore maintained a negative attitude and was clever enough to make Bismarck believe that he had some secret object in view. Bismarck pointed out that both Prussia and France could take advantage of the defeat of Austria to make territorial acquisitions and to settle all current questions in friendly agreement. Benedetti replied that there were European treaties, and their infringement would cause further wars. Bismarck denied this: if Prussia and France formally agreed to extend their frontiers, neither Russia nor England could oppose them.[1] All this shows clearly that Drouyn de Lhuys was right when he argued that Prussia was neither in the position nor the mood to oppose French demands for compensation. Bismarck put the matter still more precisely to Benedetti's secretary, Lefèvre de Behaine: if Napoleon was disturbed at the aggrandisement of Prussia he had only to make up his mind to seize Belgium and there would be no difficulty. Lefèvre replied jokingly that Bismarck, not content with establishing a new system in Germany, wanted to become the school-master of all Europe.[2]

Benedetti felt he was making no progress and the interruption of telegraphic communications cut him off from Paris; on July 16, therefore, he proceeded to Vienna, to see if he could do any better there. King William was becoming increasingly resentful of the French attempt to control his actions and lay down the conditions on which he might make peace. Bismarck's main object was to establish a Prussian hegemony in Germany which should unite all the forces of the nation; but the King wanted, above all, large territorial acquisitions; for, however highly he might value the creation of a strong federal state, some millions of new subjects and more army corps seemed to him the best guarantee of Prussia's greatness. He had gone to war unwillingly, but now he was determined to punish the kings

[1] Benedetti, 162.   [2] Harcourt, 290.

and princes whom he regarded as the originators of the
war. Bismarck worked to moderate the King's ambitions,
for he doubted if France would tolerate any considerable
extension of Prussian territory without claiming territory
for herself on the Rhine. He therefore decided to ignore
the French mediation and to try for a direct understanding with Austria, even at the price of considerable concessions.

As intermediary Bismarck chose Giskra, the Mayor of
Brünn, a man long convinced of the necessity of excluding
Austria from Germany as a preliminary to a permanent
alliance. Bismarck sent for him on July 15 and told him
that Prussia was ready to conclude peace without an indemnity or any cession of territory, except that of Venice
to Italy ; she would, moreover, be content with the line of
the Main, and would leave Austria free to make any arrangement she pleased with South Germany. Only one condition
was attached to this offer: there must be no French intervention or mediation. Bismarck was thus taking up the
negotiations at the point at which they had stood when he
had sent Gablenz to Vienna just before the outbreak of war.
It is not surprising that Giskra enthusiastically welcomed
such proposals; unwilling himself to leave his post during
the Prussian occupation, with Bismarck's approval he sent
Baron Herring, the President of the Brünn Chamber of
Commerce, to Vienna.

Meanwhile, every messenger brought more favourable
news from Paris, until finally on July 15, Goltz's despatch
of July 11 brought news more disastrous for Austria than
another lost battle. Prince Reuss had arrived in Paris on
July 10 to find Napoleon full of doubt and hesitation.
According to his instructions, he put forward the exclusion
of Austria from Germany and the establishment of a North
German Confederation as the Prussian aims; but he also
suggested the summoning of a Parliament which should
include all Germany with the exception of Austria. "The

Emperor", he reported, "only opposed me with half his strength; I missed his usual precision; he spoke like a man whose conscience was not clear and who was struggling to escape from some embarrassment he had created for himself." Napoleon promised to think over Reuss's remarks: the only thing that he was really determined to prevent was the inclusion of Southern Germany in the Prussian sphere of influence.

Napoleon had still retained some independence in the interview with Reuss, but in the next few days he collapsed completely. On July 12 Beust arrived in Paris to ask, on behalf of Francis Joseph, for French help. He only wanted to persuade the Emperor to establish an army on the frontier; that alone would suffice to compel Prussia to moderate her demands. But Beust's worst expectations were surpassed. "It was", Beust writes, "a fresh misfortune for Austria that just at this time the Emperor was suffering acutely from his prostate gland, as was shown not only in his appearance, but in his mental state. The next year at Salzburg he was physically and mentally as fresh as ever. But in 1866! The whole time he kept whining like a child: 'I am not equipped for a war!'"

Meanwhile, Napoleon had had a decisive interview with Goltz on July 11. He confessed that he had been wrong to accept Venice from Austria and to try to check the Italian advance; but he pleaded that he had only obeyed French public opinion. Now he implored the Prussian Cabinet to deal gently with him; if Prussia and Italy persisted in refusing an armistice, he would be humiliated before his own people and driven to adopt a policy completely opposed to his own inclination and plans. Something must be done to extricate him from this impossible position; at least he would like the fortress of Landau in the Rhenish Palatinate; but he added resignedly that after all it was better to renounce any gain for France. He was, in fact, still hoping, as Prince Napoleon informed Goltz, for a spontaneous offer from Prussia. Goltz assured him that William was very favourably inclined towards France and with this Napoleon was content. In any case he was satisfied on the most important point; the Prussian programme did not include the absorption of South Germany, and the only thing which still worried him was the advance of the Prussian army. On July 13 he asked Goltz: "Tell me honestly, are you trying to gain time in order to capture Vienna? Everybody is urging me to intervene against you, for your persistent advance makes me cut a ridiculous figure as a mediator." These appeals had little effect on Bismarck: he did not care how Napoleon got out of his difficulties and neither feared nor felt pity for a weakened France. Austria found herself deserted, in a position best described by a French lady who said to Vitzthum: "Do you know what history will say? I will whisper it in your ear: When virtuous Austria finally decided to yield to Napoleon's wishes, she found only an Abelard—after the operation."

Goltz made the most of his advantage and worked steadily towards an agreement with Napoleon, although he did not mention "the great annexation"—the project of annexing Saxony, Hanover, Electoral Hesse, and Nassau. Napoleon readily agreed to certain small Prussian acquisitions in the north; he longed only for the swift conclusion of an armistice, to show that his mediation had really been of some use. Goltz was later criticised in Prussian Headquarters for not producing the plan of the great annexation, but he was afraid that Napoleon would demand the Rhine as compensation. On July 14 Goltz and Napoleon arrived at a punctation which laid down the principles for the conclusion of peace. They were:

The integrity of Austria, except for Venice, and the exclusion of Austria from the German Confederation ;

The creation of a North German Confederation under the military leadership of Prussia;

Permission to create an internationally independent South German Confederation, whose relations with North Germany would be settled by a mutual understanding;

The annexation of Schleswig-Holstein by Prussia, with the exception of those districts in the north which were inhabited by Danes;

A contribution towards the costs of the war by Austria and her allies.

This programme was at once despatched by Napoleon to the Prussian and Austrian Governments with the advice to lay down arms and conclude peace on these terms. The Emperor was well satisfied with the course of events: his unselfish mediation between the conflicting powers was bound to have a good effect on public opinion, and there could be no possible objection from the French standpoint to the projected reorganisation of Germany.

These proposals were telegraphed to Vienna, and reached Prussian Headquarters somewhat later, on July 17. Napoleon soon learnt that Austria was hesitating to accept them and that Prussia was raising still greater difficulties.

The Austrian Government received Napoleon's proposals almost simultaneously with the arrival of Herring from Brünn. The Prussian offer was more favourable in two important points. In the first place, Prussia renounced any indemnity, an important consideration in view of the shaky condition of the Austrian finances; in the second, Austria would still be able to uphold her great tradition as a German power by uniting with South Germany. This possibility was expressly excluded from the French offer, because it was to France's interest to keep South Germany separate from both Austria and Prussia, and leave the way clear for French interference later. Herring's mission therefore awakened high hopes, and he was at first, as Giskra later said, "received very graciously in exalted quarters, surprised as they were by this unexpected offer, and in other quarters with positive enthusiasm". These words obviously refer to Herring's reception by the Emperor and Mensdorff.

Now, if ever, it was essential for Austria to act quickly. It is tempting to speculate what would have been the future of Germany and Europe had Austria and Prussia made peace and settled the German question between them. But the Austrian Government wanted time to think. Benedetti and Gramont were told that Austria could not accept the French proposals until it was known whether Prussia agreed to them. It soon became clear to the French diplomats that Austria had another iron in the fire; probably Mensdorff hinted to them that she could settle directly with Prussia on good terms. Gramont reported to Paris: "According to what I can learn, the preliminaries (drafted by Napoleon and Goltz) must exceed the Prussian demands in certain points, and it would be possible for Austria to secure less unfavourable conditions".[1] The French representatives felt that they were becoming unpopular with both sides: the Prussians were complaining that France was impeding their progress and the Austrians that she had abandoned them to their fate. "What we shall achieve under such circumstances", Gramont exclaimed, "will not win us a single friend", and he once more implored the Emperor to order a military demonstration against Prussia—"French mediation, which is already flagging and practically useless, would then succeed at once".

The Austrian Cabinet hesitated for some days. The idea of direct negotiations with Prussia on such favourable terms was of course attractive, but the Austrian ministers still feared to offend Napoleon by completely disregarding his mediation. Once more Esterhazy exercised a disastrous influence; to his hypercritical mind the obvious course was always the most dangerous and he suspected a fresh Bismarckian trap behind the Prussian offer. In spite of Austria's long experience of Napoleon's unreliability, Esterhazy in-

---

[1] Gramont's letter is printed in Rothan, 439-45.

sisted that there was still a chance of French support, and that nothing must be done to rouse Napoleon's resentment. In consequence Austria did nothing for some days and finally gave a half-hearted assent to both proposals. On July 18 Mensdorff and Esterhazy had an interview with Gramont and Benedetti; they announced Austria's readiness to accept the French proposals, but with one added condition—the integrity of Saxon, as well as Austrian, territory. The next day the Austrian Cabinet agreed in principle to Napoleon's terms, and Benedetti hastened with the glad news to Prussian Headquarters.

The same day Herring at last received his answer. He was to say that the Austrian Cabinet could not act merely on information from an unofficial intermediary, lest an official Austrian envoy expose himself to being snubbed by the Prussians; Austria, however, was ready to accept a formal invitation to negotiate. Herring knew that the French were straining every nerve to get themselves accepted as mediators; he did his best to forestall them and wore out his horses in the attempt to reach the King's quarters at Nikolsburg before them. It was in vain; for the position had changed completely since his departure from Brünn.

Prussian Headquarters had grown more confident with every fresh report from Paris. Napoleon and his cousin made a great mistake if they thought Bismarck could be moved to pity by the appeals of the French Cabinet. They only made him more determined than ever to ignore the vague, but boundless, French demands for German territory; he no longer even thought it necessary to allude to Belgium as a suitable compensation. Napoleon's draft terms had ceased to satisfy Prussian ambition, and Goltz was bitterly reproached by Headquarters for not advocating "the great annexation" to Napoleon. King William's hopes were rising; not content with conquests in North Germany, he wanted some Bavarian and Austrian territory as well,

and he was supported by his military advisers. It was
Bismarck who had to resist such immoderate demands, and
he had no easy task. He wrote to his wife on July 9: "We
are getting on well and we shall get a peace worth the fighting, provided we don't advance exaggerated claims and
don't think that we have conquered the world. Unfortunately we are as easily intoxicated as we are depressed, and
I have the thankless task of mixing water with the wine
and pointing out that we are not isolated in Europe, but
have three neighbours." On July 17 Goltz received fresh
and sharper instructions: Napoleon's proposals, it was declared, were only acceptable as the basis for an armistice;
they were inadequate as terms for a final peace, which
Prussia would only sign if she were assured of the acquisition of three to four million new subjects in North Germany.
Prussia was no longer bargaining over terms; she was stating
them without allowing any discussion. To please Napoleon,
Bismarck added that he and Moltke had decided to advise
the King against occupying Vienna. But there was no
mention of compensation for France; Prussia had abandoned
all thought of sharing her victory.

Once again Goltz had to extract fresh concessions from
Napoleon to satisfy his stern superiors at Headquarters.
His activities in Paris have become the subject of legend.
It is said that he was instructed by Bismarck to demand
the annexation of Hanover, Hesse, and Nassau as Prussia's
maximum demands, but that he was empowered to come
down, if necessary, to the mere annexation of 300,000 inhabitants. First, the story goes, Goltz advanced his minimum demands only to Drouyn de Lhuys, who brusquely
interrupted him with his own counter-claims for a transfer
of territory to France. Having declined to consider this,
with simulated embarrassment and a reference to the
refusal of King William, Goltz then went to the Emperor,
was announced without much formality, and impudently
advanced the most extreme Prussian claims. Napoleon,

already under the influence of the pro-Prussian party, was
weak enough to agree to everything—to the great indignation of Drouyn de Lhuys. This little tale represents clearly
enough the relations between the three actors, although
events did not follow quite so exactly the pattern of a
comic intrigue. It is a fact that on July 17 Drouyn objected to so large a programme of annexations; and that
the Emperor declared that all such details of the internal
organisation of Germany were a matter of indifference to
him, renewing the assurance when Goltz received his fresh
instructions from Headquarters.

This was something, but Bismarck wanted Napoleon's
agreement formally and in writing. Goltz was instructed to
insist that the draft terms should be amended accordingly.
"The King", Bismarck wrote on July 20, "does not attach
so much importance as I do to the establishment of a
North German Confederation and therefore lays all the more
weight on annexations, which I too regard as necessary,
as otherwise Saxony and Hanover would still be too big for
an intimate relationship. . . . I must confidentially inform
you that the King has said that he would rather abdicate
than return without considerable acquisitions of territory—
and he has to-day summoned the Crown Prince. I must beg
Your Excellency to bear the views of King William in
mind."

July 19 was the decisive day for Prussian policy. Benedetti arrived from Vienna to announce the Austrian acceptance of French mediation, while Goltz sent a reassuring
report from Paris. Prussia had thus secured the exclusion of
Austria from South Germany as well as Napoleon's consent
to large annexations north of the Main. The only question
still to be considered was whether Prussia was in a position
to fight another great battle near Pressburg before the
armistice, to secure yet more favourable terms from Austria.
Bismarck asked Moltke whether they could count on a
victory at Pressburg which would secure the passage of the

Danube, since in that case they could begin the armistice later. Moltke replied that the manœuvre was risky and the outcome doubtful, adding, however, that in war everything was dangerous.

Bismarck therefore decided to come to terms at once, but he proceeded with great caution. The French proposals of July 14 were accepted only as the basis for a five days' truce. In this interval the peace preliminaries were to be settled; and a prolonged armistice was to be granted only if Prussia was satisfied. This reservation was also made for Italy, since Prussia could not end the war without her agreement.

The decisive step had just been taken at Nikolsburg, when Herring arrived in haste to tell Bismarck that Austria was ready to negotiate directly. Bismarck replied to him: "You have come an hour too late; an hour earlier the negotiations would have taken a different course. Now we can no longer reject the intervention of France, because it has already been accepted." So ended the connection between Austria and Germany. Napoleon and Goltz had agreed on July 14 that the future South German Confederation should be internationally independent, and this barred the way to a union of Austria with South Germany. Bismarck had offered over and over again to share Germany with Austria. It may be doubted whether these offers were sincere; now, at any rate, they ceased.

In one respect Napoleon's wish was granted, for the Prussian army halted at the Danube. The truce began on July 22 at midday and was to last until July 27 at the same time. The Prussians failed in a last effort to capture Pressburg on the morning of July 22 and Benedek's army was able to join up with the Archduke during the truce. Only five days were allowed for the preliminary negotiations; but everything pointed to the end of the war and the renunciation by Austria of her great position in Germany.

In many of the minor theatres of war operations continued right up to the armistice. After the withdrawal of
the Austrian army from Venetia, the Italians had made a
serious attempt to overrun the Southern Tyrol, and General
Kuhn had but few troops with which to oppose them. But
the Italians were made rash by their superiority of numbers
and Kuhn was able to drive back more than one invading
force. More important was the Prussian campaign in South
Germany. The Bavarian army had been marching north
when it heard on June 29 that the Hanoverian army had
surrendered to General Falckenstein; it then turned west in
order to unite with the eighth federal corps, composed of
contingents from Württemberg, Baden, Hesse, and Nassau,
which was assembled near Frankfort. The allies' only chance
was to join forces, but none of the lesser princes was willing
to let his troops go far afield, and the Diet, which was still
in session at Frankfort, insisted that the federal corps
should remain to protect it. Falckenstein easily separated
the two armies and won a series of brilliant minor victories;
but he was still set on occupying Frankfort and once more
ignored Moltke's instructions to seek out and destroy the
Bavarian army. Frankfort was captured on July 15 and the
Diet fled to Augsburg, where it concluded its inglorious
existence. Falckenstein was almost immediately punished
for his disobedience by the loss of his command. He was
superseded by Manteuffel and sent in disgrace to be Gover-
nor-General of Bohemia. Manteuffel pursued the federal
forces with energy, and they were already in a state of
dissolution when the general armistice came into force on
August 2.

The last engagement of the whole war was a decisive
victory for Austria, a victory at sea in the only naval battle
fought in European waters between the Napoleonic Wars
and the Great War of 1914. The Italians had a well-equipped
modern fleet, complete with ironclads and even a three-
hundred-pounder Armstrong gun. The Austrians had a

smaller, antiquated fleet, largely composed of wooden ships; but their admiral, Tegetthoff, was a man of energy and initiative, whereas Persano, the Italian admiral, was a timid sailor, who would rather have kept his fleet safe within the harbour of Ancona. The Italian Government, however, needed a naval victory to wipe out the memory of the defeat of Custoza, and Persano was despatched to capture the island of Lissa, as a useful bargaining-counter in the peace negotiations. It was here that Tegetthoff came up with the Italians on July 20. The Italians had thirty-four ships, twelve of them ironclads, against the Austrians' twenty-three, of which seven were ironclads, but Tegetthoff determined to overcome his inferiority of numbers and armament by a concentrated attack on the Italian fleet. Tegetthoff's tactics were completely successful: two of the Italian ironclads were sunk, their wooden ships fled without firing a shot, and by the afternoon the whole Italian fleet was retreating in disarray towards its harbour. The island of Lissa was relieved and the Italian fleet did not again venture out into the Adriatic. The battle of Lissa could not reverse the decision of the battles fought on land, but it did at any rate furnish another proof that Austria was still a great power capable of defending herself.

CHAPTER XVII

PEACE

THE Austrian plenipotentiaries, Karolyi and Brenner-Felsach (the Austrian Ministers at Berlin and Darmstadt) and General Degenfeld, met Bismarck and Moltke at the castle of Nikolsburg on July 23 to negotiate the preliminary terms. Meanwhile a swarm of German princes and ministers hastened to Vienna to beg for protection. The exiled sovereigns of Hanover, Hesse-Darmstadt, and Nassau, Prince Frederick of Württemberg, Pfordten from Bavaria, and Dawligk from Baden, all besought the Austrian Cabinet not to forget them; but what could Austria do for them? She herself was looking anxiously for assistance to France, whose representatives were busily but uselessly following the negotiations.

The Prussian Cabinet had every reason to hasten the conclusion of the preliminary peace. So far French or Russian intervention had been avoided, but at any moment one of Prussia's powerful neighbours might decide to interfere. Russia was demanding a Congress to be summoned to Paris, since Prussia had no right to alter the map of Europe as she pleased: the German Confederation had been set up by all the great powers at the Congress of Vienna and a new system could be created only with their unanimous agreement. Nothing could be more unwelcome to Prussia than a Congress, which would make the prizes of her sword the subject for diplomatic bargaining.

Bismarck managed, however, to keep France and Russia apart. Napoleon, usually so enthusiastic for a Congress, left the Russian proposal unanswered, because Prussia was still holding out the prospect of a share in the spoils and he thought that this could more easily be arranged privately. He refused to be turned aside by the growing demand in France for energetic action, or by the urgent warnings of Drouyn de Lhuys against allowing German unification to endanger French safety. One thing Drouyn did accomplish: the French representatives were to declare their mediation at an end as soon as the negotiations began. The minister wanted to prevent France committing herself to a guarantee of the new German Constitution by signing the treaty. Immediately afterwards Napoleon's policy swung in the opposite direction. Goltz, in obedience to his instructions of July 20, requested the Emperor to agree to the insertion of the words, "The Emperor will recognise and support the annexation of three to four million North Germans by Prussia", in the Punctation of July 14. Napoleon agreed to all the Prussian demands, including the annexation of part of Saxony, and he even urged Prussia to take more, pointing out on the map suitable parts of Thuringia and Upper Hesse. Such kindness was positively embarrassing, for most of the Thuringian princes had stood by Prussia and there were no grounds on which they could be dispossessed.

Napoleon now felt that the time had come to ask for his reward, and on July 23 Benedetti was instructed formally to demand compensation for France: it was only fair, he was to say, that France should be strengthened, to balance the aggrandisement of Prussia. Napoleon waited anxiously for the Prussian reply, but at first everything seemed to go smoothly. Bismarck at once admitted the justice of the French claims and discussed with Benedetti how they could best be satisfied. Naturally, he said (according to Benedetti's account), victorious Prussia could not surrender any of her own territory; but perhaps the Bavarian Palatinate would provide some compensation, though it would be simplest to take Belgium. On that an agreement could easily be reached. The only thing that Bismarck asked was that no official proposals should be made to him just yet. Napoleon was quite satisfied with these non-committal suggestions, and postponed the discussion of details until after the conclusion of the preliminary peace, in order to show Prussia what a charming ally he could be. The Austrian negotiators were astonished at the French reserve, and Degenfeld complained to the Duke of Coburg that France, though theoretically on Austria's side, had in fact done nothing to help her. Thus Napoleon agreed to the "great annexation" before he got his price from Prussia. The Emperor and his ministers, Rouher and La Valette, did not yet know Bismarck: they were soon to discover the naïveté of expecting Bismarck to feel bound by the calculating generosity of his French friends.

The constant danger of French or Russian intervention was to some extent offset by Italy. True, the Italian army had not done much and was no longer even detaining a number of Austrian corps in Italy now that the army of the Archduke Albrecht had been transferred to the Danube. The Prussian generals were furious with the Italians for allowing the Austrians to withdraw undisturbed; they suspected, with some justice, that the Italian delay was due to the counsels of Napoleon.[1] Usedom, the Prussian representative at Florence, expressed his dissatisfaction so strongly that both La Marmora and Victor Emmanuel took offence; but his assurance that Prussia would not conclude an armistice without the consent of Italy had its effect, and the King resolved to disregard Napoleon's warnings and advance into Venetia. The news that Austria and Prussia had concluded a truce came as a shock to the Italians and they complained bitterly that they had been deceived. But

[1] This is proved by La Marmora's letter to Pittinengo in Chiala, *Ancora un po piu di luce*, 401.

Bismarck replied contemptuously: "We are adhering strictly to the treaty and, if we are resting for five days, it is no more than the Italians have been doing for four weeks". Bismarck now wanted peace, and on July 23 he definitely demanded from Barral, the Italian Minister, the conclusion of an armistice by Italy—Prussia, he said, had secured Venetia for her ally and there was no mention of any further acquisitions in the treaty of alliance. The Italians were forced to realise that their own efforts to conquer Southern Tyrol were belated and vain. Barral left Nikolsburg in high dudgeon, without taking leave of Bismarck; but the obstinate unwillingness of Italy to conclude peace benefited Prussia in that it induced Austria to compromise.

Against this background of intrigue the negotiations proceeded at Nikolsburg. Both sides were in a hurry for various reasons and it only needed two sessions to reach an agreement. Some of the principal points had been settled already. Austria surrendered Venice, but otherwise suffered no loss of territory. The second article contained the most vital concession: Austria gave "her sanction to a reorganisation of Germany without the participation of the Austrian Empire". Prussia was to create a federation of the North German states, and, if a South German union should be formed, it was to be allowed to unite with the northern federation. Finally Austria ceded her share of Schleswig-Holstein. Prussia was, however, committed to return to Denmark that part of North Schleswig which was Danish in language.[1]

[1] This promise was made only to Austria, as France did not adhere to the treaty of peace and Austria voluntarily renounced her claim by the Treaty of October 11, 1878. This concession was obviously the reward for the support which Germany had given to Austria over the occupation of Bosnia.

[In the session of the plenipotentiaries on July 25 Bismarck attempted to secure the omission of the clause concerning the holding of a plebiscite in North Schleswig and its eventual return to Denmark on the ground that this was something which affected only Prussia and France. Karolyi

The assessment of the costs of the war raised a much more difficult question. Prussia estimated her expenses at 100 million thalers and proposed that Austria should pay one-half of this, and her federal allies the rest. The Austrian representatives declared that the exhausted Imperial treasury could not produce such a sum; moreover Austria had a counter-claim under the peace treaty with Denmark, since the costs of the Danish war, 30 million thalers, were to be borne by Schleswig-Holstein, and Austria had not yet received her share. Prussia recognised the justice of this claim and deducted 15 million thalers from the indemnity; a further 5 million thalers was deducted in return for the provisioning of the Prussian troops on Austrian soil, and there thus remained a sum of 30 millions, which was still too much for Austria. The Prussian representatives then offered to abandon their financial claims entirely, if Austria would cede twenty square miles of territory with 100,000 inhabitants, under the excuse of adjustment of frontiers. Such a claim touched Austrian honour and provoked the answer that an adjustment could only mean an exchange of territory. The Austrians continued obstinate, and finally in the second session Prussia moderated her demands to 20 million thalers and the provisioning of the army. Austria had to thank Esterhazy for the indemnity, for Bismarck had offered from Brünn to conclude peace without one, on condition that Austria rejected the French mediation. Esterhazy had engineered the rejection of these terms and the reserve of the National Bank had now to suffer for it.

replied: "We also regard ourselves as bound towards France over the preliminaries which France proposed, and we must therefore desire the inclusion of this clause as well". Very unwillingly Bismarck agreed. Karolyi adds: "We thought we ought to insist on the retention of this clause for the sake of our relations with France". Karolyi to Mensdorff, July 25, 1866. Redlich. ii. 820.

A plebiscite was finally held in North Schleswig as one of the terms of the Treaty of Versailles.—Translator.]

The real struggle began when Prussia demanded the recognition by Austria of her conquests in North Germany.
It was hard for Francis Joseph to abandon his allies, but
there were only two to whom he was especially committed
—Saxony, because she had fought faithfully at Austria's
side, and Bavaria, because Austria and Bavaria were each
bound by the treaty of June 14 not to conclude peace without the other. Austria, however, was soon relieved of her
obligation to Bavaria, who preferred to negotiate independently. Pfordten's first attempt to come to a direct agreement with Bismarck was indeed unsuccessful—he arrived
at Nikolsburg before the armistice between Prussia and
Bavaria was in force, and Bismarck greeted him ruthlessly
with the words: "Do you know that I could have you
arrested as a prisoner of war?" But fundamentally Bismarck was very anxious to detach the South Germans
from Austria, and Pfordten shared this desire. When
Bismarck told him that Bavaria would have to surrender
the district of Kulmbach, Pfordten hastened to demand
from his Austrian ally the district of the Inn, which Austria
had acquired from Bavaria in 1779.

Saxony was in a different position and Francis Joseph
felt bound to do all in his power to protect her. Prussia was
demanding Austria's consent to the annexation of the whole
kingdom of Saxony, as well as Hanover, Electoral Hesse,
Nassau, and Frankfort. Austria would agree to everything
else, especially as Napoleon had already consented; but she
would not yield in the matter of Saxony. Francis Joseph had
promised King John and Beust to insist on the complete
integrity of Saxony, and he also wanted to secure her freedom to join the southern federation instead of the northern.
The Austrian plenipotentiaries announced that the Emperor
would appeal again to the fortunes of war rather than
abandon Saxony, and Bismarck realised that this opposition
was unshakable. He therefore reduced his terms and demanded only the cession of the districts of Leipzig and

Bautzen. This, too, was unconditionally refused by the Austrians, and the first session closed with the expectation that the war would be renewed.

The King was much more eager than Bismarck for territorial acquisitions and he considered Bismarck's efforts half-hearted. Bismarck attached most importance to the establishment of a united Germany, but William cast greedy eyes on his neighbours' territory and success increased his desire. He felt that it would be altogether too chivalrous to let Saxony emerge unharmed from her defeat, especially as he held Saxony chiefly responsible for the federal declaration of war against Prussia.[1] He was still more anxious to recover from Bavaria the original seats of his house, the old Hohenzollern margravates of Ansbach, Bayreuth, and Kulmbach. Naturally Austria was also to suffer. Prince Frederick Charles was directing the King's attention to north-west Bohemia—she was to lose the principal part of German Bohemia.

The King was suffering from an attack of cholerine, which was for a moment feared to be cholera, but his illness did not interfere with his conduct of affairs, nor did it make him less obstinate. Bismarck was aiming at a genuine reconciliation with Austria and the Southern States, and excessive annexations would endanger this object; but he was defeated at a council of war on July 23, when the generals declared in favour of larger annexations or a continuation of the war.[2] Bismarck, fully conscious of the historic im-

[1] [The King said to Karolyi on July 23 "that he regarded Beust as the special originator of the trouble which produced the war; that Saxony was the seducer, the other states, especially Electoral Hesse and Hanover, were merely the seduced, and it was unfair to let the seducer emerge quite unscathed, when Prussia would be compelled, both in order to link up her territories and to assert her rights as victor, to make territorial acquisitions at the expense of the seduced". Karolyi to Mensdorff, July 23, Redlich, ii. 818.—Translator.]

[2] Here Bismarck's memory led him astray. There was no council of war on July 23. W. Busch shows in *Der Kampf um den Frieden im*

portance of the decision and of his own responsibility for
the success of his work, felt that he was losing control of
himself; he got up silently from the discussion and withdrew
to his bedroom, where he burst into a storm of tears.

Bismarck, however, did not give up the struggle: the same
day he drew up a minute, one of his greatest and most
mature productions, in which he stated the case for a speedy
conclusion of peace on moderate terms. He reminded the
King of the dangers threatening from the neutral powers
and emphasised the fact that Austria had made every
reasonable concession. It would be a political mistake, he
wrote, "to endanger everything that has been achieved by
trying to get from Austria a few square miles of territory
or a few millions more indemnity". He warned the King
also of the cholera which had broken out in the army, and
formally declined all responsibility if "against his humble
proposal and advice" the speedy conclusion of peace was
impeded.

The next day Bismarck found the King unyielding in his
demand for Austrian and Saxon territory. The King was
so excited that it was impossible to prolong the discussion,
and Bismarck had to assume that his advice was rejected.
The solution of the conflict must be told in Bismarck's own
words, as he recounts it in his *Recollections*: "When I returned to my own room I was in such a mood that I debated
whether it would not be better to throw myself out of the
open window, four storeys high, and I did not look round
when I heard the door open, although I guessed it was the
Crown Prince, whose room I had passed in the corridor. I
felt his hand on my shoulder and he said to me: 'You know
that I was against the war; you regarded it as necessary
and bear the responsibility. If you are convinced that its
object has been attained and that peace must now be con-

Preussischen Hauptquartier 1866, Historische Zeitschrift, xcii., that the
council of war must have taken place earlier, probably on July 19. This
does not of course affect the essential accuracy of Bismarck's account.

cluded, I am ready to assist you and support your opinion with my father.' He then went to the King and came back in half an hour in the same quiet and friendly mood, but with the words: 'It has been very difficult, but my father has agreed'. This agreement was expressed in a pencilled note in the margin of one of my last minutes, which ran something like this: 'Since my Prime Minister has deserted me in the face of the enemy and I am not in a position to find a substitute, I have discussed the question with my son; he supports the view of the Prime Minister and to my great sorrow I am therefore compelled to swallow this bitter pill and accept a disgraceful peace after the army's brilliant victories.'" [1]

The King was only persuaded with difficulty by his son, although he had asked for his advice with the words: "You must speak in the name of the future". The Duke of Coburg has described how he saw the Crown Prince proceeding with hesitation and anxiety to the King's apartments. "Bismarck and I", he wrote, "awaited the decision meanwhile in the antechamber and I well remember how each minute seemed an hour. Finally the Crown Prince came out: he was exhausted, but he was able to announce that the King had agreed in principle."

At the second session of the negotiators on July 25 an agreement was therefore reached both on the question of

[1] [Max Lenz, *Geschichte Bismarcks*, 322, points out that Bismarck exaggerated the severity of his conflict with the King each time he told it, until he finally developed the story which appears in his *Recollections*. The documents show that Bismarck did not offer his resignation, but only refused to accept responsibility, and that the King did not immediately give way—certainly did not use the words of Bismarck's account; he demanded from Bismarck the "loyal support of the Prussian claims" in respect of Saxony, but added that, if these could not be obtained from the defeated, the victor must give way before the very gates of Vienna and leave posterity to judge. But on the whole, as Friedjung says, "Bismarck's account is in general a true picture of the course of events and of the feeling during these eventful days".—Translator.]

Saxony and on the indemnity. There was, however, one moment of excitement. The Austrian negotiators having got so much, Karolyi expressed the wish that Saxony should also be free to join the southern federation. This was too much for Bismarck. He jumped up and said loudly— negotiations are terminated if Austria insists on this demand. He added that he was so determined on this that he would immediately resign if the King ordered him to accept this condition. Bismarck could safely make this threat, for the King's demands were far more severe than his own.

The decision of peace or war once more rested with Francis Joseph. One stumbling-block was removed when King John himself abandoned the desire for union with the southern federation; the Saxon ministers who had remained in Dresden were now in favour of a frank co-operation with Prussia. The Emperor left the decision to his ally, adding, however, that Austria would have to consider only her own interests if the war was again unsuccessful. To this Beust answered: "To insist on war, when Your Majesty desires peace, would be to undertake a responsibility which the King cannot shoulder". But there was a party in the Austrian army which made the continuation of the war a point of honour. This view was most fiercely expressed in the military paper, the *Kamerad*: "No peace, unless it brings us as much as Austria would be entitled to demand after the defeat of the enemy". It was known in Vienna that the Prussian army was in the grip of cholera, and in fact the Prussians lost by disease half as many men as were killed in battle or had died of their wounds. Moreover, the Austrian army was now in full strength on the Danube; the first detachments of the northern army arrived in Pressburg on July 21, and by July 27 the whole of Benedek's army had completed its retreat. The Archduke had at his disposal an army of 250,000 men and 800 guns, most of which was concentrated south of Pressburg. The bridgehead north of

Vienna was strongly entrenched, the bridges at Pressburg were broken on the night of July 27, and every ship or boat for miles had been sunk. Finally ships had been equipped to hinder the Prussians if they attempted to build bridges, or to ram them. The Prussians were at a disadvantage, as they had to leave many men in garrison to protect their rear, and Moltke had therefore only 160,800 infantry, 19,700 cavalry, and 744 guns for the campaign. The Prussian army, too, was still on the march and would not be ready for some time for a decisive battle. On the other hand, it was full of confidence in its weapons and its leaders, and convinced that it could always defeat the Austrians.

It is tempting to speculate what would have happened if the war had been renewed. It is known that Moltke was planning to throw a pontoon bridge over the Danube near Pressburg, and preparations for this were made during the night of July 26. It is of course possible that this was only a diversion to distract the attention of the Austrians, while the main Prussian force stormed the trenches north of Vienna. This is, however, unlikely as the Prussians had not yet brought up their siege train and Moltke never liked to attack a strongly fortified position. The Archduke and John realised that since they could not watch every point they could not prevent the Prussians crossing the river; but they meant to drive them back into it as soon as part of their army had crossed. The Austrians were to use the bridge-heads not only for defence, but to emerge on the Prussian flank as soon as they were engaged elsewhere. If the Prussians attacked Pressburg, the Austrians would counter-attack from Vienna; if the Prussians concentrated north of Vienna, the Austrians would cross the river between Vienna and Pressburg and fall on the Prussian flank. The risk of launching the dispirited northern army on such an attack had to be taken, or the Austrians might as well surrender unconditionally at once. The morale of the two armies was indeed the determining factor. Whether the troops of the

northern army would still fight with unshaken nerve after
their experiences in Bohemia, and whether the deficiencies
in army organisation had really been made good in the
space of a few weeks—these were the questions before which
the most far-sighted officer hesitated.

The Archduke was not afraid of renewing the war, but
he realised that there were weighty reasons for concluding
peace. At the decisive council in the Hofburg he left it
to his Chief of Staff, John, to express the opinion of the
army; and John spoke unhesitatingly for peace. He exposed frankly the weak points of the Austrian position
and emphasised the dangers to which the empire and the
dynasty would be exposed in case of a second defeat; and
these arguments induced the Emperor to make peace.[1] As

[1] [This account is misleading in so far that it implies either that the
Archduke kept silent or that John spoke only of the ultimate effects of
a second defeat. At the Council of Ministers on July 26 (Minutes K. Z.
2128) the Emperor had read the reports of Karolyi from Nikolsburg
and then asked the Archduke and John for their opinions. The Archduke
declared that a continuation of the war was not impossible, although an
interval of a few weeks was eminently desirable, in view of the condition
of the northern army. "The position of the army behind the Danube
would make possible an indefinite prolongation of the war; but an
offensive, which alone could create a more favourable situation, would
only be possible if we succeeded in striking a powerful blow at the
enemy as he was attempting to cross the Danube." The Archduke then
commented unfavourably on the indemnity—clearly he was not himself
ready to advise a continuation of the war, but would have rather welcomed the advice if it had come from another.

The essential point of John's speech was that Austria could not hope
to fight on two fronts; the army on the Danube had been created only
by denuding the Italian front of troops and John declared that there
was a chance of driving the Prussians out of Bohemia only if it was
possible to make peace with Italy.

Mensdorff at once took up this argument and pointed out that Bismarck was free to make peace, whereas the Italians were completely
bound to Prussia and could not make peace without Bismarck's consent.
The only course was to make peace with Prussia and then divert all the
forces of the empire against the Italians.

Esterhazy was the first to introduce more general considerations. He

the Archduke and John went down the stairs to the Joseph-
platz after the Council, the Archduke said to John that he
was surprised that John had painted such a black picture of
the situation, since there was still a possibility of victory.
John replied dryly: "Very well, let us go back, so that the
Emperor may hear from Your Imperial Highness these
arguments too!" But however much the Archduke's heart
opposed surrender his head told him that it would be madness for Austria to appeal again to the fortunes of war, in
face of the enemy's superiority in tactics and weapons.

Both Austria and Prussia had thus good reason to desire
a speedy settlement, and at five o'clock on July 26 Francis
Joseph sent the order to Nikolsburg to compromise on the
Saxon question and sign the preliminary terms. When the
terms had been signed, William, weeping with gratitude,
embraced and kissed first Bismarck and then Moltke and
Roon. The truce, which would have expired at noon on
July 27, was extended until August 2; then the armistice

began: "If besides these two alternatives—a continuation of the war,
the success of which is highly improbable, and a rapid conclusion of
peace—there was a third alternative, the appeal to a real patriotism or to
dynastic loyalty, then there would be some hope of a successful outcome.
But this alternative does not exist, or at any rate not in a form on which
any hope can be based. One has only to look at the manifestations of
public opinion; Hungary is especially unreliable, for there the Protestants
are openly displaying their delight that Protestantism will be in future
the predominating religion of Austria." Nor could Esterhazy see any
prospect of assistance from abroad, although he hoped that the French
might later come to their senses. Esterhazy supported the armistice just
because the two enemies of Austria were hoping that Austria would
reject it and thus enable them to secure more territory—an elaborate
argument very characteristic of Esterhazy.

Belcredi also supported the armistice on the grounds that it was very
desirable to put an end to the Prussian exploitation of Bohemia as soon
as possible—another very characteristic argument.

A Council (K.Z. 2129) was held the following day to ratify the terms
of the armistice. Objection was raised only to Article V, by which
Austria agreed in advance to any changes Prussia might make north
of the Main. Esterhazy admitted that Austria could do nothing to help

was to come into force and include the South German states.
Meanwhile negotiations for a definitive peace were to be
begun at Prague.

Austria had still to conclude an armistice with Italy.
Cialdini had led his army slowly towards the Isonzo and the
Venetian frontier, and on July 18 the Italians won their
only military success of the whole war by capturing the
fortress of Borgoforte, south of Mantua. A truce came into
force on July 26 and was prolonged until August 9, but it
was impossible to agree on the terms of an armistice because
the Italians insisted on maintaining the military state of
possession during the negotiations for the final peace. The
Italians were obviously hoping to detach South Tyrol from
its loyalty to Austria, but the Austrian Government was
now free from its enemy in the north and determined to
show the Italians that Austria was still a great empire. Over
half the army of the Danube was sent back to Italy, the
Archduke Albrecht transferred his headquarters to the

her allies, but urged that there was a great difference between treatment
which one could not prevent and treatment to which one had consented in
advance. If the point was passed over in silence, Austria would be free
later to appeal to the great powers against the Prussian action.

Karolyi was then called in and at once declared that the non-ratifica-
tion of this clause would be equivalent to a continuation of the war.
Prussia had renounced her claims to annexing part of Austria or Saxony,
and was therefore all the more determined to create a unified state in
North Germany. Prussia would insist on this point, especially because
she had already got the agreement of Napoleon to a large programme of
annexations.

After such a decisive statement there was nothing for the Council
to do but to ratify the terms without reserve. It is once more characteristic that it should be Esterhazy, on the previous day the most pessimistic not only about the immediate situation but about the whole future
of Austria, who now attempted to reassert the right of Austria to interfere in German affairs—the most essential right in all the traditions
of the Habsburg dynasty, but the one the Prussians had fought the war
to destroy. Both opinions of Esterhazy contain elements of good sense,
forcefully expressed. What damns him completely as a statesman is that
it is quite impossible to reconcile the two.—Translator.]

Isonzo, and the Italians were told that the war would be resumed on August 11. Only on the 10th did the Italians give way and withdrew from the disputed area, retaining only Venetia. On these conditions an armistice was concluded.

The whole world had been left breathless by the rapid and irresistible Prussian advance, and the sudden conclusion of peace was equally astonishing to the general public. Few people knew that France and Russia were becoming increasingly impatient with the Prussian Cabinet and were threatening to intervene. On July 27, while still at Nikolsburg, Bismarck received the unwelcome news that Russia was formally proposing the summons of a Congress. There seemed to be a danger that the European powers, all hostile to Prussia, would set out to dictate the future organisation of Germany. Bismarck at once sent a forceful despatch to St. Petersburg, threatening to invoke not only the national forces of Germany, but those of Poland as well, in defence of Prussia's conquests. There was also the danger that Austria might be given new hope by the prospect of a Congress and raise difficulties against the definitive peace. Bismarck needed some weapon other than the Prussian army with which to threaten Austria, and he found it in the Hungarian legion organised by General Klapka.

Klapka's recruiting among the Hungarian prisoners of war had not been very successful. He only managed to win over about 1700 men and most of these had but little enthusiasm for the cause in which they had been enlisted. On the conclusion of the armistice the legion was officially dissolved, but on Bismarck's instructions it remained in existence, and on August 3 it embarked on the invasion of Hungary. The invasion did not proceed very far. There was not the slightest sign of a popular insurrection against the Austrian rule, and on August 6 the legion of Klapka hastily recrossed the Hungarian frontier without having fired a shot. It was kept together by the Prussians until there was no longer any danger that a war with France would provoke

a fresh Austrian attack. The Hungarian legion was one of
Bismarck's most unscrupulous weapons, for it is a fundamental rule of war that the soldier's oath of fidelity should
be respected by the enemy. But besides being unscrupulous
it was a complete failure.

The complications with Russia were solved more easily
than had at first been expected. General Manteuffel was
sent to St. Petersburg at the beginning of August and succeeded in appeasing the Tsar without great difficulty, especially as Alexander had never forgotten the help he received
from Prussia during the Polish revolt of 1863. The reconciliation was complete when William spared the Tsar's
relatives in Hesse-Darmstadt and allowed the Grand Duke
to keep Upper Hesse.

Finally Napoleon presented himself for his reward, just
as he had done with Italy in 1859. But Prussia was not
Italy. The Prussian people were exalted by their victory
and at this very moment the quarrel between King and
Parliament was brought to an end. Against the advice of
the Conservative ministers the King agreed to Bismarck's
proposal for a compromise, and on August 5 he announced
from the throne that he recognised that the military expenditure since 1863 needed the retrospective approval of
Parliament. The same day Benedetti presented the French
demand for the surrender to France of Mainz, the Bavarian
Palatinate, Saarlouis, and Saarbrücken. But Bismarck no
longer needed to treat the French gently, and a few days
later he answered uncompromisingly: "If you insist on
these demands, we shall employ every weapon, make no
mistake about it; we shall appeal to the whole German
nation, and we shall immediately make peace at any price
with Austria, abandon South Germany to her, and even
agree to the resurrection of the Diet. We shall cross the
Rhine with an united army of 800,000 men and take Alsace
from you; our armies are mobilised, yours is not, and you
may draw your own conclusions." The French Government

was rudely awakened from its dream: Benedetti, summoned to Paris, confirmed Bismarck's determination to make good his words, and Colonel von Loë brought a message from the King that he would go to war rather than surrender a single German village.[1]

Meanwhile Moltke had prepared his plan of campaign. Four army corps, about 120,000 men, were to remain near Prague in order to contain the Austrians; by the beginning of September 200,000 troops could be concentrated between the Neckar and the Main for the campaign against France and Moltke counted confidently on the support of 80,000 South German troops in this national war. But this was only a beginning: the organisation of reserve corps had already been started during the war and was now hastily completed. In a few weeks there was a reserve of no less than 30,000 men, half of them soldiers who had served their time, half of them new recruits. Moltke wrote to a friend on August 19: "Napoleon could not have chosen a worse moment for a war than when we had 640,000 men under arms. We should have had South Germany on our side and, if the worst came to the worst, we could fight both Austria and France at once. That would have produced not merely a united North Germany, it would have produced Great Germany." The King had at first doubted the military value of the reserve corps, but when he saw them parading fully equipped he said to Roon, "They tempt me to start a new war straight away".

Bismarck carefully inspired the new recruits with patriotic indignation against Napoleon and allowed the story of the French claims to leak out in the Paris *Siècle*.[2] All disputes within Germany were silenced and the various peoples of Germany, who had just been at war with one another, united in face of the common enemy. Bismarck used the

[1] Loë in the *Deutsche Revue*, xi. 166 and 267.
[2] Rothan, 358, says Bismarck used Vilbort for this skilful manœuvre. Vilbort himself is silent about it in his book, *L'Œuvre de M. de Bismarck*.

opportunity to conclude treaties with Württemberg, Baden, and finally Bavaria (August 13 to 21), under which the King of Prussia was to be Commander-in-Chief of the Germans in time of war. These treaties were secret, but the feeling of Germany was obvious and Napoleon beat a hasty retreat. On August 11 he told Goltz that this undesirable diplomatic conflict had been caused by Drouyn de Lhuys without his knowledge and rested on a misunderstanding, and he repeated this explanation in a letter to La Valette on the following day. Drouyn de Lhuys, finding himself deserted, was compelled to offer his resignation, which was coolly accepted by Napoleon.

Napoleon's friends assert that he was genuinely innocent of causing the conflict with the new Germany—genuinely the victim of a minister of the old school; and that he really only desired to establish an unselfish friendship between France and Germany. According to them, the Emperor was lying ill at Vichy and in great pain when Drouyn extracted permission from him to demand part of the Rhineland from Bismarck. Napoleon was glad enough to throw the responsibility for the disgrace of 1866 on his Ministers of War and Foreign Affairs. But Drouyn de Lhuys was not prepared to be treated as a scapegoat. He defended himself in a letter to Napoleon on October 12, 1867; coldly, almost insolently, he reminded the Emperor that he himself had read, altered, and amplified the instructions to Benedetti to demand a cession of territory by Prussia. "That is the truth", he concluded, "and it would be regrettable if it was concealed by commentaries, which ascribe both to Your Majesty and to me rôles unworthy of us." Since Napoleon made no attempt at denial, it is established beyond all contradiction that he had approved of Drouyn's proposal. His mistake lay in letting the month of July slip by before he accepted Drouyn's advice, while Drouyn carried out a policy of which he disapproved, because he hoped Napoleon would change his mind. When Drouyn finally got his way, he miscalcu-

lated the possibilities and chose the wrong moment, to be
dismissed at once when, as Napoleon had feared, he failed.
Drouyn de Lhuys said to the Prussian Minister at this time,
"I have seen three dynasties come and go; I recognise the
symptoms of the approaching fall and I am withdrawing.
You will understand me!"

In the spring of 1866 Napoleon told his favourite Nigra
that he hoped to become arbitrator of Germany by a war
between the German powers. With this object he had helped
to create the alliance between Italy and Prussia, without
which William I could not have risked a war against
Austria and the German princes. But the rapid victories of
the Prussians, and his own weakness, robbed Napoleon of
success. Ever since 1859 Napoleon had lacked the energy
needed to control the course of events. But even now he
could not abandon his plans altogether and on the evening
of August 12, the very day of Drouyn's fall, a secret agent,
a Dane named Hansen, was sent to Berlin to propose that
Prussia should annex the whole of Saxony and that King
John should be compensated on the left bank of the Rhine.
Hansen saw Keudell, Bismarck's secretary; but as he had
no official powers, he was not admitted to the minister.[1]

This, of course, was the very plan that Napoleon had
nursed before the war. The Treaty of June 12 between
Austria and France contained the clause that, in the event
of an Austrian victory, the left bank of the Rhine should
be organised as an independent state. In this way Napoleon
hoped to spare German national feeling, but at the same
time to extend French influence to the Rhine by means of
a buffer state. This was Napoleon's secret plan, and it failed
as completely as that other secret plan of Benedek and
Krismanič.

The final peace between Austria and Prussia was signed
at Prague on August 23 and ratified on August 30. Prussia

[1] Hansen, *Les Coulisses de la diplomatie*, 108.

gained 1300 square miles of territory with 3,170,632 inhabitants; but this was almost trifling compared to the
supremacy over North Germany, soon to be further extended to the South. Prussia's losses were out of all proportion to her gains: she lost in battle 3473 killed, 12,675
wounded, and 495 missing. The Austrian losses were much
greater—she lost in the Prussian war 10,404 killed and
30,300 wounded, and the 6200 missing must be added to the
killed. The cost of the war for Prussia amounted in all to
95 million thalers; but from this must be subtracted the
60 millions received as indemnity from Austria and her
allies, and the 15 millions renounced by Austria which were
due to her from Schleswig-Holstein. It is not so easy to
determine what the war cost Austria. The extraordinary
credits from April 11 to August 1 amounted to 164·5
million guelders, but this figure is not final, because the
army remained mobilised after August 1. There was furthermore the 30 million guelders indemnity, and 21 million
guelders paid to Austrian citizens as compensation for the
contributions levied by the Prussians. Against this must be
set off the 35 millions received from Italy as the Venetian
share of the Austrian national debt.

Peace was concluded between Austria and Italy at
Vienna on October 3, 1866, and ratified on October 12. The
handing over of the fortresses, which were still occupied by
Austrian troops, occasioned considerable difficulties. On the
wish of Napoleon the population voted whether it wanted
to belong to Italy: 671,757 voted in favour, 69 against, and
366 votes were invalid. Austria voluntarily restored the
iron crown of Lombardy, which had been brought to Vienna
in 1859.

Napoleon alone was not pacified. Driven on by the excitement of French public opinion, he now directed his ambition
towards the annexation of Belgium. On August 20 Benedetti produced to Bismarck the draft of a defensive and
offensive alliance, by which the one ally should receive

Belgium and the other South Germany. It was one of Bismarck's greatest strokes of genius to keep the French Cabinet in suspense—"to handle it dilatorily" as he himself said—and then to publish the draft treaty in Benedetti's handwriting on the outbreak of the War of 1870. The luck- less Benedetti, unable to deny his own hand, attempted to depict the course of events in a different light. He said that Bismarck had dictated the draft to him, but he was silenced by the publication of Rouher's secret papers, which the Prussians found at his country seat of Cercey in 1870. Bismarck had certainly played the tempter, but he had never intended to agree to the French demands. At the most he would have kept quiet if Napoleon had un- expectedly attacked Belgium, and this was what he offered in conversation with Benedetti on January 10, 1867. Bis- marck himself held that Napoleon had committed a great mistake in not occupying Belgium as a pledge during the war in Bohemia. Such a diversion of French ambition might have prevented the War of 1870; but Napoleon reached out towards his prize too late.

But these events go beyond the scope of this book. Napoleon himself was not anxious for a war: his far-sighted views and his knowledge of Germany told him that it would be better to establish a lasting friendship with Germany. As soon as the policy of aggression had failed, he set himself to prove that in fact everything had happened exactly as he had wished. His self-justification was contained in a circular despatch issued by La Valette on September 16, 1866. Napoleon declared that the former German Confedera- tion, which together with Austria had a population of 80 millions, was a far stronger barrier to France than the new Germany, split up into three. In any case a more powerful Germany was unavoidable. Napoleon pointed to the in- creasing strength of Russia and the United States and emphasised that it was a natural development for the divided peoples of Europe to draw together and form strong natural communities. The Emperor did not believe that a nation's strength rested on the weakness of its neighbours; he sought a real balance of power which should satisfy the wishes of the peoples of Europe.

These words breathed a pacific spirit, but they cannot conceal the fact that Napoleon had pursued quite other aims in the spring of 1866. Already the end of his empire was in sight. Disraeli, formerly one of his warmest admirers, said in August 1866, "Napoleon is finished. He cannot wage a war against Prussia at all; quite apart from his illness, which exercises the most disadvantageous influence on his mental ability, he is so seriously threatened at home that we shall soon experience the end of the tragi-comedy of the second Empire."

CHAPTER XVIII

THE verdict of history had been delivered and Austria had been defeated in the struggle with Prussia for supremacy in Germany. Austria had had to pay for the suppression of all independence of thought ever since the Counter-Reformation. The system of Metternich and Francis had sapped the will and energy of the people and had produced a pleasure-loving generation which shrank from any great effort. By the time of the Revolution of 1848 all energy had departed even from the very system of government. But there was a healthy tendency in the opposite direction, which prevented the empire ever sinking as low as Spain. Prince Eugene, the friend of Leibnitz and the enemy of the Jesuits, Joseph II, and his nephew the Archduke Charles, all took the lead in this struggle against the forces of tradition, which only too often led to martyrdom.

The leading men of 1866 had all grown up in the ideas of Metternich and the Restoration. They disputed the right of the peoples to control their own destinies; they under-estimated the forces of nationality; they regarded treaties and legitimate rights not only as the sources of positive law, but even as the bases of historic development. They supported the system of the Holy Alliance and so committed themselves to a sinking cause. Esterhazy was the leading advocate of this system; Belcredi provided the name of Prime Minister and Biegeleben the pen and the technical

302

knowledge; and Mensdorff, more far-sighted than his colleagues, carried out a policy of which he disapproved.
Bismarck, too, had grown up in these ideas, but he had
long abandoned them. He exploited the prejudices of
the Austrian politicians to conclude the alliance against
Denmark; but as soon as Schleswig-Holstein had been
conquered he took up a new line and so offended the
Austrian Cabinet by his disregard of their interests, and
still more of their sentiments, that Austria appealed to
the sword.

This impatience is one of the most important factors in
Austrian policy, both at home and abroad, between 1850
and 1871, between the death of Felix Schwarzenberg and
the appointment of Andrassy as Foreign Minister. Systems
of policy were repeatedly changed and Austria was ready to
go to war at the least challenge to her rights. It needed a
series of bitter experiences and the growing insight of the
Emperor to bring the foreign policy of the empire into a
quieter and more consistent course.

The decision to accept the Prussian challenge and provoke
a war in Germany and Italy was largely due to the evil
influence of Belcredi and Biegeleben, for whom even Esterhazy was too moderate. It was they who prevented the
compromise with Prussia, which Rechberg and even Mensdorff had desired. To avoid a war on two fronts, Austria
could have agreed to share her power in Germany, and so
kept Venice; or she could have established her superiority
over Prussia by renouncing her southern province. The
first alternative was rejected, and the second adopted after
Italy had committed herself to Prussia. The strength of
clerical influence was shown in almost the last act of the
old system, when Austria placed the interests of the Church
higher than the considerations of state policy. By the
Treaty of June 12 Austria surrendered Venice in the hope
of recovering the lost provinces for the Papacy. No wonder
that Cardinal Antonelli, the papal Secretary of State, ex-

claimed on the news of the battle of Königgrätz, "Il mondo casca"—"The world is falling".

The defeat of 1866 put an end to the activities of the men of the old system. But their fall was soft, for they mostly belonged to the old ruling families, and the survivors or their heirs returned to power, when Taaffe became Prime Minister. But someone had to be made responsible for the disaster and this heavy burden was thrown on Benedek. It was with the greatest reluctance that Benedek had accepted the command of the army in Bohemia and then only on condition that he should be responsible to no one but the Emperor. Immediately after handing over the command to the Archduke Albrecht, Benedek was summoned before a Commission of Enquiry, which pronounced that he should be brought before a court-martial, though the prosecution was stopped by order of the Emperor on December 1, 1866.

Benedek accepted this hard fate, because he still hoped to give an account to the Emperor of all that had happened. But it was decided otherwise; Benedek received from his Emperor no word of comfort such as Philip II gave Medina-Sidonia after the defeat of the Armada. Instead the Archduke Albrecht was sent to visit him at Graz, to point out to him how much it would damage the empire and the army if he published a defence of his conduct, which was bound to throw the blame on others. What had taken place between the Commander-in-Chief and the Emperor, and with the other generals, ought to be buried in oblivion for ever. And Benedek performed this last, and hardest, service to his Emperor. He promised the Archduke never to publish a defence of his actions, and a written confirmation of his promise was lodged in the secret archives of the Ministry of War.

Immediately after Benedek had given his word, the official *Wiener Zeitung* published an article on December 8, in which all the blame was laid on Benedek. Generals

Krismanič and Henikstein were lightly dismissed: they had
not come up to expectations, and had indeed displayed
"a lack of adaptability" during the campaign, but they had
"done their best according to their lights"; the Commander-
in-Chief was alone responsible since his were the final decisions. "There is no code of law", it continued, "which makes
the lack of the highest ability a criminal offence. . . . But
for an honourable and proud man like Benedek the loss of
the confidence of his Imperial master, the ruin of his military
reputation in the eyes of contemporaries and of posterity,
the realisation of the immeasurable disaster suffered under
his leadership by the army, and in consequence by the
whole Monarchy, must be a severer punishment than any
sentence which a court-martial might have passed on him."

Thus Benedek alone was made responsible for the defeat;
it was his fault that the army was not so successful in
Bohemia as at Custoza. Nothing could be further from the
truth. Benedek might not possess the ability to command a
great army; he lacked a proper military training and did
not know the Bohemian theatre of war. But he himself had
advanced all these objections to the Emperor before his
appointment, and the emperor had answered them by ap-
pointing Krismanič as Benedek's assistant. Krismanič at
least had not lacked self-confidence; he had cheerfully
assumed responsibility for the conduct of the war, and now
he was treated gently. He was even taken back into active
service and appointed commander of the fortress of Peter-
wardein, in which post he died on May 23, 1876. The same
spirit inspires the official Austrian history of the war: it is
almost always accurate in its details, but it is based on the
general principle that the Commander-in-Chief would have
got all the glory and he alone must bear the blame.

Benedek kept his word and suffered his fate in silence.
He was often tempted to defend himself, but his military
honour stood in the way, and before his death he burnt all
his papers relating to the War of 1866. Even the Emperor

felt the greatness of Benedek's last service to the empire and attempted to give a sign of his sympathy through his son, the Crown Prince Rudolph. In 1873 the Crown Prince visited Graz and wrote to Benedek that his Imperial father had instructed him to enquire after his health. When Benedek received the letter, he exclaimed sadly, "It is too late!" Then his pride revolted and he added, "And it is too little!" He did not request an audience of the Prince, but sent a letter with his humble thanks and with the message that he desired nothing except rest. Only at the last did Benedek reveal his bitterness: in his will he, a soldier body and soul, ordered that he should be buried in civilian clothes. Benedek never forgave the Archduke Albrecht for his harshness, but the Archduke believed that he had acted in the true interests of the dynasty in avoiding the exposures which would have followed a public discussion of the defeat, such as were produced by the trial of Bazaine in France or of Persano in Italy. The Archduke wrote in 1869 in obvious reference to Benedek: "Is it not nobler and more useful for the state, when a defeated general accepts full responsibility and bears his hard fate in silence? Does he not deserve the grateful acknowledgment of all thoughtful men? Must not every true soldier and every chivalrous man count it to him for honour and repay him with their sympathy?" The Archduke Charles had behaved in exactly the same way, when he never referred to the fact that the Wars of 1805 and 1809 had been undertaken against his express advice, and never let fall a word of complaint against the Emperor Francis.

It is understandable that the War of 1866 left a feeling of bitterness in Austria and a desire for revenge. It seemed inconceivable that the long line of German Emperors of the House of Habsburg was at an end for ever; and the alliance against Denmark, which Francis Joseph had entered without any secret intentions, appeared as a carefully laid trap for Austria. Some of the Prussian actions, such as the organisation of Klapka's legion and the attempt to seduce the Hungarian soldiers from their loyalty, deserved the indignation of the Austrian Court, and this indignation increased when Prussia kept the Hungarian legion in being for a month after the conclusion of peace. The Archdukes expressed this feeling strongly by resigning all their honorary commands in the Prussian army, and the seven Austrian regiments, which were named after the King of Prussia or any of his subordinates, were ordered to give up their titles. But this did not last long—the names of the former commanders reappeared in the official army-list of the following year.

Austria did not at first abandon her claims in Germany and undoubtedly the main reason for the appointment of Beust to the supreme direction of Austrian policy was the expectation that he would be able to organise a powerful opposition to Prussia in Germany. Beust was the only man who could revive the Austrian connections with the German princes, especially of the South. Nor were the democratic forces forgotten, as was shown by the all-German shooting contest in Vienna in 1868, the last great demonstration of the Great-German party. The Austrian Government determined also to appeal to its own peoples, especially the Germans and the Magyars, for the war of revenge against Prussia. This was the reason for the most far-reaching event in the domestic policy of Francis Joseph—the Austrian provinces were granted the Constitution of December 21, 1867, and Hungary received a measure of self-government such as it had never enjoyed since the Imperial armies freed the land from the Turk.

Shortly before this Francis Joseph and Napoleon had met at Salzburg and one of the things on which they had agreed was the necessity of introducing liberal institutions in Austria in order to satisfy public opinion in Europe. In the negotiations for an alliance which followed, Austria demanded the inclusion of Italy, in order to secure the southern frontier of the Monarchy, and the French were urged to win over Italy by withdrawing their troops from Rome and handing over the capital to Victor Emmanuel. In April 1870 the Archduke Albrecht visited Paris to discuss the joint plan of campaign with Napoleon; in June General Lebrun, one of Napoleon's adjutants, arrived in Vienna, and the Archduke developed to him his strategical plans for the co-operation of the armies of Austria-Hungary, France, and Italy against Germany, but not before the spring of 1871. During this visit Francis Joseph said to Lebrun: [1] "I desire peace above everything. I shall wage war only if I am compelled to. If I declared war at the same time as the Emperor Napoleon, Prussia could undoubtedly exploit the new German idea and provoke the peoples of Germany to revolt—not only her own peoples and those of South Germany but the Germans of Austria-Hungary as well—and that would be pretty serious for my Government. Nevertheless if the Emperor Napoleon was compelled to accept or declare war and appeared with his army in South Germany, not as an enemy, but as a liberator, I on my side should be compelled to declare that I would make common cause with him." A minute sent by the Archduke Albrecht to Napoleon also emphasised that for political and military reasons Austria must insist on France attacking first.

Unfortunately for France, but fortunately for Germany, Napoleon allowed himself to be persuaded by his ministers, his wife, and his people, to declare war before the alliance with Austria-Hungary and Italy had been concluded. Beust had already realised that the bribe of a liberal government would not induce the German Austrians to favour a war

[1] Lebrun gives an account of these negotiations in his book, *Souvenirs militaires* (Paris, 1895), 146. Cf. also the conversation of the Archduke Albrecht with Hansen in 1875 in Hansen, *Les Coulisses de la diplomatie*, 311. There is a full account of the negotiations in W. Busch, *Die Beziehungen Frankreichs zu Österreich und Italien zwischen 1866 und 1870* (Tübingen 1900).

against Germany and, probably for that reason, he turned against the German bourgeois Ministry and secured its dismissal. At the critical moment the Hungarians also refused their assistance; in the Crown Council, which was to determine the attitude of Austria to the war which had just broken out, Andrassy carried a policy of neutrality; for, unlike Beust, he expected the Germans to win, and as a Hungarian he looked with disfavour on any revival of Austrian power in Germany. The great majority of the German Austrians greeted the German victories of 1870 with enthusiasm; the most embittered Austrian patriots were silenced after the battles of Wörth and Metz, and the Emperor wisely determined that the cry of revenge should never be revived.

The freedom from prejudice with which Francis Joseph concluded the alliance with Prussia and Italy, with the very powers who had robbed him of his dynastic inheritance, is without a parallel in history. He broke further with the traditions of the old Austria by terminating the Concordat with the Pope and establishing liberal institutions in both Austria and Hungary. The rising generation may have already forgotten what progress the empire owes to these changes; but their elders still remember with what contempt Austrian learning and education was regarded by cultured Europe. The army benefited most of all from this revival of intellectual activities. Benedek, Krismanič, and Henikstein were, for good or ill, the products of the old system, and that system was for ever destroyed on the field of Königgrätz. Equally beneficial was the effect of the change on the Austrian finances. Those who experienced the three national bankruptcies of 1811, 1815, and 1867, never dreamt that the budget would be completely balanced scarcely a generation later. This was partly due to the changed position of Austria in Germany and Italy. She had no longer to defend the Rhine against France, guard her northern frontier against a jealous neighbour, and at the same time keep an army ready in Italy. The compromise with Hungary, although disadvantageous to Austria in its financial provisions, greatly strengthened her foreign policy; for the proud and patriotic Hungarians, who had served the empire unwillingly in 1859 and 1866, now became the chief supporters of its position as a great power. The division of forces, which had previously crippled the empire, was replaced by a concentration of policy directed towards the east, and as a result the empire was not really weakened by the defeats of 1859 and 1866.

But someone had to pay the price and the real sufferers by the defeat of 1866 were the Germans of Austria; they lost their political centre of gravity and have never recovered it.[1] Once their gaze, when they wished to comprehend the policy of the empire, was limited only by the far horizon of Frankfort, Milan, Constantinople, and Buda-Pest, the loss of their predominance in Germany, Italy, and Hungary confined their interests to petty questions of domestic policy, and the Government confidently assumed that their power was broken. But when Badeni acted as if the rights of the Germans had been already partitioned among the other races of the Monarchy, the German Austrians forcibly reminded the Government that they were in a different position from the Slavs and Magyars, who must of necessity regard Austria as their home. The Germans, as partners in a great national culture, have another alternative open to them, as soon as they cease to be attached to Austria by their free choice and by the loyalty they have manifested for hundreds of years. Nothing could have been more foolish than to provoke such a train of thought in a people which has no desire to probe anew into the founda-

---

[1] [These last paragraphs were written in 1897 and they contain Friedjung's own political programme. He has recounted the exclusion of the German Austrians from Germany; now, at the conclusion, he alludes to his own faith that the German Austrians could be reunited to Germany without losing their place in the Austrian Empire.—Translator.]

tions of its political and national existence, but is anxious only to live and die in its hereditary connection with the dynasty and the Monarchy.

Taaffe had already set out to increase the power of the Crown by encouraging the divisions among the German Austrians and the conflict between the nationalities, and for years this policy seemed to be successful; but it was destroyed by the mobs which swept through the streets of Vienna, Prague, and Graz, immediately before and after the fall of Badeni. It was made manifest that a policy which endangered the internal peace of the empire would in the end shake the very foundations of monarchical authority.

Austria-Hungary is, however, an empire whose destiny will always be determined by its foreign policy; and this depends primarily on relations with Germany, relations which can hardly be finally settled by the alliance of 1879: history points to a closer connection between the two countries and Bismarck himself said that the exclusion of Austria from Germany would only be the prelude to a closer union of the German race. Bismarck engineered the War of 1866 because he wanted to deprive the old Imperial House of the Imperial throne, but he sternly rejected the suggestion of seizing any part of the Austrian Empire. Like the chief of the conspirators in *Julius Cæsar*, Bismarck could refuse "to cut the head off and then hack the limbs".

In July 1866, immediately after the battle of Königgrätz, Bismarck considered whether he should not offer Austria peace on the basis of the creation of a German Confederation, comprehending the Northern Federation, Austria, and the southern states.[1] Circumstances were unfavourable to such an ambitious plan and Bismarck decided to content himself with uniting North Germany. But the idea was always present in his mind and in 1879 he proposed to Andrassy that the alliance should be made a fundamental

[1] Sybel, v. 253.

law by submitting it to the parliaments of the two countries and incorporating it in their Constitutions.[1] What he proposed was "a constitutional alliance against a coalition" which "should be brought into existence by the co-operation of all the constitutional elements, and be dissoluble only by the same co-operation, that is, with the consent of the Emperor, the Federal Council, and the Parliament in Germany, and of the Monarch and the two representative assemblies in Austria". An alliance so guaranteed would have been the logical conclusion of the movement for German unification, but the leading statesmen of Austria-Hungary were not yet ready for a revival of the old national connection, and the idea will still need many years to mature. Bismarck gave one last glimpse of his hopes for the German people in the first speech from the throne which he drafted for William II and which was delivered on June 25, 1888: "I am loyal to the alliance with Austria with German fidelity, not merely because it is in existence, but because I regard this defensive alliance as a pillar of the European balance of power and, what is more, as a legacy of German history, welcomed to-day by the public opinion of the entire German race, and in consonance with the traditions of international law, which were of uncontested validity until 1866".

Until 1888 the Prussian statesmen had carefully avoided reviving the memory of the times before 1866, when they spoke of Austria-Hungary. But William II had not fought at Königgrätz like his father and grandfather: he could refer to the old German Confederation without reopening the wounds of 1866.

When the generation of the German civil war has been gathered to its fathers, the day will come for their heirs to realise the legacy of German history.

[1] Busch, *Unser Reichskanzler*, i. 451.

APPENDIX I

(An Interview with the Author)

PRINCE BISMARCK granted the author an interview on June 13, 1890. The conversation turned on the negotiations during the visit of Bismarck and King William to Schönbrunn in the autumn of 1864, and I asked the Prince whether Austria had been at all inclined to céde Schleswig-Holstein to Prussia in return for a guarantee of her Italian possessions. The Prince replied:

"I cannot remember any such Austrian offer; and I do not think, as far as I can rely on my memory, that one was made. But according to my intentions then and later, we could easily have agreed to it; for a firm alliance with Austria was always my aim, and my royal master would gladly have given such a guarantee in order to acquire Schleswig-Holstein and remain friendly and at peace with Austria." [There follows the account quoted on page 58.]

"The Austrian statesmen", I remarked, "seem to have regarded the joint possession of Schleswig-Holstein as more important, for the position of Austria as a great power, than Milan which was already lost and could not be regained."

"I do not wish", the Prince replied, "to criticise, but merely to give an account of what happened. Rechberg was not opposed to such a solution and I had been on good terms with him ever since our time at Frankfort. I always believed that it would be necessary to reach an understanding, an alliance, with Austria, but I only succeeded in this much later, in 1879. I should have liked to have made the alliance a fundamental law. I proposed to Andrassy that it should be confirmed by the Parliaments of the two empires, so that it should not be dependent merely on the Governments. However, I could not achieve everything I wanted and it was difficult enough to get what

I did. I could certainly have arrived at an agreement with Rechberg before the war, and it was therefore very unwelcome to me that he left his post soon after the meeting at Schönbrunn. It was at this time that I advised the King to make a concession to Austria, which Rechberg regarded as necessary to enable him to remain in office. Rechberg wanted Prussia to repeat in the new commercial treaty the earlier clause, which left the way open for Austria to enter the Zollverein. I was at Biarritz, on a visit to Napoleon, and my colleagues managed to persuade my old master to reject the Austrian request. My intention to remain on friendly terms with Austria was thus thwarted."

Here I interrupted that the Prince's despatches from Frankfort clearly showed that he already regarded war as the necessary method of solving the German question.

"In general, certainly," was the answer, "but not all the time, not in the day-to-day incidents of policy. It would be a misinterpretation of the spirit of politics to believe that a statesman can formulate a comprehensive plan and decide what he is going to do in one, two, or three years. Schleswig-Holstein was certainly worth a war but you cannot pursue a plan blindly. You can only give a general indication of your aim—the statesman is like a man wandering in a forest who knows his general direction, but not the exact point at which he will emerge from the wood. It was difficult to avoid a war with Austria, but he who is responsible for the lives of millions will shrink from war until all other means have been exhausted. It has always been a weakness of the Germans to want all or nothing, but I was satisfied with any step which brought us nearer to German unification, and I should have welcomed any solution which cleared the way for the aggrandisement of Prussia and the unification of Germany without a war.

"This idea also lay behind the mission of Gablenz to Vienna in May 1866. [There follows the account printed on page 171.] The Emperor of Austria was not unwilling to accept the proposal; but Franck, the Minister of War, declared that it was impossible to make peace without firing a shot after the considerable armaments of the previous months, lest the Austrian army be accused of cowardice. Larisch, the Finance Minister, was even more opposed to it. He declared that the Austrian finances made a war absolutely essential, either to get a large indemnity from Prussia in case of victory, or to provide an honourable excuse for bankruptcy in case of defeat.

"Perhaps it was better that the affair should be settled by the sword, for the clock of German dualism has to be put right by a war once every hundred years. This dualism is older than the conflict between Austria and Prussia: first there was the conflict between the Franks and the Saxons, then between the Hohenstaufen and the Guelfs. It broke out again at the Reformation: Maurice of Saxony revolted against Charles V primarily to abolish the supremacy of the Emperor and the empire, which was what he meant by 'the freedom of Germany'. Or do you think he referred to the pitiful condition of the German peasants when he spoke of the 'beastly servitude' under which Germany was suffering? Certainly not—he meant only the obedience exacted from the princes by the Emperor. Similarly there has been the conflict between Austria and Prussia since the Silesian wars; and now it reappears in the opposition of the individual to the State. It is curious that the struggle always takes place in the middle of the century and the settlement always occurs at the turn of the century. I am not so superstitious as to see anything predestined in this: it lies obviously in the nature of the conflicting forces, which reach a point of rest roughly once in a century.

"After the battle of Königgrätz Austria made an attempt to renew the struggle with the assistance of Napoleon. The position was not without danger to us. Napoleon could indeed send only 40,000 to 60,000 men to the frontier at first, but he could have created a serious embarrassment in our rear with the help of the South German troops. It is difficult to say what would have happened if we had been defeated and if Austria had re-established her supremacy in Germany. For if we had not been completely crushed, Austria would soon have had to try to maintain her position against an alliance of Prussia, France, and Russia, and it is unlikely that she would have succeeded. However, these are speculative questions and lead us too far. The sword decided between us—but a really satisfactory position was established in Central Europe when Austria accepted our alliance. I am really and honestly satisfied with the way things have gone—it is a solution for a long time."

"Would not an alliance founded in constitutional law be desirable, such as Your Highness aimed at in 1879?"

"These are questions of future policy and I do not wish to speak of them. In Berlin they are afraid that I want to influence affairs of state, but that is not my intention. I have done enough, and now I can grant myself the ease of a country gentleman. Recently I was reading Schiller's *Robbers* and I came to the moving passage where Francis thrusts the old Moor back into the grave with the words: 'What? Do you want to live for ever?' And there stood my own destiny before my eyes."

The effect of these words was indescribable. After a short pause the Prince continued: "You must not think that I am upset by the events of the last years. I am, if you like, too proud to be affected by anything that happens after all that I have achieved. Anyone who has experienced and done so much has the right now to enjoy his rest."

APPENDIX II

COUNT RECHBERG gave me the following information in a series of long conversations:

"Buol, my predecessor, retired in 1859, not because he was opposed to the war, but because he disapproved of the moment at which it was begun, and particularly because he was not told of the declaration of war. The order to Gyulai to invade Piedmont was sent direct from the Emperor's military chancery without informing Buol and he thereupon resigned.

"My policy was always directed to freeing Austria from the isolation in which Buol had left her. I would have been glad to get on better terms with Russia, but Gortchakoff was, as I saw, a mortal enemy of Austria, and any attempt at reconciliation would have ended in failure. Napoleon III was highly unreliable and always aimed at weakening Austria in Italy. There was a pro-French party in the Foreign Office in Vienna, and Meysenbug always asserted that Napoleon would not allow Italy to attack Austria. I regarded this as folly and pointed out that Napoleon would never rest until he had fulfilled the promise he had made as a young man to the Carbonari and later to Cavour and got Venice for the Italians. I knew this through a peculiar circumstance. Palmerston had been formerly close friends with Napoleon, but the annexation of Savoy and Nice had made him distrustful, and he now sought a connection with Austria. He sent letters to me through the international spy, Klindworth, and informed me that he had bought letters from Napoleon's private correspondence for a great sum—it was said to be £100,000—which confirmed my belief that Napoleon was aiming at detaching Venice from us.

"Relations with Gramont, the French Ambassador, were very

unpleasant, as he had no respect for truth and was completely unreliable. He reported to Paris only what suited him, and his reports, which Napoleon read to Metternich, often contained the exact opposite of what I had said. In 1863, at the time of the Polish revolt, he proposed to me that Austria should give up Galicia as the nucleus of an independent Poland and surrender Venice to Italy, in return for which she should be compensated with the Danubian Principalities. That would have led to war with Russia, and I replied to him that it was odd to encourage Austria to wage war, in order to lose a province, as usually wars were fought to gain a province.

"My relations with Schmerling were very unsatisfactory. He had been jealous of me ever since 1849. When the King of Prussia was elected German Emperor at Frankfort, Schwarzenberg sent for me and said that he was very dissatisfied with Schmerling, and sent me to Frankfort, where I managed to secure the defeat of the Prussian party. Schmerling never forgave me for this.

"I could never reach a real agreement with Esterhazy, as I did not share his views on the Hungarian question. One evening he came to me and said that he knew I was not opposed to a compromise with Hungary; he then asked whether I would agree to the incorporation of Transylvania in Hungary as the Magyars wished. I replied that no Austrian Cabinet had ever abandoned Transylvania even at the time of greatest disaster. Maria Theresa had not done it, and it could not be done now. Ever after Esterhazy regarded me as the enemy of his policy. Esterhazy could be very charming when he liked, especially with women. But he was often odd in his manner, sulky, and even what the French call *maniaque*. Finally, when he took to beating his wife and set his castle on fire, he had to be sent to a lunatic asylum.

"In the Schleswig-Holstein question I kept to the firm ground of treaties; even for reasons of our own domestic policy, I could not allow that the principle of nationality alone should decide. I regarded the Prussian alliance as the best for Austria. It is true that we did not make a sufficiently definite agreement as to what was to happen to the Duchies after the war, but things happened more quickly than I wanted. At the end of the war we took the Duchies from Denmark and I wanted Schleswig to go to Prussia and Holstein to Austria, in the hope of getting a guarantee for Venice in exchange for Holstein later on. Biegeleben was of a different opinion and agreed to the surrender of Schleswig-Holstein jointly to Austria and Prussia, because otherwise, he said, 'we should have no point of conflict with Prussia'.

"My general aim was to maintain friendly relations with Prussia, because I did not believe that Austria was strong enough to wage war. This was what was in my mind during the negotiations with Bismarck at Vienna in the summer of 1864. I said to him one evening that Austria and Prussia ought to remain friendly, for then not a shot could be fired in Europe without their permission. 'I agree,' Bismarck said, 'but our domestic situation is inevitably driving us towards war abroad.' 'Napoleon', I replied, 'is in the same position and as far as I can see he will not be able to keep the opposition quiet for long without a successful war. Then there will be war in Europe and we can beat France.' Bismarck agreed to my suggestion that we should reach an agreement for the event of a French attack. It was midnight; I hurried over to Biegeleben and instructed him to draw up a draft treaty on these lines. Biegeleben, however, refused, so I drew up the treaty myself and it was approved by the two sovereigns the next day.

"Meanwhile my position in the Ministry was becoming increasingly precarious, and one day Esterhazy said to me, 'The Emperor wishes you to do him the service of resigning.' I had also made enemies at Court by strongly opposing the acceptance of the throne of Mexico by the Archduke Maximilian. My resignation took place as follows: I was invited to a Council of Ministers and was astonished to find Biegeleben there. He produced a draft note attacking Prussia, which I opposed, but I was outvoted and had to resign. I added a declaration to the minutes that the return to a policy of opposing Prussia would lead to war and that I must give a warning against such foolhardiness.

"When I resigned the Emperor asked me whether I could recommend Esterhazy as my successor. I told the Emperor that Esterhazy did not possess enough energy for the position and recommended Mensdorff, of whom Radetzky had said that he was one of the few who could replace him. Mensdorff was strongly opposed to a war with Prussia and said to me that the Prussian army was underrated and that it was better than was generally supposed.

"When I resigned, an important personage came to me and tried to persuade me to recommend Beust as my successor. I suspect that Biegeleben was behind this, but I regarded this choice as a bad one. Beust had hoped to be Buol's successor. When I was appointed in

1859, old Prince Metternich said to me: 'I am glad you have been appointed—not because of yourself, for I am indifferent who occupies the Ballhausplatz. But it would be a disaster if Beust, that political tight-rope dancer, ever became minister in Austria.' Beust was finally recommended in Austria by the Crown Prince of Saxony. He denies this in his memoirs, but it is true.

"I believed that it was possible, if not to avoid a war with Prussia, at any rate to postpone it until Austria was stronger at home. The Austrian Cabinet had the means of neutralising Bismarck's efforts towards war. The Crown Prince was totally opposed to war, and so was Manteuffel. The best thing Austria could have done was to have surrendered Schleswig-Holstein to Prussia and got a guarantee for Venice in return; that is what I worked for, and I was strongly opposed to those who wanted to cede Venice to Italy in return for pecuniary compensation.

"Belcredi and Biegeleben were in favour of war and they were joined by Esterhazy at the last moment. Esterhazy did not appear at the decisive meeting, but he knew that the other ministers had been persuaded to outvote Mensdorff. It was a monstrous thing for the Austrian Cabinet to agree to cede Venice unconditionally to Napoleon before the war and then let the blood of thousands flow for the defence of Venice. It is very probable that King William would never have been persuaded to go to war if Schleswig-Holstein had been handed over to him. In any case the Austrian statesmen ought to have made up their minds to the loss of either Schleswig-Holstein or Venice; both could not be held. Mensdorff and I agreed that Austria could not wage war simultaneously in the north and in the south."

APPENDIX III

COUNT NIGRA, the Italian Minister in Paris and later Ambassador in Vienna, was kind enough to give me the following information on September 23, 1893.

I asked him whether Napoleon wanted war and whether he had encouraged Prussia. Nigra replied:

"Yes, Napoleon encouraged Prussia. When Italy received the offer of an alliance from Prussia, I was instructed to ask Napoleon for his opinion. I told him that it did not matter to Italy with which of the two powers she allied herself so long as she got Venice. Napoleon said: 'It is advisable for Italy to conclude the treaty with Prussia, for only then will Prussia dare to attack Austria. Only then will the forces be equalised and a balance established, which will give Prussia a prospect of victory. In this way Italy will get Venice and France will enjoy the advantage of a conflict between the two powers, by whose alliance she is held in check. France can throw her sword into the scale during the struggle and will become the arbiter of Europe. If I send 100,000 men to the Rhine I shall be able to dictate my own terms of peace.' This policy was undoubtedly correct from the French point of view, but it needed energy for its execution. Napoleon had been successful as long as he had other men to carry out his ideas—Morny organised the *coup d'état* and Cavour the struggle for Italy; but Napoleon himself was incapable of seizing the right moment. The treaty between Italy and Prussia of April 8, 1866, was brought to Paris before it was sent for signature to Turin. I showed it to Napoleon and he approved of it. He imagined that the forces of the conflicting states were now roughly equal, but there he made a great mistake. The battle of Königgrätz took him completely by surprise; he had assumed that battles would be won and lost, and that he would in the meantime be free to arrange matters as he liked. I do not know whether Drouyn de Lhuys secretly disapproved of this policy; at any rate he carried it out and after Königgrätz demanded that the Emperor should take serious steps for its fulfilment. Napoleon took fright and Drouyn resigned. Napoleon was ill in 1866, but he was still in control of affairs and hardly consulted his ministers.

"When in May 1866 Austria offered to cede Venice to us I asked Napoleon what we should do. Napoleon did not give us any definite advice, he left it to us to decide what to do after the conclusion of the treaty with Prussia. I myself pointed out to him that he had advised us to conclude the treaty with Prussia, but he left the decision whether to accept Venice or not to the Italian Cabinet."

I mentioned La Marmora's assertion that Nigra himself had hesitated whether Italy should not acquire Venice peacefully.

Nigra contradicted this: "Once the treaty with Prussia was concluded it was impossible for Italy to do other than remain faithful to the alliance".

I asked whether Sybel was right in saying that Napoleon was angry with Italy from May on for not withdrawing from the Prussian alliance, because Prussia had not offered him the Rhineland as he had expected; Sybel says that it was Napoleon's wish to separate Italy and Prussia and that he ceased to favour Italy when this did not succeed.

Nigra replied: "I do not know whether Napoleon desired the withdrawal of Italy from the Prussian alliance; but I can definitely say that he never made any such demand to me and therefore that he could not be angry at our not following his advice".

"Is it not, however, remarkable", I asked, "that he concluded a secret treaty with Austria, promising among other things not to prevent the return of the Italian princes if the inhabitants themselves recalled them?"

"I have not seen this treaty and cannot say if the statement is correct. I only know that Napoleon received from Austria the formal promise to cede Venice to Italy whatever happened, and that was favourable enough for Italy. I should not be surprised if the Treaty of June 12 contained such a clause concerning the return of the expelled princes; for it would have been only a development of the Treaty of Zurich, in which Napoleon promised to be strictly neutral concerning the wishes of the people of central Italy. That clause was a blessing for Italy, because it made possible the popular movements and the plebiscites, which produced Italian unification. I did not observe that Napoleon was dissatisfied with Italian policy until after the battle of Königgrätz, when Italy refused to halt before Venice, and continued to advance.

"The battle of Königgrätz was a heavy blow to him. Drouyn de Lhuys advised him to occupy the Rhine provinces with 200,000 men and the Emperor William has himself told me that Prussia had only 6000 men on the Rhine at that moment. But Napoleon shrank from war. He had not got the men that Drouyn demanded and so he let events take their course, as he could not alter them."

I asked what could have induced the Austrian Cabinet to offer Venice to Italy at the last moment. Nigra replied with a smile: "You must ask the Austrian statesmen themselves. I cannot explain their policy; it seems absolutely topsy-turvy to me. If they had made this offer earlier, before we concluded the alliance with Prussia, we should have become their allies. That would have been the wisest policy for Austria. Probably the Austrian Cabinet did not at first know anything about the Prusso-Italian Treaty; when it heard of it, it took fright and wanted a compromise with Italy at any price. But then it was too late."

APPENDIX IV

MOLTKE ON THE WAR OF 1866

(Conversation with the Author on September 22, 1889)

"You wish to know why the Prussian army advanced in three separate armies. There was no other method of assembling our army corps except along the Bohemian-Saxon frontier. Benedek had the interior lines and therefore we had to wage an offensive war. If we had concentrated at one spot, Silesia would have had to be abandoned, and that had to be avoided at all costs."

I remarked that Govone, the Italian plenipotentiary, says that he had expostulated with Moltke before the war and received the answer that it would always be possible to concentrate at Görlitz. The Field-Marshal replied: "That is nonsense; if I said it, it was merely to keep him in the dark concerning our intentions. It would have been impossible to unite our armies at Görlitz. In any case the Italians would have done better not to criticise our operations, but to have waged war better themselves. I advised them to march past the Quadrilateral and compel the Austrians to retreat from the Quadrilateral and fight in the plain. Instead of that they marched into the Quadrilateral and were beaten by the Archduke Albrecht, although they were numerically superior! They did not even manage to detain the Archduke in Italy; he was able to withdraw undisturbed to the north and organise a large army for the defence of the Danube. The war would have had to begin all over again; our position was certainly a favourable one, but in war nothing is certain."

The Field-Marshal strongly opposed the view, current in Austria, that Benedek could have won the battle of Königgrätz if he had used his reserves against Prince Frederick Charles before the arrival of the Crown Prince. "That is certainly an error, for if Benedek had attempted such a counter-attack, an entirely fresh army corps would

324

have been opposed to him and it would have taken him some time to deal with it. Meanwhile the Crown Prince would have attacked his right flank, and probably the defeat of the Austrians would have been all the greater, for the more they advanced against Prince Frederick Charles, the more disastrous must have been the activity of the Crown Prince in their rear."

Concerning his share in the discussions before the war, Moltke said: "I was on the side of Bismarck. For me the principal point was that we must be as strong as possible in the decisive theatre of war; everything else was of secondary importance. This was why I advised sending only a small force to oppose the South German states. What could they have done even after a victory? Marched against Berlin or besieged Cologne or Coblenz? We were also assisted by the disunity among their leaders, but naturally we could not foresee that. We had to risk exposing the Rhine frontier in order to attain our main objective. At first we left a whole army corps on the Rhine, but later a division of it was summoned to Bohemia. We could therefore invade Austria with great force and were actually superior in numbers at the decisive battle."

APPENDIX V

IT has been often mentioned in the course of this work that Krismanič's plans were largely determined by the example of 1778. Like Benedek, Joseph II occupied Dubenetz with his main army, while Laudon resisted Prince Henry of Prussia roughly where the Crown Prince of Saxony and Clam-Gallas attempted to hold Prince Frederick Charles on the Iser, but with more success. Frederick the Great invaded Bohemia through the pass of Nachod on July 5 and advanced towards the Elbe. Joseph II took up a strong position and hoped the King would attack him. He wrote to his mother on July 11: "This morning I was certain we should receive a visit from the King of Prussia. He began to cannonade half an hour after midnight, but after twenty shots, which did no damage, he stopped and has since given no sign of life." It is significant that in 1778 everyone in the Austrian camp was convinced that the Emperor's position would be untenable unless Laudon held Prince Henry at the Iser, just as Benedek's position became untenable when Prince Frederick Charles crossed the Iser. Laudon infuriated Joseph II by criticising the Austrian conduct of the war. In his letter of August 10 he insisted that he could not hold the line of the Iser, but would have to evacuate it at the first attack, and then the Emperor's army too would probably be driven to an inglorious retreat.

Joseph, however, was completely under the sway of Lacy, who, as is well known, was always in favour of this form of war—the defence of long river lines and mountain ranges. Joseph empowered Laudon to act according to his own judgement in case of an attack, but urged him to remain on the Iser. Joseph and Lacy seemed to be justified and Laudon proved wrong, but only because Prince Henry did not dare with his 70,000 men to break through the long line of the Iser, defended only by 50,000 Austrians. Joseph's failure to appreciate

Laudon was a disaster for the Austrian army. Laudon could not have foreseen that Frederick the Great and Prince Henry, having grown old, would be stopped by the Austrian lines. When Joseph established a similar cordon in the Turkish War on Lacy's advice, the Turks broke through this defensive line by collecting a superior force at one point, compelled the scattered Austrian army to retreat, and laid waste the Banat. Laudon had to be summoned, and he reasserted the true rules of war by taking the offensive and storming Belgrade.

Joseph II and Lacy did, however, realise that they would have to leave their position on the Elbe as soon as the line of the Iser was abandoned. Joseph wrote to his mother on August 18: "Prince Henry has not advanced yet, but it looks as if he will march in a few days. Once Laudon is driven back, I am afraid that we shall be compelled to retreat despite our long defence." Two days later he wrote: "This cannot last long, it depends only on the will of Prince Henry; without the slightest risk he can compel us to abandon our position." Then when Laudon sent Prince Liechtenstein to show that he would have to abandon the line of the Iser, Joseph wrote on August 26: "It would undoubtedly be wisest to decide straight-away to retire behind the Elbe, but I hope and believe that I can wait one more day. Perhaps a fantasy of the King's may still bring us a day of success, which will put all our affairs in order." By this fantasy Joseph meant a frontal attack by Frederick the Great on his fortified position. But as is known, both the King and his brother took fright at the risk and left Bohemia without fighting a single battle. The campaign of 1778 therefore ended successfully for the Austrians, and it was this which seems to have dominated Krismanič's ideas when he chose the same position for the Austrian army on June 29, 1866.

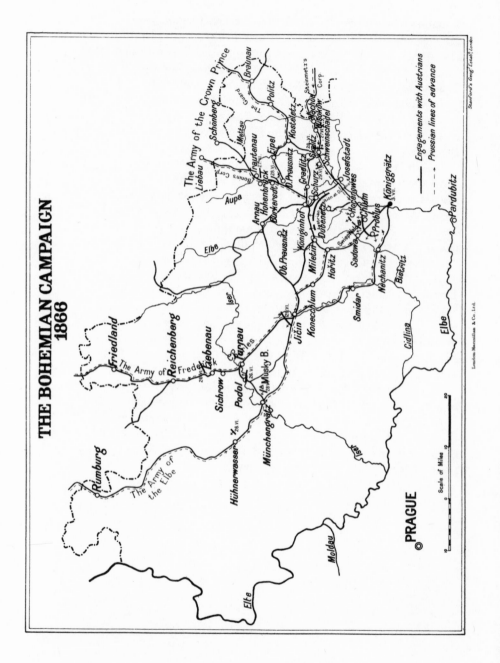

THE BOHEMIAN CAMPAIGN 1866

The Army of the Crown Prince

The Army of Frederick

The Army of the Elbe

PRAGUE

Scale of Miles

Engagements with Austrians
Prussian lines of advance

Stanford's Geog.l Estab.t London

London: Macmillan & Co. Ltd.

INDEX

Adler, Viktor, xiii, xiv, xxii

Aehrenthal, Aloys Lexa von, Count, xxii-xxvii

Albert, Crown Prince of Saxony, 166, 209, 224, 225

Albrecht, Archduke of Austria, 12, 19, 102; commands the south army in the War of 1866, 133 n., 145, 146, 148, 200, 202-204, 229, 237; commands Austrian army on the Danube, 238, 248-250, 259-261, 264, 265, 282, 289-293, 304, 324; and the armistice, 291, 292; and the dismissal of Benedek, 306; visits Paris to discuss a joint plan of campaign with Napoleon, 308

Alexander II, Tsar, 35, 295

Alsace, 172, 295

Alsen, 57

Altona, 190

Andrassy, Count Julius, 162, 163, 255, 262, 309, 311, 313

Ansbach, cession of, 286

Antonelli, Cardinal, 303

Apponyi, Count, 160

Auersperg, Prince Charles, 257

Augustenburg, Duke Christian of, 46

Augustenburg, Duke Frederick of, his claim to Schleswig-Holstein, 47-49, 52, 55-58, 62, 68-76, 93, 94, 188

Austria, the German Austrian problem and the rise of nationalism, x-xxxi, 256, 257, 263, 310, 311; and the leadership of a united Germany, xi, xii, 2-7, 17, 22, 23, 27, 28, 30-36; the language question, xvii, xviii, xxviii, 257; and the destruction of parliamentary government, xvii-xix; anti-liberal policy, xix, xx; why the empire foundered, xxi, xxiv, xxix, xxx; Socialism and Clericalism, and universal suffrage, xxii; Austro-Russian-Prussian alliance, 7; her policy of alliances, 7-10, 13 n., 302; Bismarck's distrust of (1854-57), 10, 11; attempts to force Prussia into war against France (1859), 11, 12; at war with France (1859), 11-21; works for a German national war against France, 18; concludes peace with France, 18, 20; foreign policy (1860-61), 27, 28; plan of reform (1860-63), 27, 28, 34, 35; Rechburg on Austro-Prussian alliance, 28, 29; Bismarck thinks Austrian and Prussian rivalry can only be settled by war, 33, 315; congress of princes at Frankfort to consider a plan of Federal reform (1863), 36-44; proposed enlargement of the Prussian alliance in an anti-French sense, 59-64; proposed commercial treaty with Prussia (1864), 60, 61, 314; exploitation of the state by the aristocracy, 81; Prussia prepares for war against, 85-117, 124-131; Prussian attempts to exclude Austria from Germany, 121, 123, 159, 246, 260, 261, 271; excluded from the German Federation, 283; internal situation and financial outlook (1866), 158-163; plan for the partition of Germany, and a European Congress, 170-175; Austro-French treaty (1866), 180-184, 298; impossibility of absorbing Austria into Germany, 256; foreign policy (1850-71), 302, 303; liberal institutions in, 307, 309; plan for an Austro-Hungarian - French - Italian alliance against Germany, 308; Austro-Prussian-Italian alliance, 309; the destiny of Austria-Hungary, 311; and alliance with Prussia, 312, 313, 315; war with Prussia and Italy—see War of 1866

Bach, Alexander, xvii

Baden, Grand Duke of, 42, 47, 192

Baden, treaty with Prussia, 297

Badeni, Kasimir, Count, xvii-xix, 310, 311

Ricasoli, Baron Bettino, 244
Rodich, Austrian General, 203
Rome, 111
Roon, Albrecht Theodor Emil, Count von, 26, 71, 107, 108, 212, 227
Rosenberg, Austrian general, 196
Rothschild, Baron, 91
Rouher, Eugene, 154, 155, 178, 238 n., 239, 240, 247, 300
Roumania offered in exchange for Venice, 109
Rudolph, Austrian Crown Prince, 306
Russell, Lord John, 20 n.
Russia, Bismarck and, 10, 35; demands a Congress at Paris to settle peace terms in the War of 1866, 280, 281, 294, 295

Saarbrücken, 295
Saar coalfields, 112
Saarlouis, 113, 295
Salzburg Town Council, 263
Sardinia, Austria's ultimatum to (1859), 11, 13 n.
Savigny, Herr von, 124, 193
Saxony, accepts the plan for federation (1849), 2; and the War of 1866, 101, 166, 168, 187, 206, 209, 210, 266; suggested Prussian annexation, 266, 271, 281, 285, 286, 288 n., 289, 298 ; Bismarck refuses to allow her to join the Southern federation, 289; Prussia renounces her claims to annexation, 293 n.
Schleinitz, Prussian Foreign Minister, 17, 20 n., 25, 169
Schleswig-Holstein, Prussia and Austria, and the claims of Denmark to, 46-57; Austria and Prussia expel the Danes, 53, 54; war against Denmark renewed, 57; its surrender to Austria and Prussia, 57; Bismarck aims at annexation, 58, 73; Austria and Prussia fail to agree as to its possession, 58-63, 68-76, 318; proposed treaty giving Schleswig to Prussia and Holstein to Austria, 59, 60 n.; Mensdorff proposes that Prussia takes it in exchange for part of Silesia, 68; Treaty of Gastein, 75; Prussia to govern Schleswig and Austria Holstein, 75; Austria refuses to surrender her share for a pecuniary compensation, 93, 99; Prussia complains of Austrian conduct, 93, 94; war against Austria inevitable unless she voluntarily surrenders the Duchies, 95, 98-100, 104,

105, 108, 109, 133 n. ; Prussia determined to have Schleswig-Holstein, 170; suggested that it remain an independent duchy with a Hohenzollern as duke, 171; Austria submits the question of the Duchies to the Diet, 187-189, 192; Austria decides to consult the representative assembly of Holstein, 187-190; Prussia uses armed force in Holstein, 190; its annexation by Prussia, 272; Austria cedes her share, 283; that part which was linguistically Danish to return to Denmark, 283; Bismarck on the question of its cession by Austria, 313. See also Augustenburg, Duke Frederick of
Schmerling, Anton, Baron von, xx; his career, 27; sets up a central parliament (1861), xi, xii, 27, 28; and Austria as the dominating state in a united Germany, xi, 30, 31, 35-39, 41, 43; his policy abandoned, 50; and Schleswig-Holstein, 53, 54, 57; becomes leader of Parliament, 61; his dismissal, xii, 76, 79, 80; Rechberg's relations with, 79, 318
Schneider, Louis, 168
Schönerer, Georg von, xiii, xxi
Schwarzenberg, Prince Felix, 8, 51, 53; and the Germanic Confederation, 2-5; his anti-Prussian policy, 64, 85; sends for Rechberg, 318
Schwarzenberg, Prince Karl Philipp, 197
Seherr-Toss, Count von, 33, 241, 245 n.
Sennyey, Austrian Conservative leader, 83, 160, 255
Serbia, xxiii-xxvii
Silesia, 68, 145, 146, 150, 154, 156, 157, 176, 181, 183, 186, 324; concentration of troops in, 106, 107
Skalitz, 219-221
Slavs, xxii-xxvii, 256, 257
Solferino, battle of, 15, 16
Solms, Prince Charles von, 165, 166
South Germany, Prussia and its absorption, 266, 269-271, 300; exclusion of Austria from, 276, 277; proposed South German Confederation, 272, 277, 283
Stadion, Austrian General, 14-16
Steinmetz, General, 216-220
Sternberg, Count, 225
Stockhausen, General, 3
Stosch, General, 234
Strasburg, 172
Suez Canal, 88
Suffrage, universal, 117-119

THE END

DATE DUE

APR 6 1970			
FEB 1 1972			
FEB 25 1972			
MAR 10 1972			
GAYLORD			PRINTED IN U.S.A.